Psychotherapy

A C. G. JUNG FOUNDATION BOOK
Published in Association with Daimon Verlag,
Einsiedeln, Switzerland

The C. G. Jung Foundation for Analytical Psychology is dedicated to helping men and women grow in conscious awareness of the psychological realities in themselves and society, find healing and meaning in their lives and greater depth in their relationships, and live in response to their discovered sense of purpose. It welcomes the public to attend its lectures, seminars, films, symposia, and workshops and offers a wide selection of books for sale through its bookstore. The Foundation also publishes *Quadrant,* a semiannual journal, and books on Analytical Psychology and related subjects. For information about Foundation programs or membership, please write to the C. G. Jung Foundation, 28 East 39th Street, New York, NY 10016.

PSYCHOTHERAPY

Marie-Louise von Franz

SHAMBHALA
Boston & London
1993

Shambhala Publications, Inc.
Horticultural Hall
300 Massachusetts Avenue
Boston, Massachusetts 02115

Originally published by Daimon Verlag, Einsiedeln
Switzerland, under the title *Psychotherapie,*
© 1990 by Daimon Verlag.

9 8 7 6 5 4 3 2

Printed in the United States of America on acid-free paper ⊗
Distributed in the United States by Random House, Inc.,
and in Canada by Random House of Canada Ltd

LIBRARY OF CONGRESS CATALOGING-IN-PUBLICATION DATA
Franz, Marie-Louise von, 1915–
    [Psychotherapie. English]
    Psychotherapy / Marie-Louise von Franz. — 1st ed.
        p.   cm.
    "C. G. Jung Foundation/Daimon books."
    Includes bibliographical references and index.
    ISBN 0-87773-879-3 (acid-free paper)
    1. Psychotherapy.   2. Jung, C. G. (Carl Gustav), 1875–1961.
3. Psychoanalysis.   I. Title.
RC480.5.F743813   1993   92-56454
616.89'14—dc20   CIP

CONTENTS

FOREWORD

Psychotherapy is the third volume in the series of collected essays of Marie-Louise von Franz. This volume originally appeared as a kind of celebratory volume for the author's seventy-fifth birthday. This occasion was celebrated on January 4, 1990, in the presence of many friends and former students.

The overall theme in all the articles in this book is psychotherapy. The various chapters deal with important aspects of the therapeutic and analytic process—for example, projection, transference, active imagination—as well as with essential standards for the training of therapists and analysts. All articles are characterized by a direct concern with actual practice. Clearly this is not abstract theorizing, but down-to-earth writing based on the rich experience of decades of practical work with patients and students in training. Many examples drawn from therapeutic practice accompany Marie-Louise von Franz's expositions, making this volume into a living and enriching account of the work of an extraordinary analyst in whom we find warm and earthy humor blended with intellectual stringency.

These articles appeared independently of each other over a period of twenty years. They were originally published in a variety of anthologies, professional publications, and journals, of which many are now out of print and almost impossible to find. In the list of sources that follows, the reader will find all available information on the first publication of the individual articles.

It should be pointed out that, as a matter of editorial policy, the essays in this volume have not been arranged chronologically according to the time of their appearance but rather according to their thematic content. References to and citations from the writings of C. G. Jung in all the articles previously revised by the author have been made consistent with the *Collected Works of C. G. Jung* as published by Princeton University Press. This particularly applies to footnote references. In accordance with the author's wishes, an integrated index of persons and subjects was also appended to the volume.

We would like to give special thanks to Marie-Louise von Franz, who aided the editors through word and deed, to Mr. René Malamud for his valuable assistance in gathering the articles and for his much-appreciated support, as well as to the Foundation for Jungian Psychology (Stiftung für Jungsche Psychologie), whose grant-in-aid went far toward making this publication in its present form possible.

Robert Hinshaw
Daimon Verlag
Einsiedeln, Switzerland

SOURCES

"Self-Realization in the Individual Therapy of C. G. Jung" ("Selbstverwirklichung in der Einzeltherapie") originally appeared in *Praxis der Psychotherapie* (1977). English translation by Michael H. Kohn © 1993 by Shambhala Publications, Inc.

"The Inferior Function" appeared in an earlier version in *Lectures on Jung's Typology* (New York: Spring Publications, 1971). The version herein has been revised by the author.

"Active Imagination in the Psychology of C. G. Jung" ("Die aktive Imagination in der Psychologie C. G. Jungs") appeared in *Meditation in Religion und Psychotherapie,* edited by Wilhelm Bitter (Stuttgart: Ernst Klett Verlag, 1957). English translation by Michael H. Kohn © 1993 by Shambhala Publications, Inc.

"On Active Imagination" ("Bemerkungen zur aktiven Imagination") appeared in *Zeitschrift für Analytische Psychologie* 9 (1978), pp. 161ff. English translation by Michael H. Kohn © 1993 by Shambhala Publications, Inc. (A different translation appeared in *Methods of Treatment in Analytical Psychology,* edited by Ian F. Baker (Fellbach: Bonz Verlag, 1980).

"The Religious Dimension of Analysis" ("Die religiöse Dimension der Analyse") appeared in *Die Behandlung in der analytischen Psychologie,* edited by Ursula Eschenbach (Bonz Verlag, 1983). English translation by Michael H. Kohn © 1993 by Shambhala Publications, Inc.

"The Religious or Magical Attitude toward the Unconscious" ("Religiöse oder magische Einstellung zum Unbewussten") appeared in *Psychotherapeutische Problems* (Zurich: Rascher Verlag, 1964). English translation by Michael H. Kohn © 1993 by Shambhala Publications, Inc.

"Some Aspects of the Transference" ("Über einige Aspekte der Übertragung") appeared in *Zeitschrift für Analytischen Psychologie* 4 (1973), pp. 155ff. English translation by Michael H. Kohn © 1993 by Shambhala Publications, Inc.

"Projection" ("Über Projektion") appeared in the *Schleswig-Holsteinisches Ärzte Blatt,* no. 10 (1980). English translation by Michael H. Kohn © 1993 by Shambhala Publications, Inc.

"Profession and Vocation" ("Beruf und Berufung") appeared in *Die Behandlung der analytischen Psychologie,* edited by Ursula Eschenbach (Bonz Verlag, 1979). English translation by Michael H. Kohn © 1993 by Shambhala Publications, Inc.

"Drugs in the View of C. G. Jung" ("Die Drogen in der Sicht C. G. Jungs") appeared in *Trug der Drogen,* edited by Irmgard Buck (Hamburg: Siebenstern Verlag, 1974). English translation by Michael H. Kohn © 1993 by Shambhala Publications, Inc.

"On Group Psychology" appeared in *Quadrant,* no. 13 (Winter 1973).

"The Religious Background of the Puer Aeternus Problem" ("Über religiöse Hintergründe des Puer-Aeternus-Problems") was a lecture delivered at the second International Congress for Analytical Psychology, Zurich, 1962, and was first published in 1964. English translation by Michael H. Kohn © 1993 by Shambhala Publications, Inc.

Psychotherapy

SELF-REALIZATION IN THE INDIVIDUAL THERAPY OF C. G. JUNG

Self-realization is a word that is being used today by various psychological schools, for the most part in a way based loosely on Jung's concept of individuation. Looking closely, we see, however, that they are using it in a different sense from Jung's, namely, in the sense of discovering a certain ego identity. Such an identity, as we know, arises through the ego's becoming more continuous and stable. The ego then knows something more about itself. Jung, by contrast, meant something entirely different, namely, consciously discovering and entering into relationship with another psychic content, which, drawing upon the Upanishads, he calls the Self. In this case also, a more continuous and stable ego identity develops, but of a rather different sort. It is less egocentric and has more human kindness. Here the ego does not so much realize itself, but rather helps the Self toward realization.

Initially, this certainly sounds a bit abstract. That is why, in what follows, I shall attempt to clarify this process through the interpretation of a dream that illuminates the principal aspects of our theme. I have chosen a dream because the dream is an expression of the unpreconceived, unconscious nature in human beings; thus it represents not a theory but rather a response on the part of the psyche itself to the question of self-realization.

Though the concepts of ego, Self, and the unconscious are known to most people in a theoretical way, many make use of them without knowing what they mean in terms of practical experience. That was the case also for the dreamer of our dream. He was a forty-year-old man of an English-speaking culture who had just passed his first examinations at the C. G. Jung Institute in Zurich. Theoretically, he was well informed about the concepts mentioned above. Now, however, the time had come to undertake, under supervision, his first treatment of patients. Understandably, he did not consider himself equal to this task and became frightened. His greatest fear was that he might be unable to understand his new analysands' dreams. (As is well known, a Jungian analysis is to a great extent based on the interpretation of a patient's dreams.) Everything seemed uncertain to him, and he began to ponder over what in fact a "correct" or "incorrect" dream interpretation was at all, and, even more generally, what in fact takes place in an analysis. One night, after having had a long discussion with a friend on this subject, he went to sleep and had the following dream:

> I'm sitting in an open, rectangular square in an old city. I am joined by a young man clad only in a pair of trousers, who sits down in front of me with his legs crossed. His torso is powerful and full of vitality and strength. The sun shines through his blond hair. He recounts his dreams to me and wants me to interpret them for him. The dreams are like a kind of fabric that he is spreading out before me as he tells them to me. Each time he recounts a dream, a stone falls from the sky that strikes the dream a blow. This sets pieces of the dream flying off. As I take them in my hand, it becomes clear that they are made out of bread. As the pieces of the dream fly off, they lay bare an inner structure that resembles an abstract modern sculpture. With each dream that is recounted, a further stone falls on it, and thus more and more of the basic structure, which is made

of nuts and bolts, begins to appear. I tell the youth that this shows how to expose the meaning of a dream—down to the nuts and bolts. Then it emerges that dream interpretation is the art of knowing what to throw away and what to keep, which is the way it is in life as well.

Then the dream scene changes. The youth and I are now sitting facing each other on the bank of a wonderfully beautiful broad river. He is still telling me his dreams, but the structure built up by the dreams has taken on a different shape. They do not form a pyramid made of nuts and bolts, but a pyramid made of thousands of little squares and triangles. It is like a Cubist painting by Braque, but it is three-dimensional and alive. The colors and shadings of the little squares and triangles are constantly changing. I explained that it is essential for a person to maintain the balance of the whole composition by always immediately countering a color change with a corresponding compensatory change on the other side. This business of balancing out the colors is incredibly complex, because the whole object is three-dimensional and in constant movement. Then I look at the peak of the dream pyramid. There, there is nothingness. That is indeed the only point where the whole structure holds together, but at that point there is empty space. As I look at it, this space begins to radiate white light.

Once more the dream scene changes. The pyramid remains there, but now it is made out of solidified fecal material. The peak is still radiating. I suddenly realize that the invisible peak is as though made visible by the solid shit, and that conversely the shit is also made visible by the peak. I look deep into the shit and recognize that I am looking at the hand of God. In an instant of enlightenment, I understand why the peak is invisible: it is the face of God.

Again the dream changes. Dr. von Franz and I are taking a walk along the river. She laughingly says: "I'm sixty-one years old, not sixteen, but both numbers add up to seven."

I wake up abruptly with the feeling that someone has knocked loudly on the door. To my amazement, the apartment is completely quiet and empty.

In the language of primitive peoples, this is a "big dream" or, in Jung's language, an archetypal dream, which is of supra-personal, universal human significance. We must now attempt to understand it more precisely. It is composed of four sections. The location of the first set of events is a rectangular square in an old city, which suggests tradition and human culture, in contrast to the river in the next part of the dream. This is presumably related to the fact that the dreamer has been tormenting himself with the question, "What are we doing, what would I actually be doing, in an analysis?" The answer is that the telling and interpreting of dreams is an ancient cultural tradition, which formerly used to take place in public. Already the first patient who wants to have his dreams interpreted has come. He is, however, markedly vital and healthy, not sick. His blond, sun-illuminated hair perhaps even indicates that he is a solar hero of some kind. This healthiness emphasizes that dreams, even in sick patients, arise out of the healthy level of the psyche, but it says more than that: the solar hero in mythology is a bringer of new light, new consciousness. He is already an aspect of what Jung called the Self, a still-unknown aspect of the dreamer himself that will bring him illumination.

The dreams that this man recounts have a kind of substance. They are not something frothy, airy-fairy, but something real, a piece of matter, so to speak. Stones fall on them from heaven. In that, somehow, lies their interpretation. The dreamer was very apprehensive about whether he would be able to interpret dreams correctly. In compensatory fashion, the dream image here indicates clearly that a correct dream interpretation is something that strikes the mark. Rather than being something one has contrived, it is an impersonal psychic event. The stones fall from the sky; they must be meteorites. If something comes from above, this means in mythic language that it derives from the unknown spiritual sphere of the collective unconscious. Thus, since ancient times meteorites have been highly venerated objects; they have been regarded as containing a divine spirit, as messengers of the gods. For example, the North American Arikara tribe tell us that the supreme god Nesaru sent them a black meteorite as an emissary, which taught them the ritual of the sacred pipe, the peace pipe. The famous Kaaba, the goal of the pilgrimage to Mecca, is also a black meteoric stone. Since the stones come from the sky, we see that dreams, on the one hand, and the interpretation of dreams, on the other,—the right idea that "strikes" you— both come from the unconscious. Both ultimately come from the same source, but only when the therapist and the analysand work together on the dream do the stones "strike."

The dream pieces that fly off when the stones strike turn out, upon closer examination, to be made out of bread, that is, something that one can eat, or in psychological terms integrate. It is in fact true, as we can all experience, that a successful dream interpretation, one that strikes the mark, is somehow nourishing for consciousness. A synthetic, constructive interpretation—one that does not attempt to reduce the dream content to "nothing but wish-fulfillment" or to some other "nothing but," and that instead follows the constructive thread of the dream, enriching its motifs—works like the "bread of life." Actually, in the Lord's Prayer, we are not asking for "daily bread," as the usual wrong translation runs. In the Greek text we find *hyperousion,* "supersubstantial bread."

That which cannot be eaten, or directly integrated, is the part of the dream that is left over. It is made of nuts and bolts, which gradually build up into an entire pyramid. These are, as the dream account says, the basic structure of the dream, what is left after the flesh, in this case, the bread, has been taken away. Later on we are told that we must do the same thing as we must do in life—lay bare the skeleton. This means that we must penetrate through to the deeper meaning that lies behind the dream images.

People often say, "Last night I had such a ridiculously stupid, absurd dream." They remain hung up on the surface of the dream, that combination of absurd images, without being able to penetrate through to the meaning. Jung often responded in such cases, "There are no stupid dreams, only stupid people who don't understand them."

The purpose of bolts is to hold two things together and to fasten things together, for example, tracks onto cross-ties. The sexual analogy is obvious.[1] By using bolts, things are joined. Every time a dream interpretation hits the mark, a piece of the unconscious is joined with consciousness, or else an autonomous complex is joined with the rest of the personality. In this way a continuously repeating process of *coniunctio* takes place. And from this, the strange pyramid that the rest of the dream deals with takes shape. Thus we must take a closer look at the symbolism of the pyramid.

The most important function given to the pyramid is certainly that given by the ancient Egyptians—the shape for the tombs of their kings. The pyramid was the house of the dead. The stone that crowned it shut was so placed that the first rays of the sun struck it.[2] Now, in Egypt, the supreme god, the universal god Atum, was originally represented as a cone-shaped stone, as the so-called "unknown *ben-ben* stone."[3] This name is connected with *wbn*, meaning "rise, illuminate." The same radical is found in the Egyptian word *bnw*, meaning "bird, phoenix." The phoenix symbolized the rising sun and resurrection. The most sacred temple in Heliopolis was alter-

nately called the House of the Stone or the House of the Phoenix. The same *ben-ben* stone was also considered to be the
primordial hill that rose out of the primordial waters at the
beginning of the world. Also, the same phoenix was identified
in later Egyptian history with the *ba* bird. This bird is the
immortal guide of the soul of every human being, his individuality, which after death becomes one with the universal god
without losing its quintessence of an individual earthly human
being.

In the view of Helmuth Jacobsohn, the pyramid-shaped cap-
stone of an obelisk also represents the *ben-ben* stone. It is
called a *benbenet*. When the king ritually greeted the god of
the rising sun from the base of the obelisk, the sun's first rays
fell on the obelisk's pinnacle, which in those days was gilded.[4]
At that point the *ba,* the soul guide of the god, was seen.
Benbenet, however, also meant the peak of the pyramid, which
resembled the peak of the obelisk.[5] At the moment of his resurrection, a deceased person who had become the *ba* beheld
the sun god from that point. Later such stones were also provided for ordinary people as part of their burial equipment.

As Jacobsohn points out, the *ben-ben* stone in Egypt represents a parallel to the "philosopher's stone" of Western alchemy. The philosopher's stone also symbolized the immortal
soul guide and a kind of resurrectional body of the dead. The
pyramid in our dream constitutes an amazing parallel to this,
since the dreamer demonstrably knew none of the Egyptian
associations we have been describing. All the same, the pyramid he dreamed of was also something divine; its radiant peak
was even the manifestation of God, and in its worthless garb
of matter, the hand of God could even be seen.

Perhaps it is worthwhile to remark in passing that pyramids
actually exhibit strange physical properties that have yet to be

explained.[6] Experiments with models of the Cheops pyramid made from cardboard showed that cadavers placed inside did not decay; dull razor blades placed inside regained their edge. This must have to do with the geometry of the internal space, but nothing precise is known. In any case, this is not essential for us in this context. What is important for us is only the psychological significance of the pyramid in the dream as a symbol of the Self.

Perhaps it has become somewhat clearer in the course of our discussion what Jung meant by the Self. It is not the ego, but a more embracing or eternal inner personality that is hinted at by this symbol. Jung also defined it as the conscious-unconscious wholeness of the person. Though this Self is already present in every person as his basic makeup, it is only realized in practice through understanding dreams or through active imagination.[7] Through being realized, it "incarnates" itself, so to speak, in the mortal life of the ego. If I had a gift for music like Beethoven's but never discovered or made use of it, it might as well not exist. Only the conscious ego is capable of realizing psychic contents. Even something as great, even divine, as the Self can only be realized by the ego. That is self-realization from a Jungian perspective.

Now let us return to the beginning of the first part of the dream, to the rectangular square in the city. As one can read in the work of Mircea Eliade, such a square in a city is a symbol of the center of the world, the place where heaven and earth, eternity and temporality, come together.[8] This square is thus really a symbol of the Self, but in the function of a maternal *temenos,* or protective space. And the blond dream teller is the aspect of the Self that strives toward becoming conscious, just as all mythical heroes are bearers of a new vision of the world.

At this point it becomes easier to understand why Jung always required of analysts that they should ultimately work the most on continuing to make progress in their own individuation. In so doing, they take their analysands along with them on their journey, without trying to influence them directly (which would be an abuse of power). In an early letter, Jung even goes so far as to say that the therapist should only analyze the pathological aspect of the patient's psyche.[9] This is because intellectual understanding is destructive. Understanding (Latin *comprehendere*), after all, means "taking hold of," "grasping," and thus corresponds to an exercise of power. When the patient's being and destiny are at stake, one should relate to his unique mystery with wordless respect. As Jung said, "We must understand the divine in us, but not in another insofar as he is capable of getting on and understanding on his own." Our dreamer, as we will recall, was apprehensive about his encounter with patients. His dream points him back to working on himself.

Now the image changes and the scene of the action becomes the bank of a broad river. In mythology, a river is usually associated with the stream of time, the flow of life. Thus, for example, for the Greeks, time is the god Kronos/Chronus and also the current Oceanus that encircles the earth like a ring, or that girdles the cosmos as a celestial current, with the animals of the zodiac riding upon it.

The river is also an image of eternal change. We may recall Heraclitus's statement that we can never step into the same river twice. The technical and abstract pyramidal skeleton made of nuts and bolts has now become a pyramid of infinitely numerous, mutually attuned colored squares and triangles, whose nuances of hue must continually be compensatorily balanced. This describes an advanced aspect of dream analysis. Initially every successful dream interpretation is an individual

"Aha!" experience. But now everything comes into closer contact with each other through the continuity of life, the river. One not only begins to understand individual dreams but lives with them continually. It also now becomes clear that the pyramid, in spite of its many individual facets, represents a balanced whole in which everything coheres with everything else. Colors stand for the participation of emotions and feelings. It is no longer merely a matter of seeing individual pieces, but also of relating to all the nuances of feeling in a more living way—always with an eye on the state of balance of the mysterious whole.

The basic components are triangles and squares, just as the whole itself is composed of a square base and four triangles. Those who are familiar with the work of Jung know that symbols of the Self are nearly always quaternary, more rarely triadic, structures. The models of the universe of the ancient cosmologies are quaternary, as are all natural symbols of the divine. The Catholic Church even augmented the Christian Trinity into a quaternity through the heavenly Ascension of Mary. Seen in terms of numerical symbolism, three and the triangle are masculine-dynamic, while the four and the square are feminine-static. The composition of the pyramid out of both is an indication that here the opposites are united, which indeed was already hinted at by the image of the nuts and bolts. This entire structure is in a state of ongoing transformational change of color. It is a living thing that must continually be understood anew by whoever contemplates it, in this case, the dream interpreter.

Now the dreamer discovers that the peak, the focal point of the whole structure, is empty, is empty space. Later we learn that this is the case because it is the face of God. As is well known, no human being can gaze upon the face of God and live! In many mandalas—that is, circular and rectangular religious images of the Self—in the middle there is the figure of Christ or Buddha or some other Godhead, or perhaps a symbol like the thunderbolt (Tibetan *dorje*), or a crystal, a flower, a golden ball, etc. But particularly in recent times, as Jung pointed out, there are more and more cases where the center is empty. It is, as he says, as though many modern people are no longer capable of projecting the divine image—as, for example, onto Christ or Buddha.[10] As a result, they run the risk of identifying themselves with the center, which would lead to a dissolution of the personality. The boundaries of the mandala exist in order to prevent this and to reinforce a concentration on an inner center, the Self, that is not identified with the ego. The image of the human being does not replace the deity but rather symbolizes it. In this way, the deity remains the mystery that dwells in the depths of the individual psyche.

It is the danger of any kind of atheism that the human being might place himself as the ego in the center and thus undergo an inflation that might catapult him into a psychic catastrophe. Our dreamer is not in this danger, but he still takes himself as the analyst too seriously; therefore, this image arises. When he looks at the peak, it begins to radiate. One is reminded of the *nirvana* or *satori* experience of the Far East. This is an emptiness that is not negative emptiness but rather the full power of enlightenment.

In the third part of the dream, a surprising reversal takes place, a so-called enantiodromia.[11] The beautiful pyramid is now composed of solidified shit. This makes the point of enlightenment in the emptiness visible and vice versa. The ancient and medieval alchemists never got tired of repeating that the philosopher's stone *in stercore invenitur* ("is discovered amid excrement") and that amid this refuse, the people of this world heedlessly tread it down. How many modern rationalists even today are of the opinion that dreams are "refuse," anal and genital fantasies and the like. It is true that what an analyst has to sit in his office and listen to all day is not purely edifying. One has to hear about marital strife, mad jealousies, outbreaks of repressed resentment, sexual fantasies, money needs, and endless "then he said . . . and then I said. . . ." It is horrible shit that the patients and all of us are stuck in. But when one takes a closer look, one can see the hand of God in it!

That was perhaps the greatest art of Jung himself: he could listen to such garbage and remain strangely unmoved, and then with a word or a gesture suddenly point out the hand of God that became visible in it, that is, the deeper meaning of the present crisis that made it possible to accept it. He was able to do this because he was not so much looking for the why—the personal history of the neurotic symptoms that explained how they originated—but rather for the purpose, the *telos,* or meaning of the phenomena at hand. "What does it mean for me that I have gotten myself into this slimy muck?" Through this, the peak of the pyramid becomes visible, that pinnacle that the ancient Egyptians so placed that it would be struck every morning by the first rays of the sun. In the East, particularly in Persia, the *oriens,* the sunrise, is still today a symbol of mystical enlightenment, the point where the enlightened one sees God and becomes one with Him.

The fourth part is a descent or return to everyday life. I appear (I was his analyst) and say laughingly that I am sixty-one, not sixteen, but the internal sum of both numbers is seven. Let us first examine the concrete situation. I was sixty-one, the dreamer was forty, and the women who were his new analysands were around twenty. Thus the dreamer was in the middle, about on the verge of the second half of life. Until the age of forty, he had practiced another profession, and now he was in danger of becoming frightened of his new task, like a schoolboy facing exams. The experience of life he had already accumulated, the difficult marriage he had successfully come to terms with, his three already grown children—all this he had forgotten.

What helps us here is numerical symbolism. The number one stands for divinity and cosmic unity, six for the union of the sexes and marriage. At the age of sixteen one definitively leaves behind the unconscious wholeness of childhood and turns toward sexuality and the "ten thousand things" of the world. At the age of sixty-one one has crossed the threshold toward old age, in which one turns away from the many and moves toward inner unity. But the internal sum of both numbers is seven. Seven is the number of evolution, of development.[12] We have only to think of the seven days of creation. In the number eight, the goal, differentiated wholeness, is attained. The emphasis lies here on seven, on the fact that life is development, in youth as in old age. "Everything is a transition," or *"Habentibus symbolum facilis est transitus,"* as the ancient alchemists said.

This big dream leads far away from the dreamer's fear and answers his question with an entire philosophy of life, in the center of which is self-realization. The whole is represented as purely a series of events that enlighten the dreamer. However, this should not mislead one into thinking that being an analyst does not require an achievement on the part of the ego. We know from experience that it is hard work, difficult work, and requires a lot of knowledge. The dream, which represents this work purely as something that happens by itself, indicates a compensation, because the dreamer in his ruminations of the previous day took his ego, the role of the analyst, too seriously.

The actual patients who had been assigned to him, two young women, do not appear in the dream at all. Rather the patient, the "sufferer," is an inner figure in the dreamer himself. The patient is a part of his Self.

Perhaps this dream conveys an inkling of why we of the Jungian school are skeptical of group therapy. This dream shows that the main process of inner development takes place between the ego and the Self—or, in old-fashioned language, the image of God within one. Others and their opinions have no business there. It even comes to a point where even the analyst as one's partner is too much. Ultimately, as Jung points out, a person has to "be alone if he is to find out what it is that bears him when he cannot bear himself anymore. Only this experience can give him an indestructible foundation."[13]

Such an attitude has nothing at all to do with narcissism or with egoistic individualism. These are no more than a preoccupation on the part of the ego with "the dear ego," not the Self, which is ultimately an inner mystery of the individual. The relationship between a person and the Self is not egoistic, far from it—a person can never really relate properly to other people until he has found himself, that is, his Self. All the same, Jung admitted that his position was one-sided. In reality, the extraverted path of social adaptation and the introverted path of relationship to the Self constitute a pair of complementary opposites, both justified and yet at the same time exclusive of each other. But under the pressure of overpopulation and increasing urbanization, and with the influence of Communism and of the extraverted orientation of most psychological schools, we are in great danger of focusing on just the one pole and thus of crushing the individual in his uniqueness.

Failing to take account of this could bring an unconscious counterreaction marked by unrestrained egoism and, in the

extreme case, even asocial criminality. For this reason, according to Jung's view, the time has come to pay more heed to the
inner path of the individual on the way to the Self. For only
he who is anchored in the Self can truly act ethically. Only
such a person will no longer uncritically follow the currents of
fashions and fads and political "isms." He can then also, as the
dream beautifully expresses it, perceive the hand of God amid
all the slime and muck of life—of course, only, as the dream
also indicates, if he takes a closer look.

NOTES

1. At this point the author refers to the sexual connotation of the German
   word *Mutter,* which usually means "mother" but is also the word for
   the kind of nut that a bolt screws into.—Translator
2. Cf. Helmuth Jacobsohn, "Das göttliche Wort und der göttliche Stein im
   alten Ägypten" (The Divine Word and the Divine Stone in Ancient
   Egypt), *Eranos Jahrbuch,* vol. 39 (1970): 217ff.
3. Ibid., pp. 233–34.
4. Ibid., p. 236.
5. This was a solid, precisely pyramid-shaped stone.
6. Cf. S. Ostrander and L. Schroeder, *Psi* (Bern, Munich & Vienna: Scherz
   Verlag, 1970), pp. 308ff. (Karel Drbal).
7. See the chapters on active imagination in this volume.
8. Mircea Eliade, *Kosmos und Geschichte* (Cosmos and History) (Rowohlt,
   1966), pp. 11ff.
9. C. G. Jung, letter to Hans Schmid, 6 November 1915, in *Letters,* vol. 1
   (Princeton: Princeton University Press, 1973), p. 31.
10. See C. G. Jung, *Psychology and Religion,* CW 11 (Princeton: Princeton
    University Press, 1958), para. 156, p. 95.
11. See C. G. Jung, CW 8 (1960), p. 219.
12. See R. Allendy, *Le symbolisme des nombres* (The Symbolism of Numbers)
    (Paris, 1928).
13. C. G. Jung, *Psychology and Alchemy,* CW 12 (1953), para. 32, p. 28.

THE INFERIOR FUNCTION

INTRODUCTION

Though the theme of this paper is the inferior function, one cannot talk about it without discussing the whole problem of the four functions and sketching the superior function as well, because it is all interwoven. I presuppose that the reader is familiar with Jung's book on the psychological types,[1] and will try to illustrate it by my practical experiences.

Psychological Types is one of Jung's earlier books. When he wrote it and was trying to find out about the types, he was in many respects struggling in the dark; he has since made many discoveries which are to be found in his other works, and these I intend to link up. One repeatedly meets people who do not understand how typology looks in practical life. Many people who talk about types cannot even discover what their own type is, which is generally due to their lack of practical experience. Since the book was written, the idea of the four functions of consciousness, and the functioning of the conscious human personality in this fourfold way, has proved tremendously productive, and the problem of the four functions has increasingly evolved in Jung's thought and also turns up in his thought in the religious form of the problem of three and four.

The problem of three and four, especially in the image of God, has proved so tremendously important that people tend to project the function problem onto this religious problem.

The same happens in mythological interpretation, for wherever people find quaternary symbols — say, in North American Indian mythology, where one turns to the four points of the compass or where the sand paintings are obviously of a fourfold structure — they say that that means the four functions, and they pin that concept onto the mythological theme. There are three mistakes here. First, taking Jungian concepts and attaching them with a safety pin onto mythological material is a completely sterile enterprise in itself, for it distorts basic facts. Second, it is using the concepts without thinking what they really mean and on what they are based. And third, in this special case, it is fundamentally wrong, because if you think for a moment, you realize that what we can see in mythological material is unconscious material. The Navajos, for instance, have not thought out their sand paintings and mandalas consciously; they would say that they were revealed to them, or to their medicine men. Therefore, those primitive and even evolved mythological quaternary themes are self-manifestations of the collective unconscious, so we cannot identify them with a conscious phenomenon, while the functions are modes of behavior of consciousness. We have to look at it rather in the following way.

Consciousness evolves in early childhood, as is known, from the unconscious. From our point of view, the unconscious is a primary and the conscious a secondary fact. Therefore the unconscious totality and the structure of the total personality exist in time before the conscious personality and could be looked at as in the diagram on page 18.

Consciousness in itself is a field of representations, for representations are only called conscious insofar as they are associated with the ego complex. If one says, "I know that this is so and so," that means that this is conscious to me, it is a fact

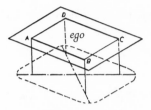

Fourfold structures
in the field of consciousness
with the ego as center

The preconscious total
quaternian structure of
the personality

in my field of consciousness. When the functions develop in
the field of consciousness—A, B, C, D in the diagram—there
comes up from below, first let us say, the thinking function,
which then becomes one of the main functions of the ego,
which uses mainly the operation of thinking in the organiza-
tion of its field of consciousness. Slowly another function appears and gradually they all—under favorable conditions—
appear in the field of consciousness. Thus you get a fourfold
structure in consciousness which mirrors exactly the preconscious fourfold structure. We have a quaternio of functions in
consciousness because there is already an inborn tendency to
build up such a fourfold structure in the unconscious. Mythological products usually mirror the basic structure (the circle),
but they do not represent its mirage in consciousness, so to
speak. This is why if we try to pin the concepts of thinking,
feeling, and so on onto mythological phenomena, we always
come to grief, for we are trying to connect in a wrong way. It
is as though we tried to identify the result with the cause. If,
therefore, we have a fourfold phenomenon in mythology, it is
better to say that it represents the general archetypal structure
of the psyche, which, among other things, has produced the
tendency always to develop into four functions in the structure
of consciousness.

The question has often been raised as to why on earth there
should be four functions. Why not three, or five? That cannot

be answered theoretically; it is simply a question of checking facts and of seeing whether you can find out more or fewer functions and another typology which would be equally justified. For Jung it was a great discovery when he later found confirmation of his more intuitively conceived idea in the fact that everywhere in myths and religious symbolism there appears the problem of the fourfold structure of the psyche and that, in studying the behavior of his patients, he had apparently hit upon a basic structure of the psyche.

Naturally, the basic fourfold structure of the psyche, which means more than only the conscious functions, is generally represented, if it appears, as a purely primitive self-manifestation of the unconscious, usually as an undifferentiated quaternion. There are just the four principles more or less of the same kind: four colors, or angels, or gods, etc. The more they are connected with consciousness, the more they tend to become three animals and one human being, or three good gods and one evil god, and then you get those more differentiated mandalas where the four poles of the quaternary structure are different from each other. This is particularly so if you are dealing with material which has been worked upon a great deal consciously, when you find the classic problem of the three and the four, about which Jung has written so much. This means that when, from this basic structure, one or the other function becomes conscious, or where under optimum conditions three functions become conscious, this has the effect that the basic structure also changes, for neither in psychology nor in any other field of reality is there ever a one-sided course of action; for if the unconscious builds up a field of consciousness, the repercussion of such a change produces an alteration in the unconscious structure as well. Therefore, in dreams and mythological material you find that this basic structure also appears in an altered form, from which it can be concluded that a part of the problem of the functions has already become conscious so that, owing to the counteraction, even the basic structure has this changed or modified form. Then again there are mandalas which are to be found chiefly in the higher civilizations, such as the images of the four Evangelists where three are animals and one a human. This theme appeared previously in Egyptian mythology in the four sons of Horus, pictured with three animals and one human head, as well as the other distorted mandalas, in which there is a certain tension within the structure, generally between the three and the four in particular.

I would like to give a brief sketch of the pattern of the four functions in Jungian psychology. Jung first differentiated two attitudinal types: the extravert and the introvert. In the extravert, the libido habitually flows consciously toward the object, but there is also an unconscious secret counteraction back toward the subject. For the extravert the hidden move toward the subject is usually an unconscious factor. In the case of the introvert, the opposite occurs, for he feels as if an object would constantly overwhelm him, so that he has to continually retire from it, for everything is falling upon him, he is constantly overwhelmed by impressions, but he is unaware that he is secretly borrowing, or lending, psychic energy to the object through his own unconscious extraversion.

Expressed briefly, that represents the difference between

EXTRAVERTED TYPE

ego   object

Threshold
of Consciousness

INTROVERTED TYPE

ego   object

the extravert and the introvert and then, if you take the four functions of sensation, thinking, feeling, and intuition, each of which can be extraverted or introverted, you get eight types: extraverted thinking, introverted thinking; extraverted feeling, introverted feeling; and so on.

Before we move on to practical examples, I would like to characterize the inferior function in its general behavior. You can say that all superior functions in an individual, whether in one case it is thinking and in another feeling, have a tendency to behave in a certain way, and the inferior function in an individual, irrespective of which it may be, has a general type of behavior. The behavior of the inferior function is wonderfully mirrored in many myths and particularly in many fairy tales, where there is a very widespread pattern of the following structure. A king has three sons. He likes the two older sons, but the youngest is regarded as being stupid or a fool. The king then sets a task in which the sons may have to find the water of life, or the most beautiful bride, or chase away a secret enemy who every night steals the horses, or the golden apples out of the royal garden. Generally the two elder sons set out and get nowhere or get stuck, and then the third saddles his horse and everybody laughs and tells him he'd better stay at home by the stove, where he belongs, but it is he who usually performs the great task. This fourth figure—he is the third son, but the fourth figure in the setup—has, according to the myths, different qualities. Sometimes he is the stupidest or the youngest, sometimes he is a bit clumsy, and sometimes he is a complete fool.

There are different versions, but he is always in some such category. In a beautiful Russian fairy tale, for instance, he is looked upon as a complete idiot, and the two elder sons ride out on wonderful horses from their father's stable, but the youngest takes a little shaggy horse and sits on it the wrong way round—with his head toward the horse's tail—and goes off, derided by everybody. He is, of course, Ivan, the Russian hero, the one who inherits everything. The story of the fool or the idiot sometimes occurs taken out of the general setup of four figures, so that he is the hero from the very beginning. Then there is the theme of the thumbling, or the cripple, or very often of the soldier who has deserted or has been wounded and discharged from the army and who is lost in the woods, where the great adventure starts. Or there may be a poor peasant boy who becomes king or inherits the kingdom, and in all these, from the very beginning of the story, you know that it concerns something more than the four functions, for the fool is an archetypal religious figure, embracing more than only the inferior function; he implies a whole part of the human personality, or even of humanity itself, and would represent what remained behind and therefore still has the original wholeness of nature, so that it has mainly a religious meaning. But in mythology, as soon as the fool appears as the fourth in a group of four people, we have a certain right to assume that he mirrors the general behavior of an inferior function.

I have often tried, in interpreting fairy tales, to go further into detail and to call the king the thinking and the fourth son the feeling function, but in my experience, that does not work. You have to twist the material and play some dishonest tricks if you force the material like this. So I have come to the conclusion that we cannot go so far, but must just say that in mythology such a third son, or such a fool, simply represents a type of the general behavior of the inferior function, whichever it may be; it is neither individual nor specific, but a general structure. That is quite correct, for if you study individual cases, you will see that the inferior function tends to behave after the manner of such a "fool" hero, the divine fool or idiot hero, who represents the despised part of the personality, the ridiculous and unadapted part but also that part which builds up the connection with the unconscious totality of the person.

There is something else to be guarded against, and that is that in the many myths where the foolish third son finds the water of life or the golden bird, or overcomes the dragon, or brings home the beautiful princess, inherits the kingdom, and so on, one is very much tempted to interpret him as the bridge to the unconscious, because the above are all symbols of what we assume to be in the unconscious. However, we must not forget that the whole mythological process represents everything in the unconscious, nor that for an introvert the unconscious very often appears outside! Therefore, it is quite right to say that the third son, or the fourth figure in the setup, makes the bridge to the unconscious, but this must *not* imply that the unconscious is always experienced as being "within," for that only applies to an extravert, as the inferior function has the opposite attitudinal type of the conscious function. An introverted thinking type will have inferior extraverted feeling, while an extraverted intuitive will have inferior introverted sensation, and so on.

One can say that the inferior function always makes the bridge to the unconscious, and in the case of an introvert it is generally by moving toward an unconscious projection which appears outside. So it could be said that the inferior function is always directed toward the unconscious and the symbolic world, but that it is not directed either to the inside or the outside; the latter varies individually. If the inferior function of an introvert moves outside, then it means that the outer realm will acquire a symbolic quality for that person. For instance, an introverted thinking type has an inferior feeling function, so the movement will be toward outer objects, that is, to other people; but such outer people will have a symbolic meaning for the person, being carriers of symbols of the unconscious. The symbolic meaning of an unconscious fact appears outside, as the quality of an outer object, *prima vista*. But if an introvert, with his habitual way of introjecting, says he need not telephone Mrs. So-and-So, for she is just the symbol of his anima and therefore symbolic, and the outer person does not matter, for it only happened that his projection fell there, then he will never get to the bottom of his inferior function or will never assimilate it as a problem. This is because the feeling of an introverted thinking type is generally genuinely extraverted, and with such a trick he simply tries to catch hold of his inferior function by means of his superior function and pull it inside. He introjects at the wrong moment so as to maintain the predominance of his superior over his inferior function. An introvert who wants to assimilate his inferior function must relate to outer objects, but bearing in mind that they are symbolic. He must not, however, draw the conclusion that they are *only* symbolic and that therefore outer objects can be dispensed with. That is a very lousy, dishonest trick which many introverts play with their inferior function. Naturally extraverts do the same thing, only the other way round. Therefore it must not be said that the inferior function is directed inward, or turned toward the unconscious within, but that the inferior function is directed toward the unconscious, whether the latter appears on the inside or the outside, and that it is always the carrier of symbolic experiences, which may come from within or without.

In the case of extraverts, I have often seen that the unconscious appears directly from within either as a vision or a fantasy. In that way I have often been impressed by the fact that extraverts, when they come to their other side, have a much purer relationship to the inner world than the introvert. I have even been quite jealous! I have seen what a naive and genuine and pure relationship they have to inner facts, for they can have a vision and take it completely seriously at once, quite naively! In an introvert, it is always distorted by his extraverted shadow, which throws doubts on it. Thus it can be said that if an extravert falls into his introversion, it will be specially genuine and specially pure and deep. That is why usually extraverts are so proud of this that they boast loudly that they are great introverts. They try to make it into a feather in their cap—which is again typically extraverted—and thereby ruin the whole thing! But actually, if they do not spoil everything with vanity, extraverts can have a much more childlike, naive, pure, and really genuine introversion than introverts. Introverts, for their part, if they wake up to their inferior extraversion, can spread a glow of life and make their surroundings into a symbolic festival better than any extravert! An introvert can give outer life a depth of symbolic meaning and the feeling of life as a magical feast of some kind, which the extravert cannot. If an extravert goes to a party, he thinks that everybody is marvelous and is ready to say: "Come on, let's get this party going!" But that is simply a technique, and the party never really reaches magical depth, or does so very rarely; it remains on the level of amiable surface. But if an introvert can come out with his extraversion in the right way he can create an atmosphere where outside things become symbolic: drinking a glass of wine with a friend becomes something like a communion, and so on. With the introvert it is linked with the outer, just as with the extravert it is really within, if he breaks through to the other side.

In *Psychological Types,* Jung speaks of the general impoverishment of extraverted and introverted thinking attitudes when these begin to wear out. He says:

> While the extravert really denies himself in his complete dispersion among objects, the introvert, by ridding himself of each and every content, has to content himself with his mere existence. In both cases the further development of life is crowded out of the domain of thought into the region of other psychic functions which had hitherto existed in relative unconsciousness. The extraordinary impoverishment of introverted thinking in relation to objective facts finds compensation in an abundance of unconscious facts. Whenever consciousness, wedded to the function of thought, confines itself within the smallest and emptiest circle possible—though seeming to contain the plentitude of divinity—unconscious phantasy becomes proportionately enriched. . . .[2]

This is just an example of the great trouble Jung took to describe how the slow overdoing of the superior function leads to its neurotic degeneration. He also alludes to a fact which plays a great role, namely that in the case of a person who has not been analyzed, the inferior function intrudes into the superior and falsifies it. Here, for instance, he describes what happens when introverted thinking is overtaxed. There was a marvelous demonstration of this some time ago in the case of a professor of philosophy who made an attack on the psychology of the unconscious in a Zurich newspaper, the *Neue Zürcher Zeitung.* He is a pupil of Heidegger and an absolute demonstration of overtaxed introverted thinking. This has the effect of his being unable to assert anything more than that life is an ontological phenomenon of existence! He enriches his statement with a few more impressive adjectives, but that is what it amounts to! This one thought, that "existence really

exists," expresses a divine plentitude for him, as it also had for
Parmenides, and he cannot cease reassuring us about such existence for several pages. And then he says, "But the unconscious would be an uncanny theater of marionettes and
ghosts." There you have an absolute illustration of what Jung
says: "The unconscious phantasy becomes proportionately en-
riched by a multitude of archaically formed facts, a veritable
pandemonium of magical factors." That is exactly what this
professor expounded in his articles — that the idea of the unconscious was awful, it was just a theatrical pandemonium, and
then he saved his conscious position by saying that it simply
didn't exist, it was just an invention of the psychologists! That
was a beautiful practical illustration of what Jung, in the sentences quoted, says. In addition to what Jung says there, if you
overdo one of the conscious attitudes, not only does it become
poor and lose its fertility, but also the unconscious counter-
function (in a thinking type it would be feeling) encroaches
upon the main function and falsifies it. That was obvious in
this professor's article, which shows that feeling was really
concerned in enlightening mankind as to the absurdity of the
idea of the psychology of the unconscious. He entirely lost the
objective style to which we are accustomed in scientific discussion, and he felt himself to be a prophet whose mission it
was to save mankind from some evil poison, so one saw that
his whole moral or feeling function contaminated his thinking.
His thinking became subjective instead of objective, and it was
obvious that he had not even read the literature on the psychology of the unconscious, not even the main books! He was
simply deeply concerned with saving mankind from such a
poisonous doctrine.

Another way in which the inferior function often intrudes
upon the superior is visible in the very down-to-earth, realistic

introverted sensation type. Sensation types, whether introverted or extraverted, are generally quite good in their relationship to money and in not being too extravagant, but if such
a type overdoes this, then his inferior intuition becomes involved. For instance, I knew a sensation type who became
madly stingy and could practically not move about in life any
longer because—well, in Switzerland everything costs something! When one tried to find out where this sudden stinginess
originated—hitherto he had been just moderately stingy like
most people in Switzerland—one noticed that he produced
any number of dark forebodings: he might have an accident
and be unable to work and support his family, something
might happen to his family, his wife might have a long illness,
his son might fail in his studies and need more years than is
usual, his mother-in-law, a very rich woman, might suddenly
get furious with him and leave her money to another family
instead of to his, et cetera, et cetera. Those are instances of
the dark fears of what might happen, which is typical for a
negative inferior intuition. Only the dark possibilities are envisaged, but he did not face the fact that he had such melancholy expectations of the future, but the first appearances of
his inferior intuition instead reinforced his sensation in a
wrong way by making him stingy. Life no longer flowed because everything was falsified by the invasion of the inferior
intuition. Thus, when the time comes for the development of
the other functions, there are generally several phenomena: the
superior function degenerates like an old car which begins to
run down and get worn out, the ego becomes bored with the
superior function, because everything you can do too well becomes boring, and beyond that, the inferior function, instead
of appearing in its own field, tends to invade the main function,
giving it an unadapted, neurotic twist. One is thus confronted

with a neurotic *mixtum compositum* of a thinking type who can't think any longer, or a feeling type who no longer shows any agreeable feeling. Then there is a transitional stage where people are neither fish nor flesh nor good red herring, but just awful! Formerly they were good thinkers, but they can't think anymore and they have not reached a new level. It is therefore very important to know one's type and recognize what the unconscious is now up to, for otherwise one is caught from behind.

The differentiation of types actually starts in very early childhood. For instance, the two attitudes of extraversion and introversion can actually be seen in a child of one or one and a half, though perhaps not always very clearly. Jung once told of a child who would not enter a room before it had been told the names of the pieces of furniture in the room—table, chair, and so on—after which it would move toward an object in the room. That is typical of a definitely introverted attitude, in which the object is terrifying and has to be banished or put in its place by a word: a propitiating gesture by which the object is made known and cannot misbehave, for a table must remain a table, so that you can walk toward it. In such little details, if one knows how to look for them, one can observe the tendency toward introversion or extraversion in a very small child. The functions naturally do not show so early in all cases, but by the kindergarten age you can usually observe the development of a main function by a preference for some occupation, or the child's behavior toward another child; for children, like adults, tend to do frequently what they can do well and not to do the things that they cannot do well. Probably most of you did as I did with your schoolwork; if you were gifted in mathematics, you did that first and left whatever you were not good at till the end and never first did the things which you disliked, which is something very few people do, for the natural tendency is to defer doing or to push off onto other people the thing in which you do not feel superior. By such natural behavior the inborn one-sidedness is increased more and more. And then comes the family attitude in which the boy who is very intelligent must study later on, or the child who is gifted in practical matters must become an engineer, so that the surroundings reinforce the existing one-sided tendencies, the so-called "gifts." There is thus an increase in the development of the superior function and a slow retardation of the other side of the personality. This is an unavoidable process and even has great advantages. Many people just fit into this pattern, and you can tell their type at once, but others may be very difficult to define. Even the people themselves have trouble in finding out their own type, which is very often due to the fact that they are distorted types. This is not a very frequent occurrence, but it does happen in cases where someone would naturally have become a feeling type or an intuitive, but was forced by the environment to develop another function. Suppose a boy is born as a feeling type in an intellectually ambitious family. His whole surroundings will exert pressure upon him to become an intellectual, and his original possibility as a feeling type will be thwarted or despised. Usually, in such a case, he is unable to become a thinking type — that would be a step too far — but he might well develop sensation or intuition, one of the auxiliary functions, so as to be relatively better adapted to his surroundings, for his main function is simply "out" in the milieu in which he grows up.

Distorted types have advantages and disadvantages. The disadvantage is that from the very beginning they cannot quite develop their main disposition, which therefore remains a bit below the mark they would have reached had they developed in the one-sided way. On the other hand, they have been forced ahead of time into doing something which in the second half of life they would have had to do anyhow. In analysis, one can very often help people switch back to the original type, and they are then able to pick up some other function very quickly and reach a developed stage, for the original disposition is a help in that direction. They are like a fish which now can return happily to its water.

What determines the original basic disposition is not known. Jung, in a brief description at the end of *Psychological Types,* says that it has probably a biological basis. He points out, for instance, the two ways in which an animal species adapts to reality: either by propagating tremendously with a very small defense mechanism, for example in fleas and lice or rabbits; or by building up the defense mechanisms tremendously, as in hedgehogs or elephants, among which propagation is reduced to a relatively small extent. Thus already in nature there are two possibilities for dealing with outer reality: either you defend yourself against it, keeping it off while building up your own life by putting up a defense against the overwhelming reality, or you pour yourself, so to speak, into it and overcome or conquer it in that way—which also corresponds with the sex and power drives. The basis is one of these two. That would be an introverted and an extraverted functioning in the biological realm.

When Jung brought out his book on types, not much had been published on animal behavior, but if you study modern books you will see that among the animals, in most patterns of behavior, there is a *mixtum compositum* of inner and outer factors. Thus some aspects of animal behavior come more from within, that is, come into play without any outer stimulus, while other animal behavior depends more on outer stimuli. It is known that the higher anthropoid apes are incapable of performing the sexual act unless they have observed another ape and learned in that way, whereas with other animals, without ever having seen animals of their species mating, the inner urge is sufficient. But if in a zoo the higher apes are brought up without ever seeing a companion mate, they remain ignorant in this way, just as a human being does. Therefore it is obvious that the behavior of an animal in part depends on an outer factor and in part is conditioned by an inborn disposition and that there is a mutual interaction between inside and outside factors.

There is also sometimes an uncertainty in animal behavior. Experiments have been made by incubating storks' eggs, allowing the eggs no contact with the social group. When birds produced from such eggs are released at the time they should fly to North Africa, those bred of eggs whose group fly over Yugoslavia will fly over that country, and those produced from eggs of birds that fly over Spain will fly over Spain to Africa — which proves that they rely completely on the inner inborn disposition which tells them how to reach Africa. But if a stork bred from the Yugoslav group is put with the birds that fly over Spain, the bird will fly with them and not follow its inborn disposition. This shows the two possibilities very clearly: being influenced by outer factors, by the social influence from outside, or simply following the inborn disposition.

Another big question always is whether when an animal performing the sexual act, or fighting or feeding, is just following an urge or acting like an engine, or does it have something like an inner representation? Adolf Portmann gives a special example which shows that while an animal is acting instinctively, it can have inner representations of what it does. *Ideas* and *representations* are dangerous words that zoologists try to avoid, but they do admit that in the so-called mind of an animal are inner pictures. Experiments have been made with a lonely bird in a cage which had no opportunity to put into practice its natural instinct to fight. Another bird of the same variety was introduced into the cage, and the two enjoyed a big fight. This is vitally important for a male animal; it contributes to his well-being if he can fight with another male of his species. After a while the enemy was removed from the cage, but much later the bird repeated the whole fight with an imaginary bird in a corner of the cage, obviously having an image of the other bird in its so-called mind. There is an analogy—though human words are dangerous, and Portmann stammers when he gives this example—but we can certainly say that there is a preform of what we would call an inner representation—a memory picture. It is just as one does oneself sometimes: one has a fight with someone and then on the way home one goes over the whole thing with this person in one's mind.

Another difficulty in defining one's own or other people's type is that if people have already reached the stage of being bored with their main function, they very often assure you with absolute sincerity that they belong to the type opposite what they really are. The extravert swears that he is deeply introverted, and vice versa. This comes from the fact that the inferior function subjectively feels itself to be the real one. It considers itself the more important or genuine attitude, so a thinking type, because he knows that everything in his life matters from the feeling aspect, will assure you that he is a feeling type. Therefore, when one is trying to find one's type, one must never ask, "What matters to me most?" but rather "What do I habitually do most?" An extravert can be constantly extraverting but will assure you, and will mean it, that he is deeply introverted and only concerned with the inner world. That is not a deception, it is how he feels, for he knows that although it may be for only a minute a day, in that minute in which he introverts he is close to himself; there he is real.

Also in the realm of the inferior function one is over-whelmed, one is unhappy, one has one's great problem, one is constantly impressed by things, and therefore, in a way, the intensity of life is very often much greater in the realm of the inferior function, especially if the superior function is already worn out, so that naturally one tends to define one's own type wrongly. Practically, it is more helpful when one wants to determine type to ask what is the greatest cross for the person, where is his greatest suffering, where does he feel that he always knocks his head against obstacles and suffers hell? That generally points to the inferior function. Many people, more-over, develop two superior functions so well that it is very difficult to say whether the person is a thinking-intuitive or an intuitive with good thinking, for the two seem to be almost equally good. Sometimes sensation and feeling are so well de-veloped in an individual that you would have difficulty in as-certaining which is the first, but does the intuitive-thinking person suffer more from knocking his head against sensation facts or from feeling problems? Here you can decide which is the first, with the other a well-developed second function.

I presuppose here that Jung's schema of the types is known, in which the two rational functions, thinking and feeling, are opposite each other, and in the same way intuition and sensa-tion, as shown in the diagram on page 35.

Very often someone will say naively that he is a thinking type and is now going to develop his feeling—what an illusion! If you are a thinking type, you can first either go to sensation or intuition; that is your choice, naturally influenced by dis-position. Then you move to the opposite of the two secondary

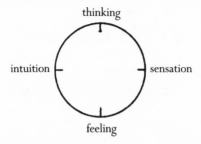

functions and lastly to the inferior one, but you cannot cross directly to the opposite function. The reason is very simple and is that they exclude each other completely; they are incompatible. Take the example of a staff officer who has to plan the evacuation of a town's population in the best possible way under given conditions. Unfortunately his own wife and children are in the same town. If he gives in to his feelings, he won't develop a good rational plan. He must simply obliterate them from his mind and tell himself that it is now his job to plan the evacuation as well as he can, and he will think of his own feelings as sentimentality—that is, he will depreciate them in order to free himself. Or else he will make a double decision in which all the others have to go one way and his family another, which is unfair; but it is a fact that in certain situations in life, feeling and thinking are quite incompatible and only one of the two can operate. One cannot make a straight jump from one to the other, but can assimilate thinking with sensation, or have them functioning relatively together very easily, and one can combine the other two very easily, so that in the jump from one auxiliary function to the other you will not suffer as much as if you had to jump to the opposite function, because when one has to move from intuition to sensation, one can still use one's old thinking as a judge, and when intuition and sensation fight like mad, one can detach from that fight by thinking.

Let us take as a practical example a thinking type who primarily couples his thinking with intuition. The philosopher Nietzsche is such a case. One is quite uncertain as to whether he had very good thinking or very good intuition; the latter is the greater in his case, but the two are very well combined and move together. Kant would also be rather on the thinking-intuition side. Such a philosopher, if he wants to enlarge his field of awareness, could bring in facts. Generally a philosopher, after in youth having evolved (the introvert draws it all from within) a certain concept of his ideas, will then have the need to check his theoretical and intuitive ideas with facts. There he will get into a certain tension between his intuition and the side with which he looks at facts, because the two do not move together either, but he will not be in complete hell, because, if the tension gets too bad, he can always detach from the situation and decide by his thinking; only when it comes to the opposite function has he to give up. The root of his former ego attitude toward life is excluded. Thus you cannot jump directly, but if you must make the leap, it is helpful if you have already developed the two auxiliaries, which do not fight so much within you, before you have to sacrifice the main function. Naturally, all your life you are knocked from one to the other, but although you can be knocked for momentary functioning into another field, that is not what is meant by assimilating or developing another function.

If I analyze a thinking type, I never push him into feeling at once; I see that the other functions are assimilated first. It is a mistake to forget the intermediary stage, for that does not work. Take, for instance, a thinking type who falls madly in love with a completely inappropriate person because of his inferior feeling. If he has already developed sensation, which implies a certain sense of reality and a certain amount of intuition—the capacity to smell a rat—then he will not fall into complete nonsense. But if he is a one-sided thinking type and he falls in love with an inappropriate person and has no sense of reality and no intuition, then there will happen what is so beautifully depicted in the film *The Blue Angel,* where the professor becomes a circus clown in the service of a vamp, because there have been no intermediary fields where he could catch himself—he is just knocked over by his inferior function. But if his analyst could see to it that, while he has not yet much feeling, at least he has developed a certain sense of reality, then he can overcome the difficulty with that intermediary function. I think that is something to keep in mind if one is an analyst—that one can never jump to the inferior function. Of course life does it, for life does not care! But the analytical process should not go that way and normally does not do so, if one follows the intimations given in dreams; for one sees that the tendency of the process is that the development should be in a serpentine movement, the normal way in which the unconscious tries to get up the inferior function.

Another difficulty of the early stages, when one is develop-

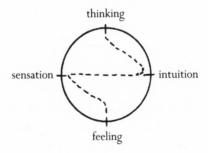

thinking

sensation   intuition

feeling

ing one's main function but not yet touching the problem of the inferior function, consists in the tendency in families to distribute the functions: one member is the family introvert and another becomes the family's practical engineer and a third the family's seer and prophet and so on, and the others happily give up because one member can do it so much better, so why bother if you are beaten from the start! This sets up wonderfully vital groups which function well and only get into trouble when they fall apart. There is a very strong tendency in most families, and also in other groups, to solve the function problem by distributing the functions and relying on the good function of the other. In marriage, as Jung pointed out, one tends to marry the opposite type, and then again one is, or so one thinks for the moment, freed from the disagreeable task of confronting one's inferior function. That is one of the great blessings and a source of happiness in the early stages of a marriage, when suddenly the whole weight of one's inferior function is gone and one lives in a lovely blessed oneness with the other and every problem is solved! It is only if one of the partners dies, or the need arises in one of them to develop the inferior function instead of just leaving those sections of life to the other, that the trouble starts. But very often in the early stages of the marriage this symbiotic solution is chosen and people are not aware of what they are doing.

The same happens again in the choice of analysts. Frequently people choose the opposite type as analyst. For instance, the feeling type cannot think and so admires a person who can think, and so he looks for an analyst with a strong thinking function. But that is not to be recommended, because if you are always with someone who knows it all so well, you just get discouraged and give up completely and just leave all the thinking to the other. You feel very happy because now thinking is taken care of, but this is no good. Jung, for instance, always liked to send people with the same blind spots to each other, because, he said, if two idiots sit together and neither can think, then they will get into such trouble that at least one of them will begin to think! It doesn't matter whether it is the analyst first or the patient! It would, of course, be the same with the other functions; the person just sits and hopes that the other will do it. Then something might happen! If one goes to the opposite type, this is something to be borne in mind, and the analyst, who should be the more responsible, should be especially careful not to display his superior function too much. He must then, against his real feeling, constantly pretend that he does not know, or feels incapable, or has no idea, and so on. He has to give up his superior function in order not to paralyze the first shy attempts his analysand might make in this field by discouraging them through his superiority. The same holds for an intuitive. The intuitive generally gets into trouble over his monetary affairs so completely that if he finds a partner who takes that in hand and does the budgeting of the income and the filling out of income tax forms for him, he will never become the hero who says: "No, I cannot do it, so I must learn, please leave it to me!" He will sigh with relief and throw it all onto the sensation type's desk and feel very happy, and then he will never get any contact with reality. You see this kind of partnership in analysis and in family life and also in primitive tribal life, where the medicine man is usually the introvert-seer of the intuitive type, who takes care of relationship with the future and the germinating of ideas and possibilities. Then there is the sensation type, who is the good and efficient hunter or scout, while the chiefs, belonging to the feeling and rational types, keep order with either the feeling or thinking function. Then nobody else needs to develop anything; people just rely on those tribal main functions of consciousness while they remain in blissful unconsciousness.

It also happens that people push off the inferior functions onto servants. In countries where there are still servants, that is done with the greatest joy! The servant is a fitting symbol for the inferior function, and naturally people tend to hire someone who can do the things they cannot and who are willing to do the things they wish to get rid of, and they will choose the servant with that view in mind. Secretaries also can perform the same function, and in this way you can shelve the problem of developing the retarded functions; but then you have other troubles, for the whole thing remains in projection, and the servant behaves to the employer as the inferior function behaves to the superior function: he apparently submits, but secretly he tyrannizes you! People who cannot cook or even sew on a button are tyrannized by a maid, who, by virtue of the fact that she can do these things, decides everything. She cannot be gotten rid of because the employers would be lost without her, thus they are tyrannized from the outside just as they would be from their own inner inferior function. Many so-called social problems are really the projected problem of the inferior function, which frequently is represented in dreams under the guise of people from the simple layers of the population, or the laborers. The unconscious uses them as a simile, to show that the inferior function has remained on that level; but people do not understand this and project, for they despise and fear the laborers at the same time. You can say that anyone who is not at ease and acquainted with his own inferior function is socially maladapted. He cannot get on with the simple people and will tend to have trouble or oppress them, because secretly he fears them. Naturally, in social setups where there are racial minorities, there is an even greater tendency on the part of the majority to project the inferior function. Then there even arises the beautiful symbolic fact that the inferior function is, so to speak, of another race, really very different from oneself; it feels strange and different from what one is, so that a person of another racial background is an appropriate hook on which to hang the projection, and that troubles social relations to a great extent. Therefore, developing one's inferior function is, in a way, also a social obligation. Until one has done this and dealt with one's inferior function, one will tend toward one-sided and asocial behavior because that is the original form. Take the four castes of India, for instance: you just distribute certain functions and then keep out of trouble yourself and keep your one-sidedness.

To the general outlines of the inferior function also belongs the fact that the inferior function is generally slow in contrast to the superior function. Jung calls it infantile and tyrannical. This slowness is in fact one of the great troubles of the inferior function, which is one reason why people hate to start work on it, for the reaction of the superior function comes out quickly and well adapted while many people have no idea where their inferior function really is. For instance, thinking types have no idea whether they have feeling or what kind of feeling it is. They have to sit for half an hour and meditate as to whether they have any feeling about something, and if so what it is. If you ask a thinking type what he feels, he generally either replies with a thought or gives a quick conventional reaction, and if you then insist on knowing what he really feels, he does not know, and pulling it up from his belly, so to speak, can take half an hour. Or if an intuitive fills out a tax form, he needs a week where other people would take a day. He simply cannot do it, or if he does it accurately, he takes forever. I know an introverted intuitive woman—to go with her to choose a blouse! Never again! It takes an eternity, until the whole shop is mad! But it cannot be speeded up, and it does not help to get impatient. It is terrible, and naturally that is so discouraging about developing the inferior function, because one has not the time.

Sometimes people have two very highly developed functions and both the others are very undeveloped. That happens where a very strong, impulsive temperament gets the development of the main function going very much. You can say that that is the disadvantage of efficiency. Lazy people never have such strongly divided functions as efficient people, so lazy people have their points — for themselves! They never overdo the one-sidedness, the efficiency of the main function, and then naturally the other functions are not quite as far down. There is also another point which one must never forget: this theory of functions does not say anything about the qualitative level. For instance, one sensation type may not be a particularly efficient or practical engineer, while another sensation type might be very highly differentiated. The total qualitative level of the personality can be very different, and there are many thinking types who do not become Einsteins, though thinking is their main function. So if we say this is such-and-such a type, it refers only to the habitual functioning and not to its quality.

The quality level seems to be a given thing. There is an old saying that you can't make a silk purse out of a sow's ear, but on the other hand, it is very dangerous to judge practically from the beginning by saying that this chap will never go very far, or will not develop very much. Sometimes quite surprising things occur. It is very difficult to judge the level practically, but I would say there is such a thing as a level which cannot be transcended and which is more or less inborn.

Sometimes by an analytical treatment you can improve the

general level unexpectedly. But then you can never prove scientifically that you have done so. You can just as well say that that level was there and was only hampered in getting out. You cannot solve the question. By the outcome you can say that analysis can develop the qualitative level, or that it was there and the process has only removed the obstacle.

Today we make too much of I.Q. tests. I would say that there is also a "feeling I.Q." The French have an expression which speaks of the *intelligence du coeur* — the intelligence of the heart. There are people who cannot think but who have a tremendous intelligence of the heart and so in general are considered highly intelligent, but their intelligence dwells in the heart, so to speak. Women very often have this intelligence of the heart and put a very intelligent husband right in their pocket with it. The same goes for intuition and sensation. They all can be highly intelligent, or rather dumb! That is why we prefer to speak of the differentiation of functions, rather than of the I.Q. of a person.

GENERAL FEATURES OF THE INFERIOR FUNCTION

There are some general qualities which characterize the inferior function, whatever it is. One of them is that the inferior function is not adapted to society. One such aspect is, for instance, its slowness. Assimilating it, and even letting the inferior function come up, takes a great amount of time. If a feeling type wants to think, he will sit eight hours to write two pages — if as much as that. If a thinking type wants to realize his feeling, he has to meditate for hours until he feels what he feels, for he does not even know what he feels, but has some strange kind of nervous sympathetic reactions in the lower part of his body and has to meditate upon these a long time till they come up as a kind of feeling. If you ask a thinking type what he feels, generally he will shoot a lot of conventional answers at you, but when you ask him what he *really* feels, he is absolutely stunned and says he does not know! If you leave him stewing for a long time, he will slowly realize what he really feels. The same is true for sensation when it is the inferior function, which is why, when intuitives begin to work on their inferior sensation, they get tremendously stiff and overly pedantic, and they have to be extraordinarily accurate in a terribly slow way. This cannot be helped; it is a stage which cannot be skipped. If people just lose patience again and say to hell with it, that they have sat the whole day and that's the result, it means they give up and that is hopeless, for it simply means that they cut the fourth function out and replace it by some kind of artificial mechanism—by a crutch. The process cannot be speeded up, or only to a certain extent, but never to the speed of the superior function, and for very good reasons, because if you think of the turning point of life and the problems of aging and of turning within, then this slowing down of the whole life process by bringing up the inferior function is just the thing which is needed. So the slowness should not be treated with impatience and with trying to educate "the damned inferior function"; one should rather really accept the fact that in this realm one has to waste time, and that is just the value of it, because that gives the unconscious a chance to come in.

Another typical aspect of all inferior functions, which is also connected with its unadaptedness and primitiveness, is its touchiness and tyranny. Most people, when the question of their inferior function is in any way touched upon, become terribly childish and touchy; they can't stand the slightest criticism but always feel attacked, for they are uncertain of themselves and, with that, naturally they tyrannize everybody around them; everybody has to walk carefully. If you want to say something about another person's inferior function, it is like walking on eggs, for people just cannot stand any criticism there, and a *rîte d'entrée* is required, waiting for the right moment for a peaceful atmosphere, and then carefully, with a long introductory speech, one might get over some slight criticism about the inferior function. But if you shoot any criticism at people, they will get absolutely bewildered and emotional, and the situation is ruined. I learned this for the first time with absolute amazement many, many years ago when I was studying. A fellow student showed me a paper she had written. She was a feeling type, and the paper was very good, but in a minor passage, where she switched from one theme to another, it seemed to me that there was a hiatus in the connection of thought. What she said was quite right, but in between the two passages, for a thinking type the logical transition was lacking, though for me it was very easy to see. So I said to her that I thought it was an excellent paper but that on one page she might make a better transition, as there was a jump from one theme to another, and if one didn't think well oneself, one did not get the connection at once. She got absolutely emotional and said, "Oh, well, then it's all ruined, I shall just burn it," and she took it out of my hand, saying, "I know it's junk, I shall burn it up!" I pulled it out of her hand and said, "For God's sake, don't burn it up!" "Oh, well," she said, "I knew you thought it would be junk," and she went on and on. When the storm was over I was able to get in a word and said, "You need not even retype it; you only need to write in one little sentence to make the transition—just one sentence between these two paragraphs." The storm started all over again, and I gave up! I saw her later, and she told me that the night after that she dreamed that her house burned down and, typically, the fire started in the roof. I thought, "My God, these feeling types!" For her, writing the paper had been such an achievement, bringing out some thoughts, and it had been just at the limit of what she could do, and then she couldn't even stand that little bit—it wasn't even criticism—but even the idea that it could be improved a bit. That's an extreme case of what always happens with the inferior function with most people. They tyrannize their surroundings by being touchy, for all touchiness is a form of secret tyranny. Sensitive people are just tyrannical people—everybody else has to adapt to them instead of their trying to adapt to the others. But people who are well adapted still generally have a kind of childish, touchy spot where one cannot talk to them reasonably and one has to adopt "bush manners," as if one were dealing with tigers and elephants.

The example concerning the paper written by a feeling type illustrates another general feature, namely a tremendous charge of emotion, which is generally connected with the manifestation of the inferior function. As soon as you get into this realm, people easily become emotional. Not only does this have the disadvantage which the above example illustrated, but there is also a very positive aspect, namely that in the realm of the inferior function there is a great concentration of life, so that as soon as the superior function is worn out—begins to rattle and lose oil like an old car—if people succeed in turning to their inferior function, they will rediscover a new potential of life. Everything in the realm of the inferior function becomes exciting, dramatic, full of positive and negative possibilities. There is great charge and the world is, as it were, rediscovered through the inferior function. But the disadvantage is that outside there is this unadapted aspect. That is why in the fairy tales which I mentioned before, the fool, the third son of the group of four royal people, is the one who can find the water of life, or the great treasure, for the inferior function brings a renewal of life, if one allows it to come up in its own realm. Many people discover relatively soon in life that the realm of their inferior function is where they are emotional, touchy, and unadapted, and they therefore acquire the habit of covering up this part of their personality with a surrogate, pseudo reaction. For instance, let us say a thinking type cannot express his feelings normally and in the appropriate manner at the right time. It can happen that he cries when he hears that a friend's husband has died, but when he meets the widow, not a word of sympathy will come out. Such a person, not only looks very cold but does not feel anything! He had all the feeling before, when at home, but now, in the appropriate situation, he cannot pull it out at the right moment. That's why, for example, thinking types are very often looked on by other people as having no feelings, which is absolutely not true. It is not that they have no feelings but that they cannot express them at the appropriate moment. They have the feeling somehow and somewhere when it pleases the feeling, but not just when they ought to produce it. It is a great error also to think that feeling types cannot think. They think very well, and very often have deep, good, and genuine thoughts, unconventional thoughts, but the thoughts come and go as they like. For instance, it is very difficult for a feeling type to pull up his right kind of thinking during an exam. There he ought to think, but thinking just goes! As soon as he is at home, he can think again, but his thinking does not comply, is not amiable enough to come up at the right time, which makes the feeling type look as though he were utterly stupid. He is looked upon by society as being stupid because he cannot produce his thinking at will.

So a minimum adaptation of the inferior function is required. I, for instance, being a thinking type, could not just go to a funeral with my hands in my pockets, whistling, and saying: "Oh, I don't care, I just don't feel anything just now! I'm sorry, I'll try again at home when I feel like it!" That excuse would not be accepted. Life has no mercy with the inferiority of the inferior function, which is why people produce a pseudo covering-up reaction. Because it is not their real reaction, they simply borrow a general form from the collective. That is why a feeling type, when pressed for thinking reactions, loves to serve up a lot of commonplace remarks or thoughts, which are not his real thoughts, but because he has to think quickly, and the real thought is not yet up to the level at which it could be expressed, he just makes a few commonplace remarks. It is very usual for feeling types to use material they have learned by heart, because something must be produced and the real thought is not yet there. The same is true for thinking types, who get into the habit of producing a kind of amiable, conventional feeling. They send flowers, bring chocolates, or use some very ordinary expression of feeling. For example, I have drawn up a type of letter of condolence with certain phrases which have struck me as being very nice and touching, and every time I write such a letter, I make a cocktail from those phrases. If I tried to express my real feelings, I would stick at such a letter for three days! The same applies to intuitives with their inferior sensation, for they simply have the habitual technical ways of dealing with it, borrowing help from the collective. One must therefore not be deceived by these pseudo adaptation reactions, but always look to see where the inferior function comes up in its own way, and not be deceived and think that someone has quite good thinking or feeling. You can always observe these covering-up reactions by the fact that they are impersonal and banal, and very collective stuff.

Another general problem connected with the inferior function is what one might call the hold which the superior function has on the inferior. When someone tries to meet his inferior function and has several times experienced emotional shock or pain in meeting real reactions, then the superior function at once says: "Ah, that is something, now we must organize that," and then the superior function, like an eagle seizing a mouse, tries to get hold of the inferior function and bring it over into the realm of the main function. For example, I know a natural scientist, a very successful introverted thinking type. Somewhere in his fifties he became very bored with his professional work and began roaming about looking for other possibilities. His wife and family could have told him a lot about his inferior feeling, a field right under his nose where he could have started some experiments! He had several dreams of collecting beautiful, rare mountain flowers, which clearly showed what the unconscious was now aiming at. He had the typical inferior feeling of the thinking type, namely rare and very special feeling—like flowers in the mountains, for the flowers there have a much more intense color than those in the plains, which is also typical for the inferior feeling of a thinking type. He thought that was a good idea for a hobby and so made friends with a botanist and went for days and all through his holidays collecting mountain flowers, and any attempts made by other people at telling him that he could do something about his feeling always met with the reply that he had given up his main function and was doing something with his other side, that he was studying mountain flowers! Thus (a) he got stuck in the concretistic interpretation instead of taking the thing symbolically, and (b) he again made a sort of science of it, for he was concerned with knowledge of those flowers, so the main function was at it again and the inferior function once more was frustrated.

To take an irrational type: there is the intuitive who gets into a situation where he should use his inferior sensation. He becomes attracted by the idea of stone-cutting, or working with clay, or something of the kind, the sort of thing which very often helps inferior sensation to come up in an intuitive, for by such means he may get in touch with some kind of concrete material, with matter. Then he will perhaps model something in clay, say a very helpless-looking, childish statue of an animal, or something of the kind, and then he experiences something improving in himself, but immediately—like an eagle—intuition jumps onto it and says that "This is it, that's what should be introduced into all the schools. . . ." And away he goes into his intuition again, into all the possibilities of clay modeling and what it could contribute to the education of humanity and what it would include, for from there one would have the key for the experience of the Godhead. You can see how the intuitive always brings in the whole world— everything is brought in, but the one thing that is not considered is the modeling of another figure! Just not that! The main function is on top again, having had this quickening and vivifying touch with the earth, off it goes, up into the air again.

The same thing happens with the feeling type who, when cornered by absolute necessity, sometimes produces a few thoughts, but then he quickly escapes this hot bath and never returns to it. But he has a lot of feeling judgment about what thinking is like and the use it has and so on, a number of evaluations instead of continuing his attempt to think. At once one skips out of it again, and then the superior function tries to get hold of the inferior function and to organize it in some way.

In fact it is absolutely impossible to pull up the fourth, inferior function, like a fisherman pulling up a fish with his rod, and all such attempts as, for instance, speeding it up or educating it so that it *should* come up at the right moment prove failures. One can try to force it to function in an exam, or in a situation in life, but this succeeds only to a certain extent and only by bringing in conventional, borrowed material. Then you can have a species of pseudo-adaptation with the three functions, but with the fourth function you cannot. It insists on remaining below because it is contaminated with the whole remainder of the unconscious and remains in that condition. Trying to fish up your inferior function would be like trying to bring up the whole of the collective unconscious, which is something you just cannot do. The fish will be too big for your rod, and if you catch it, what do you do? Do you cut it off again? If so, you regress! If you don't give in, well, there is only one alternative—your fish will pull you into the water! So at this moment comes the great conflict, which means for the thinking type, for instance, the famous *sacrificium intellectus*—in religious language—or, for the feeling type, the *sacrificium* of his feeling, and having, as it were, the humility to go down with all your three other functions onto that lower level. This then produces a stage between the two layers, about at the level where everything is neither thinking nor feeling nor sensation nor intuition. Something new comes up, namely a completely different and new attitude toward life, in which you use all and none of your functions all the time.

Really getting in touch with the inferior function is something like an inner breakdown at a certain crucial point of one's life, but it has the advantage that afterward some functions no longer tyrannize the ego nucleus, but are only used by it. If someone has really gone through this transformation, then he can sometimes think, if that is the appropriate reaction, or let intuition or sensation come into operation; but there is no longer any automatic possession by these functions. The ego can take one function up and put it down, like taking up a pencil or an eraser, according to the situation, but the ego dwells, as it were, in the awareness of its own reality outside the functional system. This breaking away from the system of the functions is achieved through the meeting with the inferior function, through which a shock is conveyed to the whole personality. One can therefore say that the inferior function is really the bridge to the experience of all the deeper layers of the unconscious. Going and staying with it, not just taking a quick hot bath in it and getting out as soon as possible, but staying in it for a long time, effects a radical change in the whole setup of the personality. That is why Jung again and again quotes an old saying of a legendary alchemist and author, Maria Prophetissa, which, translated into English, runs: "One becomes two, two becomes three, and out of the third comes the fourth as the one." One becomes two, that is, you first assimilate your main function, then the first auxiliary. This means that first you have one function and then two, and after that you assimilate a third, and thus two becomes three. But the next step does not consist of just adding another unit— going on counting one, two, three, and then adding another unit, which would make four—but now a very complicated process begins: namely, "out of the third comes the fourth as the one," for out of the third you move back toward the one, so that the *one* comes back as the fourth. Jung once told me, in a private conversation, that there is no fourth in the upper layer, but that it is just as shown in the diagram on page 53.

Field of naive ego consciousness
with three functions

Middle field where the ego-Self
relationship no longer functions
autonomously but is only instrumental

Preconscious totality with
preformed four functions

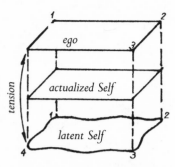

You can illustrate it in the following way: there are a mouse, a cat, a dog, and a lion. The first three animals you can get to make friends with you if you treat them well, but then comes the lion. It refuses to be added as the fourth but will eat up the others, so in the end there is only one animal left. That is what the inferior function does: when *it* comes up, it eats up all the rest of the personality, and that is why the fourth becomes the *one,* for it is no longer the fourth, there is only the one left—a total psychic life phenomenon, and no longer a function! Naturally that is a simile and just gives a kind of illustration.

There is another possibility, which is that the ego does not suffer the *sacrificium* of the main function as a sacrifice but childishly drops into the inferior function, but then there is no merit in the whole process, for then people suddenly give up their adaptedness and identify with the unadapted childish part of themselves, which is the inferior function. They try to force their surroundings to accept it, but that is not sacrificing the main function: just the opposite, it is letting the lion eat up the other three animals, which means you become childish and then you have the whole resistance in the outer world. Or, in the case of an extravert, you fade out of life and become a lonely fool. I remember, for instance, the case of an extraverted intuitive who, after a sudden breakdown in the middle of life, started to use his mystic, introverted sensation in painting. He retired from life and produced the most amazing, childish kind of lonely pictures and anonymously disappeared into this occupation. Nothing came of it because he avoided the crash of the transition; he simply threw one part away and snapped over into the other. It makes all the difference whether I just fall into my inferior function involuntarily or if I go through the whole process of suffering and then sacrifice the dominating aspect of the superior function. In the case of a sacrifice, the ego personality remains unharmed—it detaches from the functions and, in a way, can afterward use them as an instrument and put them aside again. But if you snap into the inferior function, then the former ego goes with it. It becomes identical with the inferior childish side, begins to be completely unadapted, and then, naturally, such people normally build up some kind of persecution complex because everyone is so hostile to them. They never understand why everything goes wrong, but think it must be somebody else's fault somewhere—either the Jesuits or the Communists! That is because they fell down into the fourth instead of going through the process described by Maria Prophetissa—one becomes two, two becomes three, and out of the third comes the fourth as the one.

There is a new kind of personality who has detached his ego awareness or his ego consciousness from identifying with all four functions. The nearest possible example, and a very convincing one, is found in some descriptions of the behavior of Zen Buddhist masters, where it is said that the door of the inner house is closed, but the master meets everybody and every situation and everything in the usual manner. He continues in everyday life, right in it, absolutely participating in it in a normal way: if people come to be taught, he will teach them with feeling; if a difficult problem is put before him, he can think about it; if it is the moment to eat, he will eat, and if it is the moment to sleep, he will sleep. So he uses his sensation function in the right way, and when it is a question of seeing in a flash of intuition through the other person or the situation, he will do that, so that his intuition functions. However, he will not be inwardly identical with any of these situations, he will not be tied to one of them any longer, and he will also not be tied, not only to the situation, but to his own ego functions meeting the situation. He will have lost a certain kind of childish eagerness to meet things. If you present people who are still identical with their thinking with a thinking problem, they go right into it, which is even necessary, because if they do not learn to be right in it, they will never learn to think properly and appropriately. But afterward, if you present them with a thinking problem, they remain inwardly outside it. Though they apply their thinking to the problem, they can stop thinking from one minute to another without having to continue it. Most people, when they have set themselves a problem, cannot stop thinking about it, which shows that they are possessed by their train of thought. For example, there is the absent-minded professor who even at luncheon is still thinking over his mathematical formula; he cannot stop, which shows that thinking has him. It is difficult to bring examples because there are very few people who have reached that stage, but there are very good descriptions of being detached from one's own conscious functions in certain Zen Buddhist examples.

Naturally there are also differences. We have no monastic discipline, but have to develop our inferior function within everyday life. But I think that our way of trying to approach the problem of the inferior function also imposes some kind of discipline on all individuals, which has an analogy in the monastic life, not only in the East but also in the West: for instance, remaining with a difficulty for a long time, giving up other occupations in order to have enough time and energy for this main problem, practicing a kind of asceticism. But the monastic life, whether in the East or in the West, is a collectively organized affair. You have to get up at a certain time, do certain work, obey the abbot, and so on, in contrast to which the discipline that comes upon an individual within the process of individuation is imposed purely from within. There are no outer rules, and therefore the development is much more individual. That means that if you let it happen spontaneously instead of forcing people from outside into organized discipline, then you will see that the discipline is completely different from person to person.

For a while I analyzed two men who were friends; one was an introverted thinking type and the other an extraverted feeling type. The extravert's discipline was very severe, for even if he drank a glass of wine, or stayed at a dinner party half an hour too long, he had the most awful dreams. Sometimes both would receive invitations, and the introvert would say that he had no time, but promptly dreamed that he had to go to the party, while his friend, who had received the same invitation, the same night had a dream (naturally he had already decided on his costume and knew which lady he would invite to come with him) telling him he should not go! No party, stay at home! It was really amusing to see how it was just as great an agony for the introvert to go to a party as it was sad for the other poor chap to stay away! Sometimes they would exchange notes and say, "Isn't it really nasty! Now I would like to go and may not, and you hate going but your dreams say to go!" So there is a kind of discipline, but it is invisible and very precisely adjusted. That is the advantage of our way of dealing with the problem, because you get your very appropriate private monastic discipline or military service—invisible to the outer world, but very disagreeable.

That is why there are a great many people who from time to time experience the problem of the inferior function as one of getting into the hot bath and then snapping out of it again. Then they more or less go on with their three functions, constantly slightly uncomfortable on account of the nonintegrated fourth. When that gets too bad they dive in a bit, but as soon as they feel better, they get out again, and, on principle, they remain in their trinitarian world, where the fourth is the devil who remains in a corner of their life. Now, we saw how much this has to do with even the image of God being trinitarian or quaternary because, in my experience, people who stick in this kind of phase are the people who never quite understand what Jung means by the whole problem of the fourth, and they never quite understand what individuation really means. They remain, so to speak, with little visits to the other land—in the conventional former world of identifying with one's own consciousness. Many, many people, even those who have undergone a Jungian analysis, do not get further than those kinds of visits into the fourth realm and hopping out of it again and then talking about it to others—not really trying to stay in it, because that is hellishly difficult to achieve.

As long as you do not really get into this stage there remains, so to speak, what I call the devil in the corner and the difficulty of that is that, personally spoken, this is only the personal devil, the personal inferiority of an individual, but with it really also comes in the whole collective evil as well. That means that the little open door of each individual's inferior function is what contributes to the sum of the big collective evil in the world. You could, for instance, observe that very easily in Germany when the devil slowly took over the situation in the Nazi movement. Every German I knew at that time who fell for Nazism did so on account of his inferior function. The feeling type got caught by the stupid arguments of the party doctrine. The intuitive type got caught by his dependence on money—he could not give up his job and did not see how he could deal with the money problem, so he had to stay in it in spite of the fact that he did not agree. And so on. The inferior function was in each personal realm the door where some of the collective evil could accumulate. Or, one could say that each one who had not worked on his inferior function contributed to this general disaster—in a small way—but the sum of millions of inferior functions constitutes an enormous devil! Propaganda against the Jews was very cleverly made up in that respect. For example, the Jews were insulted as being destructive intellectuals, which completely convinced all the feeling types—a projection of their inferior thinking. Or they were accused of being reckless moneymakers, and that completely convinced the intuitive, for they represented his inferior sensation and now one knew where the devil was, and so on. Thus, propaganda used the ordinary suspicions which people usually had against others on account of their inferior function. So one can say that behind each individual the fourth function is not identical with the collective principle of evil, but is just a little deficiency; yet the sum of these is really responsible for a tremendous amount of trouble.

In that way the process of individuation is an ethical problem, and someone without any morality gets stuck right at the beginning and gets nowhere, if that cannot be changed. But the word *perfection* is not appropriate; that is a Christian ideal which does not quite coincide with our experience of the process of individuation. Jung stresses that the process seems to tend not toward perfection but toward completeness. This means that you have to come down, and that means a relative lowering of the level of the personality so that this lower level may not remain quite as dark as it was before. If you are in the middle, the one side is not as dark and the other not quite as bright, and there is more a tendency to constitute a kind of completeness which is neither too light nor too dark. But one has to sacrifice a certain amount of striving for perfection in order to avoid building up too black a counterposition.

So there is a social obligation to work on one's fourth function because it makes one a less dangerous individual, and the sum of dangerously split individuals is what gives rise to wars and social explosions. Propaganda always tries to arouse this.

Someone practicing a low type of propaganda would know that it is not by reasonable talk that one gets the masses, but by arousing emotion, and emotion can be aroused in everyone at the same time if you bring up the inferior function, because that is the emotional function. Therefore, if you speak to intellectuals, you must arouse primitive feelings! For instance, if you speak to university professors, you must not use scientific language because in that field their minds are clear and they will see through all the snares in your speech if you want to get a lie across, but if you substantiate your lie with a lot of feeling and emotion—since university professors will on the average have inferior feeling—they will fall for that at once. Hitler had the art of doing this. If you read the records of his speeches, you will see that he talked quite differently to the different groups which he addressed, and he knew very well how to wake up the inferior function. A man who had been present at several of his speeches told me that Hitler did it through his intuition, or his own feeling into the situation. At times, Hitler would, at first, be quite uncertain. He would try out his themes like a pianist, mentioning a little of this and a little of that, and he would be pale and nervous, and his SS men would get all worked up because the Führer did not seem to be in form. But he was just trying out the ground, and then he would notice that if he brought up some particular theme, that would arouse emotion, so then he would just go full tilt for that! That's the demagogue! When he feels that inferior side, he knows that the complexes are there and that is what to go for, and one must argue in a primitive emotional way, the way in which the inferior function would argue. Hitler did not think that out, it was the fact that he was caught in his own inferiority which gave him that talent, but such examples are not all in the past! Naturally, emotion and feeling are not always coupled. They are connected in a thinking type. You have a very good example in the national differences between French and German. The German language has many words for feeling which are confused with emotion, while the French word for feeling, *sentiment,* conveys nothing of emotion, not a shade of it, because in general the French, as a nation, have more differentiated feeling, so to them it is not emotional. That is why the French always make fun of German feelings — they say: "Oh, the Germans, with their heavy feeling — beer and singing and 'O Heimatland,' all that sentimental stuff." But a Frenchman has *sentiment,* a clear-cut thing with no wishy-washiness about it. There you have an example of the feeling type condemning the inferior feeling of a nation whose superiority is not in feeling. The Germans *think* much better, but their feeling is rather primitive, warm and full of the atmosphere of the stable, but also full of explosives! But that is a typical instance of inferior feeling.

With a tremendous amount of devotion and training, one can build up islands where the inferior function more or less functions quite well. But even in those cases, if you get disturbed by an unconscious complex, it will happen that the devil will get you into a car accident. For instance, if an intuitive is really good at driving cars, on the one day he is dissociated and out of himself, it will be more than likely that something will happen to him in this area than it would be to another type, because even in such a case it remains that door which is not quite shut against the other impulses of the collective unconscious. But in everyday ways, one can get one's inferior function to work in certain areas quite well—with a tremendous amount of effort. This is a problem which is much greater in civilized societies.

With people who still live completely in nature, such as peasants and hunters and the Bushmen of whom Laurens van der Post wrote, there you can say that in that kind of life, one would not survive unless one used all one's functions, more or less. For example, a peasant can never become as one-sided as some town dwellers. He cannot only be an intuitive; he simply has to use his sensation. But he cannot only use that, because he has to plan the farming: when the sowing must be done and which kind of carrot or wheat must be grown, and how much, and what the prices are, for otherwise nowadays he would be ruined at once. He has also to use a certain amount of feeling, because you cannot deal with your family or animals without it, and he has to have that certain smell for the weather and the future in general—what might happen or not—for otherwise he is always in trouble. So in natural situations things are more or less arranged so that one must to a certain extent use all the functions. That is why people who live under natural conditions rarely become as one-sided as town people. Among primitive tribes and such people, you can see that they generally distribute the functions. For instance, my peasant neighbor always asks the fisherman who lives with him what the weather will be. He says he does not know how the fisherman knows, but he just does, so he himself does not bother, for the fisherman is always right. He relies on that man's intuition and does not use his own in that case, so even there people tend to push off certain functions onto others who are specialists. But they cannot do it completely as town specialists do. If, for example, you are a bachelor and work as a statistician for yourself alone, you really need practically no feeling! That, naturally, has its disagreeable consequences, but in nature you could not do that.

PRACTICAL DESCRIPTION OF THE FOURTH FUNCTION

The Inferior Intuition of the Extraverted Sensation Type

This is the end of my general outline on the problem of the inferior function. The next step will be to give you a short description of what the inferior function of each type looks like in practical life so that you can connect it with experience in your own life. I should like to start with the intuition of the extraverted sensation type. I am not going to describe the extraverted sensation type, but only how inferior intuition operates in such a type. I shall concentrate on the theme of what his inferior intuition will do in his case, and I shall go through all the possible eight types in this way. But I cannot avoid first giving you a brief sketch of the type in general and then will turn to what in this setup the inferior function does.

The extraverted sensation type is represented in someone

whose gift and specialized function is to sense and relate to outer objects in a concrete and practical way. Such people observe everything, smell everything, and on entering a room know practically at once how many people are present. You can always ask them whether Mrs. So-and-So was there and what dress she had on. If you put such a question to an intuitive, he would say he had not noticed and had no idea, and what *did* she have on? It is amazing what people normally do not see! The sensation type is, relatively, a past master at noticing such things. There is the famous story of a professor of jurisprudence who tried to demonstrate to his students the unreliability of witnesses. He had two people come into the classroom at the university and exchange a few sentences and then begin to fight each other. He stopped them and then said, "Now, ladies and gentlemen, please write down exactly what you witnessed." It then turned out that the whole quarrel had been staged, so that the professor had an exact record of what was said. But practically nobody was capable of giving an exact and objective account of what had happened. They all missed certain points. Based on this staged incident, the professor tried to show his students that they should not rely on eyewitnesses too much. This story illustrates the tremendous individual relativity of sensation: some are more and others less gifted in it. I would say that the extraverted sensation type would score highest in this field and would probably miss fewest points and give the relatively best account of the scene, while the introverted intuitive would probably just remember a few sentences and that he had seen blows exchanged, but would not know who started it all or anything else.

The extraverted sensation type is the best photographic apparatus, as it were. He can quickly and objectively relate to outer facts, which is why you find this type among the good mountaineers, engineers, business people, and so on, all of whom have a wide and accurate awareness of outer reality in all its differentiations. This type will remark on the texture of things—whether silk or wool—for he will have feeling for the material; thus aesthetical good taste is generally also present. Jung says that such people very often give an outer impression of being rather soulless. You may all have met such a soulless engineer type, where one has the feeling that the man is absolutely dedicated to engines and their oils and so on and sees everything from that angle. He produces no feeling and does not seem to think much either, and intuition is completely lacking, for that is for him just the realm of crazy fantasy. The extraverted sensation type calls everything approaching intuition mad fantasy, completely idiotic imagination, and something that has nothing to do with reality. He can even dislike thought, for if he is very one-sided, he will call that always getting into the abstract instead of keeping with the facts.

I had such an extraverted sensation type as a teacher in natural sciences. You could never put a general theoretical question to him, for he would call that getting off into abstract thinking and would say that one must keep to the facts—look at the worm and see what it looks like and then draw it, or look in the microscope and describe what you see there. That is natural science, and all the rest is fantasy and theory and nonsense. He was very good at explaining how factories make certain chemical products, and I still know the Haber-Bosch process by heart, for he hammered it into me, but when it came to the general theory of the interrelation of elements and so on, he did not teach us much. He said that that was still uncertain in science and that it was a theory which changed every year and was in constant evolution. So he skipped that side of the work. Everything which might have been a hunch or a guess, or anything intuitive, appears in a type where sensation is differentiated in an unpleasant form. That is, if this man had intuitions at all, they would be of a suspicious or grotesque kind. For example, he once in quite an amazing way ventured into graphology, and one day I brought him a letter written by my mother excusing me for not having been able to come to the course because I had had flu. He looked at the writing and said, "Did your mother write that?" I said yes, and he said, "Poor child!" He only sensed the negative! He was like that. He would get suspicious fits about his colleagues and the children in his class. You could see that he had some kind of dark intuition of something murky, for his intuition, being inferior, was like a dog sniffing in the garbage pails and such places—he was interested in dirty linen. This inferior kind of intuition was very often right, but sometimes completely wrong! Sometimes he just had persecution ideas—dark suspicions without any foundation. A type who is so accurate on the factual level can suddenly get melancholy, suspicious premonitions, ideas of dark possibilities, and one does not know how these suddenly cropped up. That is how inferior intuition came up in his case. Now, because he was an extraverted sensation type, his intuitions were more on an introverted level. That remark, "Poor child," was by chance turned toward an outer object, namely to me and my mother's handwriting, but normally, in the case of the extraverted sensation type, inferior intuition circles around the subjective position of the sensation type, very often in dark feelings or hunches or premonitions about illnesses which he might get or other misfortunes which might befall him. That means the inferior intuition is, in general, egocentric, it is turned toward the subject but with an egocentric quality in it, and it often has this kind of negative, depreciative attitude. If you get such people nicely drunk or very tired, or know them intimately so that they come out with their other side, then if they produce intuitions, they can produce the most amazing, weird, eerie ghost stories.

I knew a woman who was one of the biggest mountaineers in Switzerland. She was obviously an extraverted sensation type, and only concrete facts counted and everything was due to natural causes, of course. She could climb alone all the four thousand mountains, not only in Switzerland but in the whole range of the Alps—the French, the Savoyan, and the Austrian also. But in the dark evenings in the hut afterward, with a good fire burning, she would switch over and tell you the most eerie, horrible ghost stories of the type you would normally hear among the shepherds and peasants. It was quite wonderful to see this primitive, weird fantasy coming out of her. The next morning when she put on her boots, she would laugh it all off and say that was all nonsense! For then she would snap back into her superior function and laugh about what she had said the evening before. The same was true for the man I mentioned earlier, for at school excursions he would suddenly switch over and tell you extraordinary, fantastic events that he apparently had experienced. It is always a kind of personal experience, a personal event, aimed at the person himself, which shows the introversion of the intuition; what such a person intuits in such a situation is part of his personal problem and situation.

Another aspect of inferior intuition in an extraverted sensation type is a sudden attraction for Anthroposophy, Theosophy, or some other cocktail of Eastern metaphysics, generally of a most otherworldly and metaphysical type. Suddenly very realistic engineers and people who you would think are the most unlikely persons would join such a movement and with a completely uncritical mind get quite lost in it. That is because their inferior intuition has such an archaic character. On their writing desks, to your great amazement you will find mystical writings, but of a rather second-class quality. If you ask them if they read that, they will say that it is just nonsense but that it helps them to go to sleep—that is when the main function still denies the inferior function! If, for example, you ask the Anthroposophists at Dornach who supplied the money for their buildings, you will find that it came from just such extraverted sensation people. As a whole, you can say that the American nation, for instance, has a very great number of extraverted sensation types, which is why, on the other hand, such strange movements flourish especially well in the United States, to a much greater extent than in Switzerland, for example. In Los Angeles you can find practically every kind of fantastic sect, and you are told a host of unrealistic stories of a rather dubious character.

I remember once analyzing such a type, and during the day, in the middle of another hour, I suddenly had a telephone call from him. The man was sobbing over the telephone and said he was overwhelmed: "It happened—I cannot tell you, I am in danger!" Now, this was not a hysterical person, and he had no latent psychosis or anything of the kind, so you would never expect him to behave in this way. I was absolutely astonished and asked him if he would be able to go to the station and buy a ticket and come to Zurich—he was living in another Swiss town. He said he thought he could manage, so I told him to come. By the time he arrived he had snapped back into his superior sensation and brought me a basket of cherries, which we cheerfully ate together. I said: "And now what?" But he could not even tell me! Because by getting to the station and buying the cherries, he had gotten back onto the upper level again. He had been attacked for a minute from the other level, and the only thing I got out of him was when he said: "For a minute I knew what God was! It is as if I realized God! And it shook me so much that I thought I would go mad, and now it is gone again. I remember it, but I cannot convey it anymore, and I am no longer in it." There, via the inferior function, intuition, he suddenly had the whole collective unconscious and the Self, and everything. For a minute—like a flash—it all came up and completely shook the upper part of his personality, but he could not hold it. That was the first beginning of the coming up of inferior intuition, which shows its tremendously creative and positive, as well as its dangerous, aspect. Intuition has that quality of conveying a tremendous amount of meaningful contents simultaneously. You see the whole thing in one minute, in one second, and that had come up for a minute—and then it went again. There he was, munching cherries, back in his rather flat, ordinary, extraverted sensation world. That would be an example of the first genuine appearance of inferior intuition in such a type.

Then comes the great danger from what I call the grip of the superior upon the inferior function. I knew an extraverted sensation type, a very efficient builder and good businessman—a parvenu—who had made a tremendous amount of money. He was very practical but built horrible houses. Only the gadgets in them were perfect, so that people liked to live there, even though from an artistic point of view the houses were awful. He was a good skier, dressed very well, admired women, and had the kind of refined sensuality which an extraverted sensation type can display, with good taste in food and so on. This man fell into the hands of an intuitive woman twenty years older than himself. She was a wild, fantastic mother figure, and enormously fat, which in her case represented lack of discipline; introverted intuitive types are often terribly immoderate and exceed their reasonable limits both physically and psychically, which has to do with their inferior sensation. This woman lived only in her fantasies and was absolutely incapable of supporting herself financially, so it was the typical union where the man provided the money and looked after the practical side of life and the woman the whole fantasy aspect. I once went skiing with him, but never again— I was bored to tears! The only thing which he might have talked about in an interesting way was his business, but he did not talk of that to women, and otherwise he had nothing to say except that the sun was nice and the food not bad! To my great surprise, this man invited me to the Anthroposophs at Dornach to see a play. The theater called the Goetheanum was his other "spiritual" mother and held a great attraction for him. He was absolutely gripped by the play, so moved that he was completely knocked out. I watched him from time to time and wondered what was the matter with the man, for he was completely carried away. Afterward I was tactless enough to say that the play was too high up for me and that what I was longing for was a good steak! He was shocked out of his wits by my materialism! I was only about eighteen at the time and would be wiser now and not make such remarks. But that was how this type of inferior intuition worked. On the one side it was projected onto this woman and on the other side there was Dornach. He tried to break with the woman, having realized the mother-son relationship, and hoped to park his inferior intuition in Dornach instead. That was certainly a step forward from just having it projected onto a mother figure, for at least it was an attempt to assimilate it on an inner level, which was why my remark was so especially tactless. How the attempt worked out I have no idea, for I lost contact with him, but one should never make depreciative or hurtful remarks if people come out with their inferior function.

Another example of inferior introverted intuition, but this time really inferior, illustrates the disgusting form and desperate abyss into which the inferior function can lead. Recently, in an American science fiction publication, I read the story of a man who invented an apparatus by which people could be dematerialized and then rematerialized. With it the operator could be in one place and could send electronic waves through space which would rematerialize people at the other end. He could, for instance, be in Zurich and then materialize in New York. By means of such an apparatus it would be possible to dispense with airplanes, ships, and the like. First he experimented with ashtrays, but that did not quite work, and then later with a fly. A few mistakes occurred at the beginning, but after the adjustment of a few wires it seemed to work with the fly. In case anything went wrong, he wanted to be the first victim, so he put himself into the apparatus. Unfortunately, the experiment got stuck on the way and he came out at the other end with the enormous head of a fly! He tried to contact his wife and, covering up his head with a cloth so that she could not see it, told her that she must try to free him, and gave her various instructions, but nothing worked. Finally, in desperation, he asked her to kill him, out of kindness to him, which she did. Afterward the story just becomes one of the usual criminal type. When he is dead and buried, the woman goes mad and gets put into an asylum, but then the fly is found, so that it might have come right after all, but it is too late. The prosecution, out of pity, has the fly put into a matchbox, which is sentimentally deposited on the tomb, and an inscription states that the deceased was "a hero and a victim of science." I have spared you most of the disgusting and perverse details in the story, which are expounded with great gusto.

There you see how inferior intuition takes shape in a sensation type. Since the story is written by a sensation type, it gets disguised as completely practical sensation. The fly would represent inferior intuition which gets mixed up with the conscious personality. A fly is a devilish insect. In general, flies represent involuntary fantasies and thoughts which annoy one and buzz around in one's head and which one cannot chase away. Here, this man gets caught and victimized by an idea which involves even murder and madness, since he induces his wife to murder him. In order to save her life she is put into a lunatic asylum where she spends her time trying to catch flies, hoping to find the one which might be a part of her husband. At the end of the story the commissioner of police talks to the author and says that the woman was, after all, just mad, and one sees that he would represent collective common sense — the verdict finally adopted by the writer, which says that all this is just madness.

If, instead of projecting again, the writer had established the continuity of his inferior function in his consciousness, and had got it free from his extraverted sensation, then a really pure and clean story would have come out. In genuine fantasies such as those of Edgar Allan Poe and the poet Gustav Meyrinck intuition is established in its own right, for these fantasies are highly symbolic and can be interpreted in a consistent way. But a sensation type always wants to concretize his intuitions in some way.

The Inferior Intuition of the Introverted Sensation Type

First I must discuss the main function of the introverted sensation type. Many years ago, in the Psychological Club, we had a meeting at which members were asked to describe their type in their own words, instead of just quoting Jung's book on the types. Members were to describe how they experienced their own superior function, and I have never forgotten an excellent paper which Emma Jung gave, for it was only after hearing it that I felt that I now understood the introverted sensation type better than I ever had done before. In describing herself, she said that the introverted sensation type is like a highly sensitized photographic plate. When somebody comes into the room, such a type notices the way the person comes in, the hair, the expression on the face, the clothes, and the way that person walks. All this makes a very accurate and tremendous impact on the introverted sensation type, who is so highly sensitized that every detail is absorbed. The impression comes from the object to the subject. It is as though a stone fell into deep water: the impression falls deeper and deeper and sinks in. Outwardly, the introverted sensation type looks utterly stupid. He just sits and stares, and you do not know what is going on within him, for he looks like a piece of wood with no reaction at all—unless he reacts with one of the auxiliary functions, thinking or feeling; but inwardly the impression is being absorbed.

The introverted sensation type therefore gives the impression of being very slow, which is not the case; it is only that the quick inner reactions go on underneath and the outer reaction comes in a delayed way. These are the people who, if told a joke in the morning, will probably laugh at it at midnight. The type is very often misjudged and misunderstood by others in their surroundings because one does not realize what goes on within. If such a type can express his photographic impressions artistically, then they can be reproduced either in paintings or in writing. I have a strong suspicion that Thomas

Mann was such an introverted sensation type. He can describe marvelously every detail and give the whole atmosphere of a room or personality, as, for instance, in *The Magic Mountain.*

The inferior intuition of this introverted type is in a way similar to that of the extraverted sensation type, for it also has a very weird, eerie, fantastic inner life, but it is more concerned with the impersonal, collective outer world. With the builder I mentioned, for example, you can see that he is an extraverted sensation type. He picks up intuitions that concern himself. In his extraverted sensation he is concerned with the collective outer world—with road building, or the building of big houses, but his intuition is applied to himself and is mixed up with his personal problems. With the introverted sensation type, the movement from the object comes toward him. The novels by Thomas Mann have a very subjective character, while his intuition is concerned with events which go on in the background—he picks up the possibilities and the future of the outer world.

I have just seen in the material of an introverted sensation type material which I would call very prophetic—archetypal fantasies which mainly represent not the problems of the dreamer but those of his time. The assimilation of these fantasies is very difficult because there is the same difficulty as with the extraverted sensation type, namely that sensation is a function with which we comprehend the here and now. The negative aspect of sensation is that the type gets stuck in reality. As Jung once wrote: for them the future does not exist, future possibilities do not exist, they are in the here and now, and there is an iron curtain before them. They behave in life as though it will always be the same as it is now; they are incapable of conceiving that things might change. The disadvantage of the type is that when his tremendous inner fantasies well up, the person has great difficulty in assimilating them because of the accuracy and slowness of the conscious function. If such a type is at all willing to take his intuition seriously, he will be inclined to try to put it down very accurately. But how can you do that? Intuition comes like a flash, and if you try to put it down, it has gone! So he does not know how to deal with the problem and goes through agonies because the only way his inferior function can be assimilated is by loosening the hold of the superior function.

I knew an introverted sensation type who for many years had very accurately painted the contents of her unconscious. It took her about three weeks to complete a painting. The paintings were absolutely beautiful and worked out in every detail, but, as I heard from her later, she did not paint the contents of her unconscious as they came, but corrected and improved the colors and refined the details. She would say, "I naturally improved them aesthetically." Slowly the need to assimilate the inferior function became imperative, and she was told by her dreams that she should speed up her paintings and take the colors exactly as they were, however crude, and just put them on paper quickly. When I translated the message of her dreams in this way, she got into a panic and said she could not, it was impossible. To have this put to her was like being knocked out; she could not do it but continued to paint in her usual way. Japanese Zen paintings can give the essence of an image from within, which would be the opposite of this woman's work. She did not get the accuracy from within and could not do what her dreams indicated and had a tremendous battle, for she could not give up the superior function and accurate detail. So again and again she missed the coming up of the inferior intuition for she could not put it down when and as it came.

That is how the fight looks between the superior and inferior function in the introverted sensation type. If you try to force them to assimilate intuition too quickly, they get symptoms of giddiness or seasickness. It is rather like being on the sea or in an airplane; they feel carried away from the solid ground of reality, and because they are so stuck there, they get actual symptoms of seasickness, or get giddy from a purely psychological background. I knew one introverted sensation type who had to go to bed to do active imagination, for otherwise she felt exactly as if she were on a boat and became seasick. She felt as if the solid ground were dissolving under her feet. Naturally, if you are not that type, you are rather amused, but again here there is the possibility of the superior function getting hold of the inferior. A marvelous example is the Swiss painter Heinrich Füssli, who became famous in the last century and went to the English court. He was obviously an extraverted sensation type, and his inferior function came up in the most fantastic themes. He painted a wonderful picture of Shakespeare's *Midsummer Night's Dream* — this light and fantastic fairy tale. The theme attracted him because it *was* completely fantastic, but instead of painting it as it would have come up from within, he made a minute study of it and fixed and glued his intuition into a very sensuous form. In the picture Titania is waking up and looking at the ass with whom she is in love and she just looks amazed! The fairies and witches and her lover are all there watching her. It is a beautiful picture but painted in such a classic way, with so much detail of flesh and garments, and even with every hair painted in on the ass's head, so that the picture loses just the atmosphere it should convey, namely that of the dream world. Thus, in a way, it fails completely, and Füssli, in spite of his gifts, never quite became a really famous painter. The picture shows how he ruined his own chances by not giving up his superior function. He should have painted quickly with all the vagueness of a dream world, but instead he fell into his superior function and made a painting, putting in the toenails of every figure and so on, so that the picture became frozen and lost its dynamic character.

Because the introverted sensation type's superior function is introverted, his intuition is extraverted and therefore is generally triggered off by outer events. Such a type might, while walking down a street, see a crystal in a shop window, for instance, and his intuition might immediately get its symbolic meaning, or the whole flood of the symbolic meaning of the crystal would come into his mind, but that would have been triggered off by the outside event, since his inferior intuition is essentially extraverted. Naturally, he has the same bad characteristics as the extraverted sensation type, for in both types intuitions are very often of a sinister character, with dark premonitions — that an atomic war will soon break out, that people around them will die of cancer, and they also pick up negative gossip. The fantasy material tends to be of a sinister character and if it is not worked upon, the prophetic contents which break through will be pessimistic and negative.

All split-off inferior functions have a tendency to be compulsive and create persecution ideas. You find that also in the thinking type, for instance. The inferior function is always the vehicle for persecution ideas, so always first watch out for it. If intuition goes astray, one is possessed by sensual fantasies of the most coarse and sexual type, like a rat sniffing around in dustbins. Always, when people feel undermined and persecuted, it is likely that the inferior function has gone underground and is persecuting and undermining the superior function, for the former is always the door by which such dark things come in. Intuitives are bottled up with coarse sensation fantasies too, because they neglect sensation so much. But when the hunches or intuitions of the sensation type appear, they give this dark feeling of something impending somewhere and are therefore colored with fear. But one must be careful because only the event can show whether a prophecy was right or not. Premonitions of an atomic war cannot be said to be incorrect and just inferior intuition; they might be right! Only by looking backward in history can you see if they were wrong and just negative intuition. The prophets in the Bible became immortal just because they were right, so they were probably not sensation types but genuinely intuitives with relatively correct intuitions. In the sensation type, intuition can be absolutely right *or* wrong. I cannot tell you how often in my life I have been rung up by sensation types who "knew" that Jung was dying or dead, or that So-and-So had gone into the hospital, or was hopelessly ill, when there was nothing of the kind!

What is worse about negative intuition is that it sometimes does hit the nail right on the head. Jung says intuition is anyhow a problematic function because it gets right to the core of the situation. It either hits the bull's eye, or goes absolutely astray, right outside even the realm of the target. In general, when intuition is the main function and one of the other functions—either thinking or feeling—has been developed, the person has an intuition that it might be either the bull's eye or off in the woods, and therefore he holds back. But inferior intuition is just primitive, and it either hits the bull's eye or goes extremely wide of the mark. And the sensation type sometimes surprises you by hitting the bull's eye, which you can only admire, or else with hunches in which there is no truth—just pure invention! The type has sudden inner intuitions, and the great difficulty for him is to know how to deal with them, for they may be complete nonsense or absolutely right.

The Inferior Feeling of the Extraverted Thinking Type

The conscious personality being extraverted, I will try to describe the way in which inferior introverted feeling works. The type is to be found among organizers, people in offices and government positions, in business, in law—many good lawyers are of the extraverted thinking type—and among scientists, when they are the type who organize scientific investigations where they can build up teamwork. They can also compile useful encyclopedias. They dig up all the dust in old libraries and do away with inhibiting factors in science due to clumsiness or laziness or a lack of clarity in language, and the confusions which arise from having a different terminology. The extraverted thinking type brings order here by taking a definite stand and saying, "If we say so-and-so, we mean so-and-so," or "If we mean that, we mean that," and so on. They put clarifying order into the outer object, the outer situation. It is a rational function, and as its direction is outward, it is an activity which tends to establish logical order. At a business meeting, such a man will say that one should get at the basic facts and see how to proceed. A lawyer who has to listen to all the chaotic reports of contending parties is able, with his superior mind, to see which are the real conflicts and which the pseudo contentions and then arrange a solution satisfactory to all parties. The type has a great faculty in this way and is socially creative. They can cut through with creative clarity of mind and bring things into acceptable order. The emphasis will always be upon the object, not the idea. Such a lawyer will not fight for the idea of democracy or domestic peace or anything of that kind. His whole mind will be absorbed with and swallowed up by the outer objective situation. If you were to ask him about his attitude or ideas about something, he would be absolutely amazed, for he is not concerned with that and would be completely unconscious of any personal motive. Generally, if you search for them, the unconscious motivations will consist of a childlike, naive belief in peace, charity, and justice. If pressed into saying what he understood by "justice," he would be quite bewildered and would probably throw you out of his office, because he was "too busy," so the subjective element remains in the background of the personality. He never thinks about what he understands; he fights for justice but never considers what he understands by justice! His premises of high ideals remain within the realm of his inferior function, which is feeling. For his ideals he will have a strange mystical feeling attachment which he will not show, and you would have to drive him into a corner to find out about it. Feeling attachments to certain ideals or to people are present, but never appear in daytime activities. Such a man might spend his whole life in settling problems, in reorganizing firms, or in situations where there was a necessity for putting things clearly, and only at the end of his life would he start to ask himself mournfully what he had really lived for. And then he falls into his inferior function. Hitherto everything has made demands on his main function; he has never considered what he lived for, for the dark background has remained unclear.

I once talked to a man of this type who was terribly overworked and needed a good holiday. He gave *me* a lot of good advice, saying *I* should go on a holiday, and when I asked him why *he* didn't, he replied, "My God, I should be much too much alone and get much too melancholy!" Such a person will ask himself whether his work is really important. He may remember how he once saved someone from being robbed and so on, but had the world improved? Such feelings would have come up in him, and he would have felt like falling into an abyss. He would have had to recheck his whole evaluation of things. Naturally, therefore, he avoided taking any holidays—until he fell and broke his hip and had to stay six months in bed—and that is how nature imposes the inferior function on such people!

The extraverted thinking type has, in a hidden way, a kind of mystical, loyal feeling attachment to ideals and often also to people, but this deep, strong, warm feeling hardly ever comes out, but is entirely hidden. I remember an extraverted thinking type who really moved me when he once came out with his feeling for his wife. Its genuineness, depth, and warmth were really touching, but when I talked to his wife, it was deplorable to see how very little idea she had of that, because as a mad extravert, he would spend the whole day in his profession, milling around in life, and those deep feelings were never expressed. If his wife had been dying of consumption he would not have noticed it until he was at the funeral and it was too late, and *she* did not realize the depth of his feeling for her and that, in a very deep sense, he was very loyal and faithful to her, for all that was deeply hidden and not expressed in his life; it remained inside and was introverted and did not move toward the object. It took quite a few talks to get a better understanding in the marriage and make the wife realize that her husband really loved her. He was so terribly occupied with the outer world and his feeling was hidden and neither expressed nor accepted in his life, so that his wife did not realize it, though actually it played a tremendous hidden role within him.

I remember the dream of the approaching transference of an extraverted thinking type. He dreamed that while he was coming to me (he was a foreigner), an old coachman with an old coach and four horses had also left the town where he lived and was slowly moving toward Zurich, but had not yet arrived. This man had come to analysis for all sorts of outer reasons — to learn about Jungian psychology, etc. — but his feeling was also on the way, but it had only come a few kilometers, and I teased him by asking when his coachman was going to arrive! If people can begin to laugh about their inferior function, that can be redeeming, for then everything is twenty times better. When a sense of humor is established and you can pull the other person's leg, as they can pull yours, a lot of trouble is cleared away, which is why I mentioned the archetype of the fool at the beginning of this chapter. This man had a sense of humor and was able to laugh about his coachman.

Introverted feeling, even if the main function, is very difficult to understand. A very good example is the Austrian poet Rainer Maria Rilke, a feeling intuitive type, who wrote: "Ich liebe dich, was geht's dich an?" ("I love you, but it's none of your business!") That is just love for love's sake! The feeling is very strong but does not flow toward the object; it is rather like being in a state of love within oneself. Naturally, this kind of feeling is very much misunderstood, and such people are considered to be very cold. They are not at all cold, but the feeling is all within them. On the other hand, they have a very strong hidden influence on the surrounding society, for they have very secret, strong inner ways of establishing values. For example, such a feeling type may never express his feeling but behaves as though he thinks one thing is valuable and another not, which exerts a certain impact on other people. When the feeling is inferior, it is even more hidden and more absolute. The lawyer I described has his idea of justice, which would have a very suggestive effect on other people; that is, the hidden feeling at the back of his mind of what he considers to be justice would unconsciously influence other people in the same direction without his ever noticing it. It would really dictate not only his own fate but that of others, invisibly, but through his activity. The hidden, introverted feeling of the thinking type establishes strong invisible loyalties. Such people are among the most faithful of all my friends, even though they may only write at Christmas, if at all, and there is no other contact. I know that they are absolutely reliable in their feeling, but one has to move toward it to get to know of its existence.

Outwardly, the extraverted thinking type does not give the impression of having strong feeling. In a politican, his inferior feeling might unconsciously manifest in a deep-rooted and steadfast loyalty to his country and would seem to him to be completely evident—but it might make him throw the atom bomb or commit some other destructive act. Unconscious and undeveloped feeling can be barbaric and absolute, and therefore hidden destructive fanaticism sometimes suddenly bursts out of the extaverted thinking type and, if unchecked, can be very destructive and manifest in some sudden fanatical action. These people are incapable of seeing that, from a feeling standard, other people might have another value, for they do not question the inner values which they defend. Where they definitely feel that something is right, they are incapable of showing their feeling standpoint, but they never doubt their own inner values.

In that point inferior feeling is different from inferior intuition. Intuition is an irrational function which grasps facts, future possibilities, and possibilities of evolution, but it is not a function of judgment. Inferior intuition might have presentiments about a war, or illnesses of other people, which might happen or might not, or of archetypal changes in the collective unconscious. Introverted intuition has sudden hunches about the slow transformation of the collective unconscious in the flow of time. Every age has a certain atmosphere about it. For example, in art or in literature, there are sudden breaks with former themes, and introverted intuition has a feeling for them. A German writer named Bruno Goetz wrote a book about the Third Empire, meaning by it a Kingdom of God in which paganism and Christianity would be mixed. He wrote it long before the Nazis came to power. The Nazis tried to get hold of him and make him write for them, but he flatly refused. He even foretold in this book much of what the Nazis actually did, even to the extent of describing bands of young people between eighteen and twenty who devastated everything. The scenes he described came out practically in detail later in Nazi Germany, but at the time he wrote the book there was nothing of the kind; it was still the time of the Socialist Weimar Republic, but Goetz's introverted intuition just knew where the archetypal constellation was moving, and he expressed it. But this can also happen when introverted intuition is inferior. There are sudden flashes of insight into the background processes which come up and disappear again, but there is no judgment, just as Goetz describes facts without judging them. As a writer, he simply puts them before you, and you do not know whether he approves or disapproves. That is what intuition does, it presents facts, with no valuation, but feeling is quite different. In Jungian terms, it is a rational function (Latin *ratio* = order, calculation, reason), a function which establishes order and judges, saying this is good and this bad, this agreeable and this disagreeable to me. So the inferior feeling of a thinking type would judge the values of people and ideals and not just represent facts; that would be the difference.

For example, an extraverted sensation type who neglected his intuition to a great extent had a recurring dream of poor people and laborers of a disagreeable type who broke into his house at night. He was terrified by this ever-recurring dream and began to go around in his circle of friends and at dinner parties saying that there was absolutely nothing that could be done, that he knew the Communists would win out. As he was a very able politician, this had a bad effect, for people listened to what he said. This was a bad, wrong kind of inferior intuition, based on personal projection. That is an instance of inferior intuition. Yet someone with inferior feeling might suddenly start a lawsuit, convinced that he was fighting for the right and good, but if someone else could shoot this conviction down, he would throw the whole thing over, including the lawsuit which he had himself begun. The sudden change in his judgment would indicate the sudden intrusion of inferior feeling, and this brings in another point. People are very easily influenced when it is a question of their inferior function, because since it is in the unconscious, people can easily be made uncertain, while in the realm of their superior function they generally know how to act when attacked, for they have all their weapons ready and are broad-minded and flexible and feel strong. As soon as you feel strong, you are quite willing to discuss things or change your attitude, but where you feel inferior, you get fanatical and touchy and are easily influenced. The expression on a friend's face can affect the feeling of a thinking type, because his feeling is in the unconscious and therefore open to influence. Therefore, as mentioned before, the extraverted thinking type can make a very loyal friend, but you can suddenly lose him because he has been poisoned against you and may drop you one day like a hot potato and you don't know why or what has happened! Somehow, something poisonous got into his system, someone said something, or even just made a face when your name was mentioned! The feeling is unconscious. Such effects can only be cured when they are taken up consciously. If you objected, in thinking terms, about his policy in having the lawsuit, the extraverted thinking type would be willing to discuss it and to ask your reasons. He would be approachable and not influenced in a wrong way, while in the realm of feeling he would break off suddenly and without reason and without quite knowing why himself.

These hidden introverted feelings of the extraverted thinking type are sometimes very childish. After the death of such people you sometimes find notebooks in which childish poems have been written to a faraway woman whom they never met in their lives and in which a lot of sentimental, mystical feeling is poured out, and these they ask to have burned after their death. That feeling is hidden. It is, in a way, the most valuable possession they have, but all the same it is sometimes strikingly infantile; still, it has this kind of mystical inner religious quality about it. Sometimes the feeling remains entirely with the mother and never comes out of the childhood realm, and you may find touching documents about the attachment to her. In such cases the introverted feeling function has never moved out of the childhood place.

The Inferior Feeling of the Introverted Thinking Type

The main function of this type is not so much trying to establish order in the outer world, but is concerned with ideas. Someone who says that one should not start with facts but should first clarify one's ideas would belong to the introverted thinking type. His wish to bring order into life starts off with the idea that if you are muddle-headed from the very start, you will never get anywhere. You must first know what ideas you wish to follow and where they come from; you must clean up your own muddle-headedness by digging into the background of your thinking. For instance, all philosophy is concerned with the logical processes of the human mind, with the building up of ideas, and so on, and this is the realm where introverted thinking is mostly at work. In science those are the people who, for example, are perpetually trying to prevent their colleagues from getting lost in experiments and who, from time to time, try to get back to basic concepts and ask what we are really doing mentally. This explains why, in physics, there is generally a professor of practical physics and another for theoretical: one lectures on the building up of experiments and the other on mathematical and other principles and the theory of science. In all the different sciences there are always those who try to clarify the basic theories of their scientific realm. The extraverted historian of art will try to find out about the facts and try to prove, for instance, that a certain type of Madonna was painted earlier or later than another type and will try to connect that with the history and background of the artist, while the introvert might even ask what right one has to judge a work of art. He would say that first we should understand what we mean by art for otherwise we will get into a muddle. The introverted thinking type always goes back to the subjective idea, namely what the subject is doing in the whole matter.

The feeling of the introverted thinking type, as far as the attitude is concerned, is the other way around for the extravert, which means that the introverted thinking type has that same kind of strong, loyal, and warm feeling described as typical for the extraverted thinking type, but with the difference that the feeling of the introverted thinking type flows towards definite objects. While the extraverted thinking type deeply loves his wife but where Rilke, for instance, says: "I love you, but it is none of your business," the feeling of the introverted thinking type *has* an outer object. He would therefore say, in the Rilke style, "I love you and it *will* be your business; I'll make it your business!" Otherwise the introverted thinking type's feeling has very much the same characteristics as the inferior feeling of the extraverted thinking type, with very black and white judgments, either yes or no, love or hate. But it can be very easily poisoned by other people and by the collective atmosphere and in that way can be made uncertain. The inferior feeling of both types is sticky, and the extraverted thinking type has this kind of invisible faithfulness which can last endlessly. The same is true for the extraverted feeling of the introverted thinking type, except that it will not be invisible but visible faithfulness. If you evaluate it positively, it will be faithful, but to negative evaluation it is sticky. It resembles the gluelike flow of feeling in an epileptoid person; it has that kind of sticky, doglike attachment which, especially to the beloved object, is not always amusing. You could compare the inferior feeling of an introverted thinking type to the flow of hot lava from a volcano—it only moves about five meters an hour, but it devastates everything on its way. That is why, naturally, an introverted thinking type will very soon experience that with his extraverted feeling he is always putting his foot in it, for the feeling is so primitive, sticky, and childish; but it also has all the advantages of a primitive function, for it is very genuine and warm. When an introverted thinking type loves, there is no calculation in it. It will be for the sake of the other, but it will be primitive. That is true for both types, for the thinking types have primitive feeling, but on the other hand it is never calculating. The inferior feeling of a thinking type is like a lioness that would like to play with you. She has no other intention than to play, but she rubs herself, purring, against your leg, or eats you up, or gives you a great blow so that you fall over when she licks your face. But there is no calculation or intention about it; it is just an expression of feeling, just as a dog wags his tail! What touches people in the feeling of domestic animals is just this lack of calculation.

So in both thinking types, inferior feeling is without calculation, whereas people who have differentiated feeling are, in a hidden way, calculating, and they always put a little bit of ego into it. I once saw the boss of a typist who was a feeling type and wondered how she stood such a horror for a single day! But she smiled and said that he was her boss, so she made the best of it, since she must put up with it, and by looking at him closely she could find that he had this and that positive quality. One could say that to see good possibilities and recognize them is admirable, but on the other hand there is a little calculation in it: she wanted to keep her place with her boss, so she made that positive feeling effort. That would never happen to the inferior feeling of a thinking type! I could never have stood it—I would rather not eat and could not have stuck it for twenty days! I was struck here by the difference between inferior and differentiated feeling. The feeling type had found a few positive qualities in that horrible man and put up with him. She did not deny all the negative things I saw in him, but she said he never demanded overtime and he gave merit to those who worked for him, so she discovered a few positive factors and stuck there.

In his book, Jung explains some of the misunderstandings

between the types. If I had said that this office girl was calculating and acting out of opportunism, it would have been absolutely wrong, because that was only a background motive in her case—that would be the negative projection of the other type. It is not that she is just an opportunist, or is acting in a calculating way in having such positive feeling, but that she has differentiated feeling. She therefore never has strong feeling reactions but knows that where there is value, there is always something negative; nothing is quite black or white, but everything is grayish in reality. She has that kind of philosophical attitude. It was only I who suspected the calculation and opportunism because the introverted thinking type always knows consciously on which side his bread is buttered. But that is not right. On the other hand, you can say that inferior feeling has the advantage that there is really no calculation in it. The ego has nothing to do with it, but naturally this can create unadapted situations. Think, for instance, of the film *The Blue Angel,* in which a professor falls for a vamp and faithfully and loyally gets ruined by her. That would be the tragedy of the inferior feeling function. One could honor him for his faithfulness, but one could just as well say that he was a damn fool and that his inferior feeling had very bad taste. That is also true for the inferior feeling of a thinking type: the feeling shows either very good or very bad taste. A thinking type can sometimes choose very valuable people for his friends, or he can pick absolutely the wrong one, for the inferior function has both aspects and rarely fits into conventional patterns.

Another way in which infantile feeling can manifest in thinking types is instanced in the case of Voltaire, the French philosopher, who was, I think, an introverted thinking type. He fought the Catholic Church with all his might and was the author of the famous saying *"Ecrasez l'infâme"* (Root out the infamy). He was an intellectual and a typical representative of the age of enlightenment. On his deathbed, however, he got very jittery and asked for the extreme unction and took it with a great upwelling of pious feeling. There he showed at the end of his life that he was completely split: his mind had left the original religious experience and his feeling had stayed there invisibly, and when it came to dying and death—which one has to meet as a whole person—the feeling came up and overwhelmed him in a completely undifferentiated way. All sudden conversions have this quality, or they are due to the sudden appearance of the inferior function in a type.

In the case of inferior feeling, just as in the other cases, the inferior function is very much coupled with emotion. Whenever people have very emotional feeling, it is a sign that the feeling is undifferentiated. As soon as tears come into their eyes in a feeling situation that has been constellated and everything is flowing heavily and passionately, you know that the inferior function has been touched. But this is also true for the inferior intuition of the sensation types. You will remember my description of the extraverted sensation type man with whom I went to the Anthroposophic tragedy play. When I said that I had had enough of that and wanted a good steak, he did not think that was a joke. He had been so deeply emotionally touched by the play we had seen together that it was hitting at his emotion when I made this tactless remark. He was not an emotional man, but a very cold fish and very down to earth; yet at this moment he was moved to the core of his heart, and therefore one could not joke about it.

All inferior functions have this tendency to make people deadly serious and emotional and pathetic. You can see it very clearly in the feeling of the thinking type. Introverted thinking may show very pathetic if not hysterical qualities in the manifestation of feeling. On the other hand, as Jung writes in *Psychological Types,* people who know thinking types well know that you can have very warm feeling and intimate and reliable friendships with them, because if there is feeling, it is true and genuine.

The Inferior Sensation of the Extraverted Intuitive Type

Extraverted intuition is a function by which we conceive outer possibilities. A sensation type could say about a bell, "This is a bell," but a child would say that you could do all sorts of things with that, it could be a church tower, and a book could be the village, and something else could be another object, and so on. In everything there is a possibility of development; thus intuition in mythology is very often represented by the nose. One says, "I smell a rat," that is, my intuition tells me that there is something fishy about. I don't know quite what, but I can smell it! We perceive such possibilities, and then three weeks later the rat, or the cat, is out of the bag, and you say: "Oh, I smelled it, I had a hunch there was something in the air!" These are not yet materialized, unborn possibilities, the germs of the future. Intuition is therefore the capacity for intuiting that which is not yet visible, future possibilities or potentialities in the background of a situation. The extraverted intuitive type applies this to the outer world, and therefore will be very gifted and score very high in surmising the outer developments of the external situation in general. Such types are very often to be found among business people who have the courage to manufacture new inventions and put them on the market. You find them also among journalists and frequently among publishers. They are the people who know what will be popular next year and will do big business because they will bring out something which is not yet the fashion but soon will be, and they are the first to put it on the market. You find them also among stockbrokers who, beyond the normal calculation based on the reading of newspapers and financial reports of commercial concerns, will have a certain something which tells them that a certain stock will go up, the market will be bullish, and they will make money through sensing the rise and fall of stocks. They will realize what is in the air and will be the first to speak of it. You find them wherever there is something new brewing, and you find them also in the more spiritual realm. They will always be in the advance movement, interested in the advanced aspects of a science, and they are full of enterprise and will speculate as to the outcome of this, and how something else could be used, and another thing disseminated among people, and so on.

Because intuition needs to look at things a little bit from afar or vaguely in order that it may function, you have to half shut your eyes and not look at facts too closely in order to get this hunch from the unconscious. If you look at things too precisely, you focus on facts and then the hunch can't come through. That is why intuitives tend to be unpunctual and vague, always rushing about a little bit too late, arriving too late, and not focusing on any fact too exactly. Another disadvantage of this main function is that the intuitive type generally sows but rarely reaps. For instance, if you start a new business, there are generally initial difficulties, the thing does not work yet; you have to wait for a certain time for it to begin to be profitable. The intuitive very often, tragically, does not wait long enough; he starts the business, but that is enough for him, so he resells it and loses on it, but the next owner makes a lot of money out of the same business. The intuitive does not reap what he has sown. He is always the one who invents, but who

in the end gets nothing out of it if he overdoes his main function, for he is, as it were, rushing through things and incapable
of waiting till what he has sown comes out of the soil and he
can gather the fruit. If he is more balanced and can wait a little
while, and if he does not dissociate completely by identifying
with his main function, then he is a person who can stir up
new things in all the corners of the world.

Naturally, the extraverted intuitive tends specially not to
attend to his body and his physical needs: he absolutely does
not know when he is tired. He does not notice it and needs a
breakdown to show him. Also he does not know when he is
hungry; he does not know that he has any endosomatic per-
ceptions, if he is an exaggerated one-sided type. He tends also
to lose himself in the object. You find such people, for instance,
following in the trail of creative people, promoting the creativity of others, absolutely losing their own possibilities in the
other. This is especially the case with publishers and art dealers
and such people who admire the creative artist and try to
promote his work, without realizing that they lose themselves
in the object, in the other person, and forget about themselves.
Inferior sensation, like all inferior functions, is in such people
slow, heavy, and loaded with emotion and completely—because introverted—turned away from the outer world and its
affairs. It has, like all inferior functions, a mystical quality about
it.

I once analyzed an extraverted intuitive type, a businessman
who had started a great many businesses in some faraway
country and had also speculated a lot and bought gold mines
and the like. He always knew where possibilities were and
made a large fortune in a very short time, absolutely hon-
estly—quite decently—and simply because he just knew! He
knew what was coming, what would happen in a few years,

and he was always on the spot first and got the whole business
in hand. His introverted sensation—he was rather a split personality—came up first in dreams as a very dirty, bad-tem-
pered tramp who sat around in inns in a bad, nasty temper
and in dirty clothes, and one did not know what this fellow
wanted of the dreamer. I induced the dreamer to talk to this
tramp in active imagination, and the tramp said that he had
been responsible for some physical symptoms (psychogenic
symptoms of a compulsory character), on account of which he
had come to analysis, and that they had been sent because he,
the tramp, did not get enough attention. So in his active imagination the man asked what he should do, and the tramp said
that once a week, dressed in clothes such as the tramp wore,
he should go for a walk in the country with him and pay
attention to what he had to say. I advised the dreamer to
follow the advice precisely, with the result that he took long
walks through many parts of Switzerland, staying in the most
simple inns, unrecognized by anybody. He would wander
along, and during this time he had a great number of overwhelming inner experiences which came through contact with
nature: the sunrise and small things like seeing a certain flower
in a corner of a rock, and so on. It hit him right to the core of
his personality. I can only describe it as experiencing, in a very
primitive way, the Godhead in nature. He came back very silent and quieted down, and one had the feeling that something
had moved in him which had not moved before. His compulsory symptoms disappeared completely during those weekly
walks. Then came the problem of how he could keep this
experience and avoid slipping back when he got home to his
own country. So we consulted the tramp again, who said that
he would let him off the symptoms if he would take an afternoon off each week and go alone into nature and continue his

talks with him. The man then left, and from his letters I learned that he did this for a while, but then slipped back because there was too much business, too many possibilities of starting three other businesses, and too many meetings to start all these three other businesses. So, he put the tramp off, always saying, "Next week, next week—sure, I am coming, but next week"—and then he promptly got his symptoms back! That taught him, and he switched back and walked regularly and was all right again. It then crystallized into buying a little farm and having there a horse of his own, and one afternoon a week he attended to this horse, with what you could only call religious devotion. He cleaned it and nursed it by brushing, washing, and looking after it, and the horse was his friend. Like a ritual he went to visit it and ride about on it and look after it every week. From then on he had peace, and I have not heard much. I am sure a lot is going on inwardly with this horse, but I haven't heard much except for Christmas cards saying that he was getting on all right—and photographs of the horse!

There you see how the inferior function, introverted sensation in this case, was the door to experiencing the deeper layers of the unconscious, its superpersonal aspects. He got out of his ego and ego purposes via this contact with nature and the horse, and one sees also very clearly that even if the introverted sensation appears outside—in the horse, in this case— it obviously carries a symbolic meaning. Attending the horse was for him attending to his own physical and instinctive personality: the horse was a first personification of the impersonal collective unconscious for him, but it was very important just for an intuitive type to do this completely concretely and very slowly and not go off, for instance, and say, "Oh, the horse is a symbol of the unconscious," but really to stick to the concrete horse which he had and attend to it even though he knew it was a symbol. It carried the meaning of his life, but he had to attend to it in this concrete form. He had a lot of little accidents at first because he was very helpless in sensation matters, so he broke a lot of bones, one after the other, rather a harmless business—his collarbone and such things—until he was capable of really attending to a horse properly, because he was not at all good at sensation matters, being accustomed to rushing about and to having servants for all the concrete facts of life.

Two factors are very big problems for this type: money and sex, especially insofar as they really have to do with sensation, though I must say I have seen the same thing with the introverted intuitive, for in general this is typical for inferior sensation. Money imposes a certain amount of sensation: we must know about how much we have and how much we can spend; a certain accuracy and realism is needed. Sex, in its physical aspects, is also a sensation experience. Very often intuitives have great difficulty in these areas because they have great numinosity for them. But sex or money complexes do not appear only in intuitives; other people can have a sex complex or a money complex, but with the intuitives there is the additional trouble that it touches their inferior function, which means that physical sensation is numinous, is a *tremendum numinosum,* something which touches their emotions. Therefore they cannot, for instance, often go near it; it is sacred and exciting, or the other way around—very coarse. The inferiority of sensation in an extraverted intuitive sometimes shows in the very coarse vulgarity of their sexual fantasies and acts. It is completely primitive and undifferentiated. Some act it out completely, and others suffer from very vulgar sexual fantasies of a very primitive nature. But this, in a way, is not so bad with an

extraverted intuitive because the inferior sensation is introverted and so not turned toward the outer object and therefore
also not meant to be lived on a great scale but rather to be
touched as a carrier of inner meaning.

The person who is really in touch with the future, so to
speak, with the germs of the future, is the creative personality.
Now, the extraverted intuitive, because he is capable of sniffing
the wind and knowing what the weather will be tomorrow,
will see that this perhaps completely unknown painter or
writer will be the man of tomorrow, and therefore he will be
fascinated. His intuition can recognize the value of such a creative person.

He will attach himself to creative people and try with his
intuition to get them started and support and back them, because his intuition rightly tells him that there is the future,
that is what is going to succeed, even if today it is completely
ignored or not yet recognized, and in that way he has sometimes great merit. Creative people are often introverted and
are so occupied with their creations that they cannot be away
from their work in order to promote it. Their work takes up
so much of their energy that they cannot be bothered with
how it should be presented to the world, how to advertise it,
or anything of the kind. Moreover, any kind of purposiveness
poisons creative processes, so they may not even do it, but very
often then the extraverted intuitive comes and helps. But, naturally, if he does that all his life, then, as happens very often,
publishers and art dealers who are would-be creative people
project a minor creative ability which they have in themselves
onto the creative person and then they lose themselves. So,
sooner or later, such people will have to pull themselves out of
their extraversion and say, "Now, even if it is on a minor scale,
what is *my* creativity?" And then they will be forced down into

their inferior sensation, and instead of attending to other people's creativity they will have to attend to their own inferior
sensation and what might come out of that.

The same thing applies to this businessman whom I took as
an example: he always started up new factories and new enter-
prises and got a lot of other people to work and make money,
but when he consulted me, he was the poorest devil of all poor
devils. He had nothing out of it except a lot of money! But he
was so much occupied in rushing along making money that he
couldn't enjoy having it; he had not the time! It was only when
he discovered that he could buy a farm and a horse that he got
a little out of his money. For the first time in his life he had
something, because he was able to have a farm and a horse!
But if analysis had not gotten him to start this, he would have
had just nothing from money, it would have remained an abstract thing in the bank! But as he did not know how to enjoy
life—how to live in the here and now, to look after his body
and to pay attention to this world, to see the beauty of the
world, to see the sun rise and the trees blossom—what was
the use of having money? It needed the turn to his inferior
function to have all that; before, it had been of no use to him.
His wife was a sensation type and he first told me he was
earning all the money for her! Now, she knew how to enjoy it,
but he was making it for her! It was not her fault; she did not
really want him to make so much money, but he projected
sensation onto her, and so he was doing it for her. And he got
nothing out of it; he was just pale and always haunted, rushing
about in airplanes and trains to make more money! Even when
he had realized a bit, every time he saw the possibility of big
business, it was so difficult to let it go, to leave it for someone
else to take. It was a battle with his greed. He would see a
possibility that nobody else had noticed and could just take it

and make all that money. But he had to leave it alone so that somebody else could take it—that was hell! That is the sacrifice of the superior function. For an extraverted intuitive it means letting some business go down the drain and thinking, "Oh, well, other people need money too, let them have it, I have enough!" They just cannot resist the possibility which they, with their clever intuition, saw first! But you can't develop the inferior function without giving up, to a certain extent, the superior function. In his case it meant that he had to give up a great deal of money. There it was, just lying in front of him, he could just have taken it if he wanted, and that naturally was very disagreeable, because he knew that if he did not take it, somebody else would. But for the extravert it is always giving up a certain amount of worldly advantage, if he wants to turn toward introversion, and in the extraverted intuitive it meant giving up these possibilities, seeing them and not using them in any way! Just letting them go!

The Inferior Sensation of the Introverted Intuitive Type

The introverted intuitive type has the same capacity as the extraverted intuitive for smelling out the future, having the right guess or the right hunch about the not yet seen future possibilities of the situation, but his intuition is turned within, and therefore you can say that he is primarily the type of the religious prophet, of the seer. On a primitive level he is the shaman who knows what the gods and the ghosts and ancestral spirits are planning and who conveys that to the tribe. In psychological language we should say that he knows about the slow processes which go on in the collective unconscious, the archetypal changes which take place in the unconscious, and he conveys that to society. The prophets of the Old Testament, for instance, were people who, while the people of Israel were happily asleep—as people always are—from time to time told them what Yahveh's real intentions were, so to speak, and what He was doing just now, and what He wanted His people to do, which the people generally did not enjoy hearing.

Many introverted intuitives are to be found among artists and poets. They generally are artists of the type which produces very archetypal and fantastic material, as in Nietzsche's *Thus Spake Zarathustra* or in Gustav Meyrinck's *The Golem* and Kubin's *The Other Side*. This kind of visionary art, as one could call it, is generally only understood by later generations as a realization of what was going on in the collective unconscious at that time. The inferior sensation of this type also has difficulties in noticing the needs of the body, or being very uncontrolled about it. You know that Swedenborg even had a vision in which God Himself told him he should not eat so much! He ate, naturally, without the slightest self-discipline and with complete unawareness. Swedenborg was a typical introverted intuitive, the prophet or seer type, and he was coarse and uninhibited and impossible about overeating, and so once he had a vision of God telling him that he should stop that! The introverted intuitive also suffers, as the extraverted intuitive does, from a tremendous vagueness where facts are concerned.

As an illustration of the more ridiculous aspect of the inferior sensation of an introverted intuitive, I could tell you the following story. An introverted intuitive woman was present when I gave a lecture on early Greek philosophy and was terribly moved and impressed by it and asked me to give her private lessons about the early Greek pre-Socratic philosophy, as she wanted to get deeper into this field. She invited me to tea and, as happens very often when you have to give lessons to introverted intuitives, she wasted my first hour—this was many years ago—in telling me all about how she was moved and what she conceived to be at the back of my mind and hers and what she believed we could do together and so on. She talked and talked, as we say, "the devil's ear off," so the first hour got wasted and the second hour got wasted, and as I felt that really I had to earn my money and get her going somehow, I insisted that we should look at the book which I had brought and proceed in a systematic way. She suddenly got that and said, yes, she would look at it now, but that I should leave her alone, for she had to do that quite her own way. I noticed that she was getting very nervous. The next time when I came she said that now she had found the real way to get into the problem, namely, that, naturally, she could not study Greek philosophy without knowing about the Greeks, and she could not know about the Greeks before knowing quite concretely about their country, so she had now started to draw a map of Greece, and she showed me the map! That had taken a lot of time! With her inferior sensation she had first had to buy paper and pencils and ink, and that excited her enormously. She was absolutely in heaven about her discovery, and she showed me something which I must say was very beautifully done. She had made a map of Greece and really done it slowly and accurately. She said that she could not now go on with philosophy; she first had to finish this map. So the next time she had colored it! That went on for a few months, and then her intuition picked another theme she was very enthusiastic about, and we never got down to Greek philosophy! She left Zurich, and I did not see her often, but I did meet her about fifteen years later, and then she told me a long story of how she was still impressed and moved by the lessons on Greek philosophy which I had given her and all that she had conceived from them. She had just drawn a map! With immense devotion! She was a very extreme case of introverted intuition, but I must admit in looking back that I see that it was a really numinous thing for that woman to draw this map of Greece, because there, for the first time, she had gotten in touch with her inferior sensation.

Introverted intuitives are sometimes so completely unaware of outer facts that their reports about things have to be treated with the greatest care, for though they do not lie consciously, they can tell the most appalling stories, simply because they do not notice what is right under their noses. I very often distrust ghost reports, for instance, and reports about parapsychological phenomena, for those reasons. Introverted intuitives are very much interested in such fields, but because of their absolute weakness in observing facts and lack of concentration on outer facts, they can tell you the most appalling nonsense and swear it is true, simply because they have not noticed what was going on. They pass an absolutely amazing amount of outer facts unnoticed and just do not take them in. I remember, for instance, driving with an introverted intuitive type one autumn, and in all the fields the potatoes were being dug up and there were bonfires. I had noticed that long ago and was enjoying the sight. Suddenly the introverted intuitive person, who was driving, stopped the car in horror, sniffed, and said: "Something is burning! Is it coming from outside?" She looked at the brakes and everything was all right and then she decided it was outside and was the bonfires! I had noticed those bonfires long before; they were everywhere and it was absolutely obvious that the smell of burning came from them! But introverted intuitives can drive for an hour through such a country with such a phenomenon and not notice it—and then *suddenly* be struck by the fact and then, of course, make something out of it which it is not. They will make a wrong guess! It had, naturally, also the quality which all inferior functions have, namely that the sensation of an introverted intuitive comes up into consciousness in bits: sometimes it functions and then it disappears. For example, suddenly a smell is intensely realized. Three-quarters of an hour before, it was not realized at all, but then suddenly it is taken in with great intensity. The inferior sensation of an extraverted intuitive is extremely strong, but it breaks through here and there and then fades again out of the field of awareness. Of course, the introverted intuitive also has particular trouble in approaching sex because it involves his inferior extraverted sensation. You see it most tragically mirrored in the works of Nietzsche, where, toward the end, shortly before he went off his head, very coarse, vulgar sexual allusions more and more penetrate some of his poems and had already also appeared in *Thus Spake Zarathustra.* When he went insane, he apparently produced material of that kind, which unfortunately was destroyed after his death because of its distasteful character. Extraverted sensation in his case was very much connected with women and sex and in a completely outer concrete way, and he didn't know how to deal with the problem at all.

The positive aspect of inferior extraverted sensation in the case of an introverted intuitive is also to be found in an interesting way in the illumination experience of the German mystic Jakob Boehme, an introverted intuitive. He had a wife and six children for whom he never earned any money and with whom he was in constant trouble because his wife always said that instead of writing books about God and fantasizing about the inner development of the Godhead, he would do better to see that his family had something to eat. He was really crucified between these two poles of life, but his greatest inner experience, a revelation of the Godhead upon which all his later writings are based, came from seeing a ray of light being reflected in a tin plate. The sun suddenly came in through the window and reflected in the plate, and his eye was hit by the ray of light, and that outer sensation experience snapped him into an inner ecstasy, and within a minute he saw the whole mystery of the Godhead. Then for years and years he really did nothing except slowly translate into discursive language what he had seen inwardly in one second! He carried out his vision by describing it and circumambulating it many many times, which is why his writing is so emotional and chaotic, for he tried to describe this one experience in so many words and in so many amplifications. But the actual vision was set in motion by seeing a ray of light striking a tin plate on his table, which implies extraverted sensation — an outer fact started off the process of individuation in him; all his deeper realizations were started in that short moment. There you see, besides the inferior aspect of extraverted sensation, this strange character of wholeness, the mystical aspect which the inferior function often has. It is interesting that even Swedenborg's overeating connected him with the Godhead — it had to be the Lord Himself who told him that he should not overeat, so that the problem of his inferior sensation is connected with his deepest or greatest concern. That little silly detail is connected with his greatest concern — it is the Lord Himself who takes the trouble to warn him.

Something interesting about Boehme is that as long as he was crucified between inner needs and his nagging wife, who said he had better make good shoes and feed his six children and then speculate about a Godhead, he was very productive, but after his first book was published, a German baron was so sorry for him and felt so much that he was the great seer that he removed all his outer troubles by paying for his and his family's support, and from then on Boehme's writing got full of resentment and repetitions. It sterilized his creativity, and on his tomb is an image of the Godhead like this:)(, which is really tragic, as it shows that he could not unite the light and the dark sides. That remained an insoluble problem to him, and in my experience it is connected with the simple fact that he accepted money from this baron and thereby escaped the torture of his inferior function.

I once analyzed a woman of that type who came from a simple sector of the population. She had great inner visions, and she too, naturally, was in a constant muddle about money and outer life and just didn't know how to function. She was in trouble with the landlord and with the dairy because she forgot to give the bottles back or swore she had given back five when the shop swore it was only one—the usual sensation trouble which such prophets have. They just stumble about in reality and are quite sure they have done something which the others say they have not and so accuse them of lying. They simply do not know what they are doing. They can't count bottles or remember whether they brought the bottles back to the shop or not. Now, this person too had a secret hope that one day someone would discover her capacities and pay for her support and she would escape those troubles. But when she got out of them, she went completely off her head! As soon as she got back into her worries and accepted them, she was all right. So to be crucified between the superior and the inferior function is vitally important, and I can only tell you that if you ever feel like saving such artists or prophets, for God's sake look at the case first very circumspectly and see how much you can afford to help them, because if you buy them off reality, then they go off reality! And then you have not helped them in the least. Just that type will *beg* you to help them out of their trouble, on their knees they will beg you to save them from the torture of outer reality with which they can't cope. But if you save them, the creative core of their personality is destroyed. That does not mean that if they are starving you cannot give them something so that they can survive and help them from time to time, when the situation is bad. But don't let them off the problem of reality because, strangely enough, that sterilizes the inner process as well. That happened to Boehme, and because of it he was not able to unite the opposites, not even in his system and not in his life either, so what Baron von Merz did destroyed him by unwise charity.

The Inferior Thinking of the Extraverted Feeling Type

The extraverted feeling type is characterized by the fact that his main adaptation is carried by adequate evaluation of the outer object and adequate relation to it. The type will therefore very easily make friends, will have very few illusions about people, but will be capable of evaluating their positive and negative sides appropriately and of knowing how much or how little they and the situation means to them. So people of this type are generally very much liked by those around them. They are well-adjusted, very reasonable people who roll along amiably through society and can get what they want very easily and can somehow ensure that everybody is willing to give them what they want. They lubricate their surroundings so marvelously that life goes along for them very easily. You find them frequently among women, and they generally have a very happy family life with a lot of friends. Things are easy in the surroundings, but this does not mean that they have the slightest illusion or are calculating; they are just amiable, seeing the good in situations and people. Only if they are in some way neurotically dissociated do they become a bit theatrical and a little bit mechanical and calculating. If you go to a luncheon party with an extraverted feeling type, she or he is capable of saying little things like, "What a nice day it is today, I am so glad to see you again, I haven't seen you for a long time!" And the person really means it, and with that the car, so to speak, is lubricated and the party goes! You feel happy and warmed up. They spread a kind of atmosphere of acceptance, and it is agreeable: "We appreciate each other, so we are going to have a good day together." They make those in their surroundings feel wonderful, and in the midst of that they swim along happily and create a pleasant social atmosphere. Only when they overdo it, or if their extraverted feeling is already worn out and they therefore start to think, do you notice that this becomes a little bit of a habit, that it becomes a phrase which they say mechanically. For instance, I once noticed an extraverted feeling type on a dreadful day when there was a horrible fog outside saying mechanically, "Isn't it a wonderful day?" I thought, "Oh dear, your main function is rattling off; you overdo it!"

In general people of this type have very good taste in the choice of partners and friends, but are a little bit conventional about it. They wouldn't risk choosing someone too much out of the ordinary, but would remain in a socially acceptable framework. The extraverted feeling type dislikes thinking, because that is the inferior function, and what they dislike most of all is introverted thinking, which means thinking about philosophical principles or abstract things or basic questions of life, such as: What is the meaning of life? Do I believe in God or not? What is my attitude toward the problem of evil? Such deeper questions are carefully avoided, and there is the reaction that thinking about such problems would make one melancholy. The unfortunate thing is that, naturally, they do think of such things but are not aware of it, and because their thinking is neglected, it tends to become negative and coarse. It consists of coarse, primitive thinking judgments without the slightest differentiation and very often with a negative tinge. I have also seen that introverted feeling types sometimes have very negative thoughts about the people around, very critical, I would say overcritical judgments, which they never allow really to come out. That is why Jung says that the extraverted feeling type can sometimes be the coldest person on earth, and it may happen that if you get lured into this well-lubricated car of their extraverted feeling and feel, "We like each other and get along well together," then suddenly one day they will say something to you which is like smacking you on the head with a block of ice! One sometimes cannot imagine what cynical negative thoughts they have. They are not aware of them, but they pop out when they begin to have the flu, or when they are rushed, or in such moments when the inferior function wells up and where control of the superior function fails.

An extraverted feeling type dreamed that she should establish a bird observation station. She saw in the dream a kind of cement building, a tower built high up in the air, and on the top was a kind of laboratory where one had to observe the birds. So we thought she should try to be aware of autonomous thoughts which would, as it were, alight on her head and go again. That is how thoughts operate in a feeling type; she has thought-birds alighting on her head and flying off and before she can say, "What am I thinking?," they are gone again. The woman agreed, and I asked her how it could be done technically. She said she should take a little notebook and a pencil and carry them around with her, and when she had a sudden thought, she should just jot it down! Nothing more, and we would see afterward how the thoughts were connected. Next time she brought only one piece of paper, and on it was: "If my son-in-law died, my daughter would come back home." She got such a shock through that thought that she never put a ring on a second bird!

That one bird was quite enough for a long time! She then confessed something even more interesting and said that in a way she knew she sometimes had such thoughts but always thought that if she didn't write them down, then they would not have any effect, but if she did, then they would act like black magic and affect the surroundings, so she avoided looking at them. Now, that was completely wrong; it is the other way round! If the feeling type is aware of his negative thoughts, then they don't act like black magic; they are depotentiated of any destructive effect. It is just when these thoughts are left alone to fly around his head without being caught that they actually have a destructive influence on their surroundings.

If one analyzes extraverted feeling types and is a little bit sensitive to the atmosphere, one very often gets a bit frozen or cooled down in spite of their amiability, because one senses these critical negative thoughts swarming around in their heads but never expressed; they hit one in a disagreeable way. One sees a kind of cold flash sometimes in the eyes, and one knows that there is some very negative thought about, but the next minute it is gone! It gives one the creeps! For instance, thoughts such as, "If you die . . . ," are generally based on a very cynical outlook on life: the dark side of life is illness and death and such things, and the thoughts circle around these factors, but the person doesn't "allow" them to come through, so a kind of second philosophy of life, cynical and negativistic, creeps around in the background. The worse thing about these negative thoughts in the extraverted feeling type is that they are introverted and thus very often turned against themselves. I have never caught so many absolutely destructive judgments as extraverted feeling types have about themselves. At bottom they allow themselves to think that they are nobodies and worthless, that their lives are worthless, and that everybody else might develop and get on the path of individuation, but they are hopeless, and so on—absolutely destructive condemning ideas of themselves, but which they do not think consciously. These thoughts dwell in the back of their minds, and from time to time, when they are depressed or not well off, or especially when they introvert (that is, when they are alone for half a minute), then this negative thing whispers at the back of their mind: "You are nothing; everything is wrong about you." These thoughts are coarse, primitive, and very undifferentiated; they are generalized judgments which are like a cold draft which goes through the room and makes you shiver. The effect is that extraverted feeling types naturally hate to be alone when such negative thoughts could come up in their minds, so as soon as they have realized one or two, they quickly switch on the radio or rush to meet other people. Therefore, the worst thing about them is that they never have time to think. But they carefully arrange their lives in that way!

Because extraverted feeling types have such a tremendous capacity for objectively feeling the other person's situation, they are usually the people who genuinely sacrifice themselves for others. If you are alone in the flat and have the flu, it is certainly an extraverted feeling type who will turn up first and ask who is doing your shopping and whether he can help you. The others couldn't be so quick and practical about feeling into your situation, for they feel how you feel at every minute and then naturally cannot resist lending a helping hand. To the others, even though they might like you as much, it would not occur that they could do this or that for you, either because they are introverts or because another function is dominant in their system. So you find the extraverted feeling type always jumping into the breach, for wherever something does not function, they realize it at once and see the importance of it. Feeling is seeing the value of something, and they see the importance or the value of what should be done and then just do it. Naturally, if they overdo this, they pile up negative resistance against the outer situation. If this woman who had the one little thought—"My only daughter would come back home"—had dug deeper, she would have had to say to herself, "O.K., let's face that thought! What am I after? If I have such a thought, what is the premise, and what is the conclusion to be drawn?" She could then have developed the thought and said that the premise is something like a devouring mother's attitude, and the conclusion is that she wants the son-in-law removed. Why? For what purpose? She could, for example, have said, "Assuming that my daughter does come home, what then?" And then she would have seen that she would have hated to have a sourpuss old maid of a daughter at home. And in continuing that thought, she would have seen that there was a contradiction in it, and then she would have probably dropped into a deeper layer and said, "And what then? If my children have now left home, what is the real purpose of my life?" And then she would have had to philosophize about the future purpose of her life after forty-eight: "Does life still have a meaning once one has brought up the children and started them into life, and if so, what is it, and what is the meaning of life altogether?" She would have been confronted with the deep but human philosophical questions which she never had faced before, and that would have brought her into deep water. She naturally could not have solved the problem, but then she might have had a dream to help along a whole process, a quest for the meaning of life which her inferior thinking function would have started. Now, because the case was that of an extraverted feeling type, the quest would be a completely introverted inner thing, like developing an introverted philosophical view of her own life. That would have required that she spend a long time alone in her room and really become slowly aware of the dark underground of her thoughts.

The easy escape which I have seen in several extraverted feeling types is that they get out of the difficulty by simply selling their souls to some already established system. One person I remember got converted to Catholicism and simply adopted, unchecked, that basic Scholastic philosophy and from then on only quoted Scholastic authors. That was, in a way, taking up the thinking function, but taking it up in an already established form. The same thing can be done with Jungian psychology, just repeating the concepts by heart in a mechanical way, but never working out one's own standpoint. It is a kind of pupil-like, uncreative attitude which just takes over the system unexamined and never asks, "What do *I* think about it? Does this really convince me? Are the facts upon which this thought is based convincing to me? Does it coincide with the facts I have checked? Can I take it over myself with my own conviction? Does it coincide with my own inner experiences?" Instead, it is taken over wholesale, so that if such people then meet others who themselves know how to think—for instance, thinking types—they get fanatical because they feel helpless. They then fight for the system they have chosen with a certain apostlelike fanaticism because they feel uncertain about the basis of the thinking system: how the system developed, its basic concepts, and so on; and because they are uncertain and have the feeling that the system could be thrown over by a good thinker, they adopt an aggressive attitude.

Another danger is that if an extraverted feeling type starts to think, he gets completely caught up in it. Either he cannot cut off his relationships sufficiently to go and sit and be alone and think, or, if he succeeds in cutting off all outer ties, in having enough time alone to get down into the problems of his own thoughts—which is already great progress—then he gets terribly caught by them and really loses sight of life and disappears into books, or into a library, and gets covered with dust and is no longer able to switch to any other activity. He gets swallowed by that one thought task.

If you want to have a very world-famous example of the inferior thinking of an extraverted feeling type, read Goethe's *Conversations with Eckermann*. It is just an amazing collection of platitudes—*aperçus* of so-called depth, but really just plain platitudes. There you see the inferior function of Goethe very visibly exposed to the world. He has also published maxims, general reflections, which—and that is very typical for their level—you meet on the back leaf of every calendar! They are very true, you can rarely object to them in any way, but they are just so true that any sheep could have thought them just as well. That is Wagner at work in the great poet.

Naturally, the inferior thinking of the feeling type is threatened by such generalities and platitudes, which are typical for undeveloped thinking. If, for instance, you give students of fourteen to eighteen years of age a theme to write about, you will see that at that age they usually cannot produce any differentiated or special thought but write generalities—which, at that age, is already an achievement. The way in which we educate children in school in writing such generalities is most idiotic. I remember that in my own youth we got such themes as "Does the individual or do the masses decide the course of history?" Now, imagine! How can a girl of sixteen know anything differentiated or factual about that? You just write generalities! I must confess that it is only hearsay, but I have heard that many debating clubs in American colleges seem to move on those levels, without the slightest differentiation of thought as to facts, or anything extraordinary or above level, or anything focused on one theme; there are just evident platitudes and generalities which anybody could think. The inferior thinking of the extraverted feeling type has therefore a very disagreeable way of secretly making one feel uneasy. The feeling type likes—unconsciously—to throw a wet blanket on his surroundings with his secret negative thinking. There is a kind of skepticism which can exert a repressing effect upon others. If you get into discussion with the negative thinking of such an extraverted feeling type, you see that, in general, he has jumped to conclusions too quickly and thereby has not gotten to the bottom of things. There are all kinds of negative thoughts and rather sweeping statements which are also a typical feature of inferior thinking.

The Extraverted Thinking of the Introverted Feeling Type

The introverted feeling type mainly adapts to life by feeling, but more in an introverted way, that is, mainly toward the orientation of the subject with a differentiated scale of evaluation. This type is very difficult to understand. Jung says that the saying "Still waters run deep" applies to people of this type. They have the same reactions of a very differentiated scale of value, but unlike the extravert, they do not express them outwardly, but are affected by them within. You often find introverted feeling types in the background where important and valuable events or setups are taking place, just as if their introverted feeling has told them that that setup was really important and was the real thing. With a kind of silent loyalty and without any outside explanation, they turn up in places where important and valuable inner facts, archetypal constellations, are to be found. With inconspicuous constancy they will stick, for instance, to important archetypal ideas, and they generally exert a positive secret influence on their surroundings by setting standards. The others observe them and, though they say nothing, for they are much too introverted to express themselves much, they set certain standards because they have them within themselves. Introverted feeling types, for instance, very often form the secret ethical backbone of a group, for without irritating the others with moral or ethical precepts, they themselves have such right standards of ethical values that they secretly emanate a positive influence on those around. One has to behave correctly because they have that kind of right value standard, or good taste, which always suggestively forces one to be decent if they are present, and that is because their differentiated introverted feeling sees what is inwardly the really important factor.

The thinking of this type is extraverted, flowing toward the outer object. In amazing contrast to their silent and inconspicuous outer appearance, the introverted feeling types are therefore generally interested in an immense number of outer facts. In their conscious personality they do not move about much, but sit in their badger's hole, while their extraverted thinking, their more unconscious mind, roams about among an extraordinary amount of outer facts. They read, for example, about the most unexpected things: the natural sciences and God knows what. They are interested in practically all outer facts of life, but this is a kind of hidden interest, whereas with the

extraverted thinking types, that would be right in the foreground of their interests. If introverted feeling types want to
use their extraverted thinking in a creative way, they have the
usual extravert's difficulty of being overwhelmed by too much
material, too many references, and too many facts, so their
inferior extraverted thinking sometimes just gets lost in a mo-
rass of single outer objective references and facts through
which they can no longer find their way. The inferiority of
their extraverted thinking very often expresses itself in a certain monomanic way, in that they have only one or two
thoughts with which they race through a tremendous amount
of material. This is very obvious and is why Jung characterizes
the Freudian system as a typical example of extraverted
thinking.

Jung has never said anything about Freud's type as a human
being; he has only said in many of his books that Freud's system represents extraverted thinking, so what I add now is my
personal conviction, namely that Freud was an introverted
feeling type and that therefore his writings bear the characteristics of his inferior extraverted thinking. There you typically
have the fact that the basic ideas are few and that they are
raced through, and that the writer has beaten through an
enormous amount of outer material and is completely oriented
toward the outer object, so that a rather poor biological outer
setup of facts is connected with the basis of his thoughts. If
you read biographical notes about Freud, you see that as a
person he had a most differentiated way of treating people. He
was an excellent analyst and had a very differentiated way of
treating his patients. He had also a kind of hidden gentleman-
liness which had a positive influence upon his patients and in
general upon his surroundings. One must really in his case
make a distinction between his theory and his personality as a

human being. I think, from what one hears about him, that he belonged to the introverted feeling type.

The advantage of inferior extraverted thinking is what I now characterize negatively as racing with a few ideas through a tremendous amount of material. (Freud himself complained that his dream interpretation felt awfully monotonous—the same interpretation of every dream was boring even to him.) If this is not overdone, and if the introverted feeling type is aware of the danger of his inferior function and keeps a check on it, it has the great advantage of being simple, clear, and intelligible. It has a few comprehensive thoughts which have a kind of obviousness, in a positive sense of the word. But this is not enough, and the introverted feeling type is obliged to drill a bit deeper and try to specify and differentiate his extraverted thinking, if he does not wish at some time to fall into the trap of this kind of monomania of ideas. Therefore he has to specify his thinking, that is, make the hypothesis that each fact he cites in proof of his ideas illustrates them with a slightly differentiated slant, and with this object in view, his idea should be reformulated each time. In that way he keeps up the living process of contact between thought and fact instead of just imposing his thought upon facts. Inferior extraverted thinking has just the same negative tendencies to being tyrannical, stiff, and unmolded, and in that way not quite adapted to its own object, that all inferior functions have.

THE RELATIONSHIP OF THE INFERIOR FUNCTION
TO OTHER CONTENTS OF THE UNCONSCIOUS

We have now to ask how the inferior function relates to the shadow, the anima, and the Self when it appears in dreams. It relates to and gives a certain quality to all these figures. For instance, the shadow in an intuitive type will often be personified by a sensation type; you can say that the inferior function is contaminated by the shadow in each type, for in a thinking type it will appear as a relatively inferior or primitive feeling person, and so on. Thus, if in interpreting a dream you ask for a description of this shadow figure, people will describe their own inferior function. When you try to make the shadow conscious, or to become conscious of your own shadow, the inferior function will give the animus or the anima figure a special quality. For example, the anima figure, if personified by a particular human being, will very often appear as a person of the opposite function, the fourth function. Again, when personifications of the Self appear, the same thing will happen. You can therefore say that the inferior function is the door through which all the figures of the unconscious enter.

Our conscious realm is like a room with four doors, and it will be the fourth door by which the shadow, the animus, and the anima and the personification of the Self will come in. They will not enter as often through the other doors, which in a way is self-evident, because the inferior function is so close to the unconscious and remains so barbaric and inferior and undeveloped that it is naturally the weak spot in consciousness through which the figures of the unconscious can break in. In consciousness it is experienced as a weak spot, as that disagreeable thing which will never leave you in peace but always causes trouble, for every time you feel you have acquired a certain inner balance or inner standpoint, something happens from within or without to throw you off again, and it is always through that fourth door, which you cannot shut. You can keep the three doors of your inner room closed, but on the fourth door the lock does not work, and there, when you do not expect it, the unexpected will come in again. Thank God, you can say, for otherwise the whole life process would petrify and stagnate in a wrong kind of consciousness. It is the ever-bleeding wound of the conscious personality, but through it the unconscious can always come in and so enlarge consciousness and bring forth new experience.

As long as you have not developed your other functions, your auxiliary functions, they too will be open doors, so in a person who has only developed one superior function, the two auxiliary functions will operate in the same way and will appear in personifications of the shadow, animus, and anima. It is only when you have succeeded in developing three functions, in locking three of your inner doors, that the problem of the fourth door still remains, for that is the one which is apparently not meant to be locked. There one has to succumb, one has to suffer defeat, in order to develop further. So if you attend to your own dreams, you will see that these inner figures, if they appear personified as real persons, tend to choose such personifications. Another kind of personification, which naturally has to do with the shadow, is that the fourth function is contaminated with personifications from the lower levels of the social strata of the population or by the underdeveloped countries. That is a beautiful expression—the "underdeveloped" countries. It is just marvelous how we Westerners in our superior arrogance look down on the underdeveloped countries and project our inferior functions upon them! The underdeveloped countries are within ourselves, and therefore, naturally, because this is such an obvious symbolism, the inferior function for a white person often appears as a wild Negro or a wild Indian. Frequently also the inferior function is expressed by exotic people of some kind: Chinese, Russian, or whoever may give that quality. The unconscious tries in this way to convey the quality of something unknown to the conscious realm, as if it would say: it is as unknown to you as the Chinese are unknown in your culture. The shadow, animus, and anima appear very often projected onto Asian or African or "primitive" people.

This dream simile for the inferior function is also particularly fitting in that this function tends to have, in a negative way, a barbaric character and to cause possession. If, for example, introverts fall into extraversion, they do so in a possessed and barbaric way. I mean barbaric in the sense of being unable to exert conscious control, being swept away, being unable to put a brake on, unable to stop. This kind of exaggerated, driven extraversion is rarely found in extraverts, but in introverts it is like a car without brakes that goes on without the slightest control of consciousness. That is a rather well-known fact, because the inferior extraversion of introverts has to manifest outside, socially. An introvert may become disagreeable and arrogant, pushing and shouting so loudly that the whole room has to listen and everybody must notice. Such inferior extraversion may suddenly pop out in this way when an introvert is drunk. The introversion of the extravert is just as barbaric and possessed but not so socially visible because an extravert disappears right out of life if possessed by barbaric introversion. He goes completely mad in his own room, but it is not visible to other people. Extraverts who fall into their primitive introversion walk about looking very important. In dark allusions they assure everybody that they are having very deep mystical experiences about which they cannot talk, they are so important and so deep. In an important kind of way they indicate that they are now deeply steeped in active imagination and the process of individuation, and you know that you must leave at once, because they have to work on that. And then they sit in a possessed way for hours, unable to relax and unable to pull out of it. If you ring them up, they say they are deep in their process of individuation and cannot go to a tea party just now, and this is thrown at you with a kind of defensive attitude. You have a strange feeling of a barbaric kind of possession. If this happens to them in the form of yoga, or Anthroposophy, then there will be that same display of something mystical of great importance going on and of an unfathomable depth into which they have now dived. There is a mixture in it, for actually they are constantly threatened with switching back to their extraversion, which explains their over-emphasis on lack of time and wanting no contact with anybody. They would love to switch over to their extraversion and go to every tea party and every dinner party, so in a kind of defensive way, they say, "No, this is absolutely forbidden; now I am in the depth of the psyche." Very often in this phase people are sure that they *are* the type that they now have to live. For instance, extraverts who are in the phase where they should assimilate introversion will always swear that they are and always have been introverts and that it has always been an error to call them extraverts. In this way they try to help themselves to get into this other side, which for them is so difficult to acquire. If they try to express their introverted inner experiences, they generally do so with overexcitement. They become terribly emotional and want to take the floor and have everybody listen. That is because to them it is so tremendously unique and important.

This barbaric quality of the inferior function which is mixed up with the other attitudinal type is one of the great practical problems and constitutes the great split of the human personality, for not only has one to switch from one function to another, but with the fourth function one definitely has to switch to the other attitudinal type, and then one risks (or even cannot avoid) being temporarily possessed by the opposite attitude and thereby become barbaric and unadapted. One can thank God if one's opposite function is only personified by primitive people in dreams, for it is very often represented by Stone Age people or even by animals, so that the inferior function has not even reached a primitive human level; it is still completely on an animal level. The inferior function in that stage dwells, so to speak, in the body and can only manifest in physical symptoms and not yet on a human conscious level, not even a primitive one. When you see, for example, how sometimes an introverted intuitive stretches in the sunshine with such enjoyment of his inferior function, you have absolutely the feeling that he is like a dog sitting in the sunshine enjoying the sun or food; his sensation is still on the level of a dog or a cat or some other domestic animal.

Feeling in a thinking type very often does not go beyond the dog level. It is more difficult to imagine that the feeling type thinks like an animal, but even that is true; these people have a habit of making banal statements which one feels any cow, cat, or dog could have made if they could speak, for they move in a realm of complete generalities. Dogs sometimes make helpless attempts to think. My dog sometimes drew some terribly wrong conclusions. He always lay on my couch, and I used to try to chase him down, and from that he concluded that I did not like him to sit on anything above the ground. So whenever one put him on something, he became bewildered and thought he would be punished. He couldn't understand that it was only the couch and not any other raised piece of furniture which was forbidden. He had simply drawn the wrong conclusion! It is just the same when you try to teach dogs to be clean in the house. They conclude that the same applies to any kind of paved floor, and they and their owners get into all sorts of trouble until at last the poor dog realizes that it is only in the house that he must be careful. There you see that a dog has a kind of halfway undeveloped thinking which tends to draw the wrong conclusion. I have often been struck by the fact that feeling types think in exactly the same way, for when you try to explain something to them, they may draw a completely general conclusion, some sweeping assertion which does not fit the situation in any way, and they do the most stupid things. Primitive thinking started in their heads, and they drew some kind of amazingly unadapted conclusion, which led to entirely wrong results. Thus you can often say that the thinking level of the feeling type is about on the dog's level; it is as general and helpless and stiff as you can observe it in the higher animals.

In general, in most normal societies, people cover up their inferior function with a persona. One of the main reasons why one develops a persona is so as not to expose inferiorities, especially the inferiorities of the fourth function, which is contaminated with one's animal nature, one's unadapted emotions and affects.

When Jung founded the Psychology Club in Zurich, he had in mind to try to find out how a group, or a society, would work in which the inferior function would not be covered up, but where people would contact each other by it. The result was absolutely amazing. People who came into this society from outside were shocked out of their wits by the rude, bad behavior and the absolutely unending quarrels this group displayed. I visited the Club many years ago and till then had never made a move toward becoming a member because I felt too shy. One day Jung said to me, "Do you not *want* to join the Psychology Club, or do you not *dare* to join it?" I said, "I did not *dare* to join it, but would love to." So he said, "All right, I will be your godfather"—we need godfathers to get into the Club—"but I'll wait first to see if you have a dream, if the right moment has come." And what did I dream? I dreamed that a natural scientist, an old man who looked very much like Jung, had made up an experimental group to find out how animals of different species got along with each other! I came into the place, and there were aquariums with fish in them, enclosures with tortoises, newts, and such creatures, and cages with birds and dogs and cats, and the old man was sitting in the middle, taking notes on how the animals behaved socially with one another. I discovered then that I myself was a flying fish in an aquarium and could jump out. I told my dream to Jung and he said, with a grin, "I think now you are mature enough to join the Psychology Club; you have got the central idea, its purpose."

In this rather humorous way the unconscious took up the idea, namely that it is really a great problem, for as conscious beings we can contact each other, but in this inferior function, one person is a cat, another is a tortoise, and a third a hare—there are all those animals! Such social adaptations present a great difficulty. There are all the problems of having one's own territory, one's own ground, for every animal species has a tendency to have a few meters of homeland. Every bird and every animal defends its territory against intruders; one may not step on the other's ground, and all these complicated rituals build up again as soon as human beings join together and discard the persona and try really to contact each other. Then one really feels as if one is moving in the jungle or the bush: one must not step on this snake or frighten that bird by making a quick movement, and things become very complicated. This need for bush manners has even led to the belief that psychology causes social behavior to deteriorate, which to some extent is quite true. At the Jung Institute, too, we are in a way much nastier and more difficult a group to get along with than, say, a society for breeding dogs or hares, or a club for fishermen, for there the social contact is in general on a much better level. Such an accusation has often been made not only of the Psychology Club but also of the Institute. But the truth is simply that we tend not to cover up what is going on underneath. In all other societies or groups of people, that is covered up and plays under the table; underneath there are all these difficulties, but they are never brought up to the surface and discussed openly. But, in fact, naturally, facing the shadow and the inferior function has the effect that people become socially more difficult and less conventionally adapted, and that creates more friction. On the other hand, it also creates a greater liveliness: it is never boring, for there is always a storm in a teacup and excitement, and the group is very much alive instead of having a dull, conventional, correct surface. It has even gone so far that in the Psychology Club, the animal tendencies to have one's own realm became so strong that people started reserving seats; there was So-and-So's chair, and you couldn't sit on it; that was a major insult, because So-and-So always sat there. I have noticed that there are also papers on certain chairs on which people write their names: this is my chair — in other words, there the dog or the cat So-and-So sits! That is a very good sign, and I thought: "Well now, that is better, matters are improving!" It is a restoration of an original and natural situation. But it is amazing how deeply the inferior function can connect one down into the realm of animal nature within oneself.

Apart from the humorous way in which I have just described it, it is a very important fact, for the inferior function is actually the connection with one's deepest instincts, with one's inner roots, and is, so to speak, that which connects us with the whole past of mankind. Primitive societies perform dances with animal masks which are meant to connect the tribe with their ancestral ghosts, that is, with the whole past of the tribe. We have, for the most part, lost such masked dances, though there is still Carnival as a remnant. Anyone who doesn't know his inferior function yet should go to a masked Carnival and find out how he feels then! On such occasions you can often reconnect with your animal past and with your inferior function.

Theoretically one can naturally have all the functions all ways, but it won't be a problem, and there would not be much intensity of life in it. Jung once said that your *opposite* type is not the hardest thing to understand. That is, if you have introverted feeling, it *is* very difficult to understand an extraverted thinking type, but it is even harder to understand someone of the same functional type with the other attitude. That means that it would be most difficult for an introverted feeling type to understand an extraverted feeling type. There one feels that one does not know how the wheels go around in that person's head; one cannot feel one's way into it. Such people remain to a great extent a puzzle and are very difficult to understand spontaneously. That is why the whole theory of types is tremendously important practically, for it is the only thing which can prevent one from completely misunderstanding certain other people. It is a clue, at least theoretically, to some understanding of a person whose spontaneous reactions are a complete puzzle, which you would, if you reacted spontaneously, misunderstand completely. Just the other day I observed such a case. An intuitive brushed aside facts to such an extent that it gave a sensation type the idea that the other was the worst liar he had ever met his in life. Everything that intuitive person said was not quite right; the sensation type checked it all, and every single fact was twisted or in some other way not quite right, and so on. So the sensation type got the idea that this was just awful, that this person lied from morning to night—not one fact she had cited was right! Now, in that special case it was not a question of lying, but of tremendous one-sidedness and complete inaccuracy on the factual side. But the accusation of lying was incorrect, and in that sense it is very important to understand the types, because then a lot of very difficult misunderstandings can be avoided. I was called in to settle the dispute and tried to explain that in this case it was just the classical inaccuracy of the intuitive type. You must pin down such a person, interrupt every sentence, and say, "How was it exactly?" But it is even more difficult, as I said, to understand the same function type with the other attitude. There one can really only use theory to understand the other, because with one's spontaneous reactions one cannot.

In general, in the realm of the inferior function, people are afraid of each other, terribly afraid, because they feel helpless. I remember once I quarreled with a woman of my same type—introverted thinking—and we shouted at each other. The night after, I dreamed that a hare and a budgerigar were put together in a cage, and the budgerigar was sitting on a perch shivering with fear and the hare in the other corner of the cage doing the same. So the comment of the dream was: on the surface you quarrel, but underneath you are both deathly afraid of each other. The feeling personality is deathly afraid of the other feeling personality. So I would say that the only way to relate on the level of the inferior function is by what Jung calls bush politeness. In the bush, if people meet each other, they stop ten meters off and put down their spears ostentatiously to show that they have no evil intentions, and then they bow, and sometimes kneel down, and then slowly they move toward each other, and stop again and bow again, and then assure each other that they have no intent to harm, and then only do they shake hands, which is very similar to the way in which animals that do not know each other approach each other. They take a look from a distance, advance a little, and then stop again, and then try to read in the other's eyes what the other is going to do. We do exactly the same thing! As soon as we fall into the inferior function, we behave like primitives to each other and therefore need all the rituals of the primitive in meeting each other. One can only compensate for the fierceness and unpredictability and unadaptedness of the inferior function by bush politeness.

I have just read in Van Gennep's *Les Rîtes de Passage* examples of how explorers approach a primitive village. They have to stop when they are so many miles away, and then three messengers from the village come, and the villagers have to be assured that the explorers have no evil designs and especially that they do not intend to use black magic against the inhabitants. The messengers then go back, and when they return, gifts are exchanged, sometimes even women are exchanged or may be given to the guests, who sleep with them, because that establishes a kind of kinship; if a man sleeps with another man's wife, he is akin to him, he has been taken into his family. The Naskapi people of the Labrador peninsula did that, and many Eskimo men used to lend their wives to foreigners for the night, to prevent any kind of evil outburst, any thought that a guest might murder the people in the house, or that the latter might murder the guest, which could happen at any time in those countries where there were no police, for one could just disappear forever if one visited such people. Among many primitive people there is an exchange of blood; they cut each other and exchange blood. There is also a special way of kissing and of exchanging gifts — all those *rîtes de passage* come into play as soon as you have to relate to people on the level of the inferior function.

We can see the same thing in everyday life. For instance, you may have known someone for two or three years, but only on the conventional level of having tea or dinner together and talking about the weather and politics and theoretical questions, but never having dared to touch the sore spots in each other or to bring the conversation around to some ticklish point. But then one day you feel that it is not a real relationship, that you are not getting really close, and then you have a little wine or, if the atmosphere is favorable, you come out with your sore spots and invite the other to come out with his, and so through all the precautions of bush politeness you slowly really approach! I don't know any other formula than bush politeness, for that is the formula with which to approach the other side, because the sore spots generally are connected with the inferior function.

There is a difference between personal politeness and bush politeness. Let's take a practical example: I was once driving home with an intuitive type late at night, and he forgot to turn on the ignition and tried over and over again to start the car, and it would not go. I ventured politely to ask whether he had switched on. "Naturally," came the reply, but with such an affect that I didn't dare say any more! Now, that was his inferior sensation! So there we sat for half an hour, and I felt sure of what the trouble was but didn't know how to tell him! The slightest tone of knowing better, or of the governess, would have produced a similar reply. I felt so helpless because I knew all the time what was wrong but didn't know how to get around the sore spot. So you see, there the inferior function and the sore spot are absolutely connected. If he had not had inferior sensation, he would not have been so touchy. If I had said, "Have you switched on?" He would have said, "Oh, my God!" and done so and off we would have gone, but instead we sat for an hour on the road, guessing what the trouble could be, and I just didn't know how to approach this sore area of the inferior function.

You see, there was the question of his prestige. I must say, a lot of alcohol added to the *abaissement,* which made the affects much more explosive, and then the man was older than I, and there was the question of being impolite. The kind of politeness that was called for was not of the persona; it is a matter of having real feeling and understanding for the other person's weakness and not daring to touch that weakness. If you trigger off an affect, there is always the risk of a complete break, it is the razor's edge, for there may be a definite split. I know, for example, that once a group of twelve people left the Psychology Club in a mad affect. They wouldn't discuss the thing anymore but just left, and among them were quite valuable people. I met one of them later—an old man who was terribly sorry about it—and I asked him why he did not come back now, but he could not; he said it would be against his feeling of honor. The affect had gone too far! He had said such awful things in his rage that he felt he could not now come back; his pride made it impossible. That is tragic and very unfortunate, and that is why bush politeness is necessary in dealing with the inferior function, because the affect very easily goes too far and then the relationship is broken forever. The same can happen with two people as well as with a group; they very easily burst so far apart that they cannot be reconciled again. The inferior function plus the load of emotion behind it is a really dangerous business.

The assimilation of functions is such a serious business that people generally spend a very long time in assimilating their auxiliary functions and sometimes, say for at least eight to ten years, become a type which was not their original type. I once, for example, knew a woman who was an introverted feeling type; that is, in the past she had been a feeling type, but in the stage at which we met, she had already switched the process to developing intuition and at that stage had as much trouble with her sensation as if she had been a genuine intuitive. She was in the stage of being an intuitive; she even swore that that was her type! But if you looked at her past history carefully, you saw that that was not true. In the years before we met she had been living mainly by intuition, for her feeling was already worn out and contained no more life. And then she went through all the crises of having to switch from intuition to sensation which you see with a primarily intuitive type; for example, she became completely inaccurate about facts and had trouble relating to them, exactly as an intuitive does. She then stated with great emphasis that it had always been an error to call her a feeling type, for she was an intuitive, but she was wrong! She was right and wrong for at the stage at which she was, she was exactly like an intuitive, but that was because she was at the stage of living in her second function and was just in the crisis of getting over to the third.

The process of assimilating the functions is not in any way easy. To assimilate a function really means to live at least a few years completely with that one function in the foreground before you can claim that you have assimilated it. If once you do a little bit of cooking or sewing, that does not mean that you have assimilated your sensation function, and if you do a little bit of thinking on a Sunday afternoon, it does not mean that you have assimilated your thinking function. People often have great illusions about that. It means that the whole emphasis of life, for a while, lies on that one function. Switching over to the next function takes place when you feel that the way you are getting along now has become lifeless, when you get bored with yourself and your activities, or constantly have the feeling that this is not it—then you have again reached the stage where you have to make a switch over to another function. Generally it happens that you do not have to make up your mind theoretically. The best way to know how to switch over is simply to say, "All right, all this is now completely boring; it does not mean anything to me anymore. Where in my past life is an activity which I feel I could still enjoy? An activity out of which I could still get a kick?" And then just genuinely pick that one up, and in that case you will see that you have switched over to the inferior function.

ARCHETYPAL PARALLELS TO THE MODEL OF THE FOUR FUNCTIONS

With this model of the four functions, Jung wanted to set up a heuristic model which allows us to understand better the functioning of human consciousness. This is a working hypothesis, not a dogma. Surprisingly enough, however, quaternarian models have also come up in physics and in theology, models which seem to have a relationship with Jung's function model. In physics there are, for instance, the four Wilkinson principles. According to Wilkinson, you can look at physical phenomena in four ways, explaining all phenomena from the standpoint of energetic processes. That would be analogous to the sensation function, or sense perception, which is an energetic process—photons hit our eyes, and so on. The principle of gravitation would have a certain analogy with the thinking function—arranging facts in a certain order, an upper and a lower realm. You can explain material phenomena to a great extent from that principle or from that angle. The principle is cohesion within the nucleus of an atom. Particles of the same charge repel each other at a certain distance, but if they approach beyond that, they attract each other with a specially strong cohesion. That would correspond to the feeling function of relationship and relatedness. Finally, the fourth principle is what the physicists call the "weak interaction," which is a constant, very slow, diffuse process which dissolves all material phenomena. This dissolution would correspond to intuition, which always tends to blur or dissolve facts and can only operate if it does so.

That is an interesting new viewpoint which shows that Jung, with his intuition, when he set forth this principle of the four functions, touched a very archetypal idea to which now an analogy from a completely different angle reappears in modern physics and is expounded by people who have not been influenced by Jungian thought whatsoever. My attitude toward this is that the idea of the four functions is an archetypal model for looking at things and that it has the advantages—and disadvantages—of all scientific models. Wolfgang Pauli, the physicist, once said something which seems to me very convincing, namely that no new theory, or new fruitful invention in the field of science, has ever been put forth without the working of an archetypal idea. For instance, the ideas of three-dimensional or four-dimensional space are based on an archetypal representation, such as has always worked, to a certain degree, in a very productive way and has helped to explain many phenomena. But then comes what Pauli calls the self-limitation of that archetypal hypothesis, namely that if one overexpands the idea to phenomena where it does not apply, then that same fruitful idea becomes an inhibition for further scientific progress. The idea of three-dimensional space, for example, is still completely valid for ordinary mechanics, and every carpenter and mason uses it when he makes a drawing or a plan, but if you try to apply the idea to microphysics, then you go off the track. So it can be said that that was an archetypal idea which originated, as can be clearly proved in the scientific mind of Westerners, through the dogma of the Trinity. Kepler, when he made his planetary models, said that space has three dimensions because there is the Trinity! Or take Descartes, who asserted the idea of causality by saying that it was based on the fact that God never has whims but always proceeds in a logical manner, and therefore everything must be causally connected. If God had sudden whims and sudden ideas, then there could not be causality. So all the basic ideas even of natural science are archetypal models, but they work in a fruitful way only if one does not force into them facts or areas of facts where they do not fit.

I think that this theory of the four functions has a kind of practical value but it is not a dogma, which would make it completely rigid. That is why Jung very clearly puts it forward as a heuristical standpoint—a fruitful hypothesis by which you can find out things, but not something which you can in any way pin down as an absolute dogma. But we know now that in all scientific investigations we cannot do more than put forward thinking models and see how far the facts fit, and if the facts do not coincide, then we have to correct the models. Sometimes we do not have to revise the whole thinking model, but must say that it only applies in a certain area and that as soon as you switch over to another area of facts it becomes a distortion. I personally am convinced, especially with this new confirmation from the Wilkinson principles, that we have not yet exhausted the fruitfulness of the model, but that does not mean that there are not facts which do not fit into it and would force us to revise it.

The problem of the third and the fourth in religious symbolism also connects with the problem of the four functions. To refer to the diagram on page 18, the archetypal constellation would be at the basis of the psyche, the structural tendency to develop four functions which you find in all mythologies of four persons, four directions of the compass, the four winds, the four angles at the four corners of the world, and all these symbolisms of four groups. It is in Christian symbolism also, for instance, in the symbols of the four evangelists, where three are animals and one a human being. There are the four sons of Horus, with three animal and one human head. Those are manifestations of a basic structural archetype in the human psyche, of the disposition in a human being which, as soon as he tries to cast a model of a total existence—of the total cosmic world, total human life, or something like that—tends to use a fourfold model. The choice just naturally falls upon a fourfold model more often than on any other. In China, it is to be found everywhere. These fourfold mandalas always arise from an impulse to cast a model of total existence, where people do not want to face a single fact but want a mapping out of general phenomena. It would therefore be an inborn structural disposition in the human psyche to use such fourfold models for totalities.

The problem of the four functions in the consciousness of an individual would be a secondary product of this more basic model. That is why, as I tried to explain in connection with the diagram on page 18, it is not advisable to use the factors of the conscious functions to explain functions in the archetypal structure. Rather, one should say that the problem of the four functions in the consciousness of an individual is *one* of the many manifestations of this more general archetypal disposition. If, for instance, you try to explain the model of the four mountains in the four directions of the world in China, or the four winds in the four corners of the world, if you try to pin them down by saying that one *must* be thinking, the other *must* be another function, you never get anywhere; it does not click. So I would say the archetype of the *quaternio* as a model of the explanation of the total situation is more general than the four functions. There is in the human being an inborn disposition always to cast this model when attempting to establish a general orientation toward inner or outer life. It would therefore be dangerous to reduce the dogma of the Trinity and the problem of the fourth person of the Trinity, whether the Virgin Mary or the devil, to the problem of functions. I would rather turn it the other way around and say that it is a more general archetypal problem *but,* in the individual, does assume, among other things, the form of—or touches on the problem of—the four functions. For example, in the Christian religion, the Devil is the symbol of absolute evil in the Godhead, but it would be very presumptuous if you accorded your inferior thinking or inferior feeling such a great honor as to call it the devil in person! That would be rather an inflated explanation of your inferiorities—just as you could not say that your three relatively developed functions were identical with the Trinity! As soon as you put it as bluntly as that, you see how ridiculous the idea would be, but you *can* say that there is some connection, since evil, negativity, and destructiveness do connect in the individual with the inferior function. As a practical example, let us say that you have an inborn tendency to intrigue, yet you will rarely intrigue, or your intriguing shadow will rarely interfere with your main function, because it is so much under your ethical control that it cannot sneak in there; yet it connects very easily with the inferior function.

I can give you an instance of something that happened to me the other day. An intuitive person had to send me a letter with some very agreeable news for me, but she was very jealous and mislaid that letter. Now, did her inferior sensation function make her mislay the letter with the good news for me, or was it her intriguing, jealous shadow? It was both! The intriguing, jealous shadow got her via the inferior function. You can never pin down such a person; you can only say, "Oh, that's your inferior sensation, don't let's mention it again." But it is typical enough that the shadow or the negative impulse sneaks into the inferior function. I remember the case of a man, a feeling type, who was terribly jealous because a woman in whom he was interested had a tremendous transference to Jung, so that the feeling type felt snubbed by her. She just wouldn't look at him, and that cut him to the heart. He could not get over it for a long time and even wrote a book against Jungian psychology, full of errors and misquotations in which he put forth a so-called better new philosophy—much better than Jung's—*nomina sunt odiosa.* On the feeling level—his superior function—this man could not do a nasty thing; he could not attack Jung, for instance, by getting nasty because his feeling was too differentiated. He saw too clearly that Jung, who could not help this woman's transference, had nothing to do with it, so his feeling remained decent, but his inferior thinking picked the motivation—which was rotten jealousy and nothing else—and produced the most amazing junk, even to the extent of misquoting certain sentences in Jung's books. He was not even able to copy out the quotations properly because he had been blinded and swept away by a shadow impulse. Shadow impulses, destructive impulses, jealousy, hatred, and so on, generally get one via the inferior function, because that is the weak spot, that is where we are not in constant control of ourselves, are not constantly aware of the operations of our actions, so that in this corner, any destructive or negative tendencies attack and there you could say that the devil does have to do with the fourth function because it gets people through it. In medieval terms, we could say that the devil wants to destroy people and will always try to get you by your inferior function. That is the problem of the fourth door of your room, where angels can come in, but also devils! In that way I think the problem of the Trinity and the devil, as Jung comments in his paper "A Psychological Approach to the Dogma of the Trinity," does connect with the function problem, but you cannot *reduce* it to the function problem. The function problem is a subdivision, not the explanation of the problem, but practically, in the individual case, it is, in my experience, connected in this way. But you could not call, for instance, such an archetypal figure as the Virgin Mary or the devil a personification of the inferior function.

However, the problem of the fourth function has in some ways a religious archetypal dimension, and the integration of the fourth element into a trinitarian system has occupied the minds of many alchemists. Jung has commented extensively on a remarkable text of the Middle Ages which is concerned with this problem.[3]

This alchemical text mirrors, in a projected form, the problem of the fourth function and a way of establishing a middle ground for this insoluble problem. It is called the "Treatise of the Alchemist Aristotle addressed to Alexander the Great about the Philosophical Stone." It is probably of Arabic origin and was translated into Latin. The following recipe is given:

Take the snake and put it on the car with the four wheels and let it return so often to the earth that the whole car sinks into the depths of the sea and nothing is left visible but the blackest dead sea. There you must leave that car with its wheels until so many vapors arise from the snake that the whole plain dries out and becomes completely sandy and black. This is the earth which is no earth, but a stone without weight. But when the vapors return in the form of rain, then you can pull the car out of the water onto dry land and at that moment you will have put your four wheels upon the car.[4]

That is a very strange image. You take the wheels off the car and load them on it. It is interesting that completely independently you can find the same image in the *I Ching,* where it is sometimes said that one has to take off the wheels from the carriage. As far as I know, that cannot have any connection with Western alchemy. When you have put your four wheels upon the carriage, you can, if you wish, "go on towards the Red Sea, running without running, moving without movement." Jung then comments that the snake in alchemy is the symbol of Mercurius, the *prima materia,* the matter with which you start the process and which further on personifies a kind of nature spirit full of opposites. As shown in Jung's paper "The Spirit Mercurius," Mercurius was thought of as a kind of double ambiguous nature spirit. This Mercurius snake is here placed upon a carriage. The wheels are interpreted in the text as the wheels of the elements, and the carriage or the car is called a spheric tomb, a round tomb or sepulcher. That means that the simile of the car in our text represents the alchemical vessel in which the spirit of the unconscious is contained. Jung says the symbolism describes briefly the essential phases of the *opus:* the snake of Hermes, the cold side of nature (that is, the unconscious), is caught in a round vessel which is made of glass and which means the Cosmos as well as the soul. If one looks at it from a psychological standpoint, it would represent consciousness of the outer and inner world. The putting of the wheels onto the carriage indicates a cessation of all four functions: one withdraws them inward, so to speak. The later transformation of these four wheels corresponds to the psychological assimilation of the integration process through the transcendent function. This function unites the opposites, which, as alchemy shows, are ordered in a *quaternio,* if they concern a totality.

We have not solved the problem which I touched on with the diagram on page 18. I said then that the ego assimilates its first function and is for a while content with that. After a time it assimilates a second conscious function and lives contentedly with that—it has pulled up both from the unconscious. Then it pulls up a third onto the plane of consciousness which contains the life activities. Now three functions are assimilated on the upper, civilized level upon which we try normally to live. I have said that one cannot bring the fourth function up to this level, no matter how much one tries. On the contrary, if one tries too hard, the fourth function will pull one down to a completely primitive level. You can simply drop down suddenly onto a low animal level if you want to, and then live your inferior function in a concrete form without having assimilated it in any way, because in such a case you lose the whole upper structure of your former personality, all that you have developed up until then. You just forget about it; it does not mean anything any more to you.

The fourth function is always the great problem: if I don't live it, I am frustrated and half dead and everything is boring. If I live it, it is on such a low level that I cannot do it. Most people have not the courage; others would have it, but they see that it is not a solution either. So what do you do? This is *the* great problem, which generally comes only rather late in life, thank God, because it only comes really in a strong form when the three other functions have been assimilated, and at that moment this chemical recipe comes into place: namely, the effort to assimilate the fourth function by putting it into a spherical vessel, that is by giving it a frame of fantasy. It comes at the moment when one can only get on, not by living the fourth function in a concrete outer or inner way, but by giving it the possibility of a fantasy expression, whether in writing or painting or dancing, or any other form of active imagination.

Jung found that active imagination was practically the only possibility for assimilating the fourth function. He discovered that after having assimilated three functions, he couldn't get on with his inferior function, and he began to play—to give his inferior function an expression through symbolic play. There in the choice of the means of active imagination you generally see best how the inferior function comes into play. For instance, an intuitive type will generally have a genuine desire to fix his active imagination with clay or in stone or by making it materially visible in some way, perhaps by making constructions. Otherwise it will not be real, and the inferior function will not come into play. Jung, being an intuitive, dis-covered it first by the need to build little clay and stone castles, and he saw that that was how to realize the problem constel-lated by the fourth function. Dancing is a rare form of active imagination which I have usually seen done by people whose feeling is the fourth function. Sometimes thinking types, when they have to assimilate their feeling function, have a genuine wish to express it in dancing in certain primitive rhythms, so dancing as an expression of active imagination is, as far as I have seen, typical for that inferior function. Inferior feeling can also express itself in very colorful paintings, color in general expressing strong feeling moods. A sensation type will conceive of weird stories or wild, fantastic novels into which intuition can run. So we can say that when there comes the problem of how to assimilate the unconscious psychological problem by fantasizing, the choice is generally connected with the inferior function, and usually it is only through active imagination that one can establish the middle lane upon which, so to speak, the three superior functions fall down and the fourth comes up.

At that moment there are no longer four functions because one transmits one's feeling of life into an inner center, and the four functions remain only as instruments which can be used at will, taking them up and putting them down again. The ego and its conscious activity are no longer identical with any of the functions; one moves out of them altogether, which is what the alchemical text represents by the putting of the four wheels upon the car. There is a complete standstill in a kind of inner center, and the functions do not function anymore toward the outer or inner world; they are not wheels which turn. There comes a standstill of all four functions, and then one can bring them out at will, as, for instance, an airplane can let down its wheels in order to land and then draw them in again when it has to fly. This is really the whole essence of the process of individuation. Then the four functions are like wheels which have been put upon the car but which you can sometimes at will put on again if you wish to use them. At that moment the problem of the functions is no longer relevant; they have become mere instruments of a consciousness which is no longer rooted in them or in a driven way active within the functions, but has its basis of operation in another dimension, a dimension which can only be created by the world of imagination. That is why Jung calls this the transcendent function. Fantasizing this inner ground is what he calls the transcendent function; it creates the uniting symbols. This coincides strangely with the alchemical symbolism, which always speaks of the problem of the four elements — water, fire, air, and earth — which are, as in our text, represented as wheels which have to be integrated. Then there is the fifth essence, which is not another element but is, so to speak, the gist of all four and none of the four; it is the four in one and not the four. There you have the same idea: onto the four comes a fifth thing which is not the four but is something beyond them and consists of all of them. That is what the alchemists called the fifth essence, the *quinta essentia* or philosopher's stone. It means a consolidated nucleus of the personality which is no longer identical or identified with any of the functions. Here one steps out, so to speak, of identification with one's own consciousness and with one's own unconscious, and dwells or tries to dwell on this middle plane in which all four are integrated. From then on, as the text says, one moves without movement, runs without running (*currens sine cursu, movens sine motu*), and then another kind of development begins because in alchemy, as well as in the development of the personality, this problem of the four functions is only the first step — it is quite difficult enough to get even as far as that!

What we call active imagination is different from what generally is used in other therapeutic systems where you let people just fantasize. It is fantasizing with ego consciousness taking its standpoint. You could call this fifth thing the urge toward individuation. When it is still unconscious, it is simply that urge toward individuation, that element of constant dissatisfaction and restlessness which nags people till they reach a higher level again and again in life. The *principium individuationis* is identical with the transcendent function, but in the special form of Jungian psychology one does not let it just bite one till one has to take the next step, but one turns toward it directly and tries to give it form by expressing it through active imagination. And that, in a way, then leads to an evolution which transcends the problem of the four functions, so that the constant battle of the four functions comes to a rest.

With your inner nucleus of consciousness you stay in the middle place and no longer identify with what goes on in the upper or lower planes. You stay within your active imagination, so to speak, and you have the feeling that that is where your life process goes on, or really takes place; all the rest are illustrations of it. For instance, on the one plane you very often notice synchronistic events happening, and on the other are the dreams, but you keep your consciousness turned toward the events which happen on the middle plane, that is, on the events which evolve within your active imagination, the thing with which you move along through life. The other planes still exist for you, but you are not centered in them.

Wholeness forms the center of consciousness and the parts one can visit at will, but they are no longer essential. Actually, when you talk to people who have not yet done this, you feel that they are identical with one function: one minute they talk of thoughts and are right in what they think, or they tell you about dreams and are right in them, not outside. Their ego— the flow of life—is absolutely identical with one of their functions. By contrast, when the other process has happened, the central part of the personality has stepped out of the functions. You can still think or feel at will, according to the requirements of the situation, but your self-awareness is no longer identical with the function. The center of gravity shifts away from the ego and its functional functioning into an interim position, into attending to the hints of the Self.

By the understanding of the four functions, Jung has created an instrument by which a lot of unnecessary quarrels and mis-understandings can be removed. It is especially helpful to ap-pease marital quarrels. What remains a task for future generations is to apply it to ethnic groups. The latter are also often predominately ruled by a function: for instance, the Irish by intuition, the British by sensation, the Germans by thinking, and the French by feeling. So there is a lot more to investigate in the future.

NOTES

1. C. G. Jung, *Psychological Types,* CW 6 (1971).
2. Ibid., paras. 628ff.
3. C. G. Jung, *Mysterium Coniunctionis,* CW 14 (1963), paras. 26off.
4. Ibid., para. 260.

ACTIVE IMAGINATION IN THE PSYCHOLOGY OF C. G. JUNG

It is my task here to give an account of "active imagination" in the psychology of C. G. Jung. As is well known, this is a particular dialectical way of coming to terms with the unconscious. Jung began to discover it around 1916 in his work on himself.[1] He described it for the first time in detail in 1929 in his introduction to Richard Wilhelm's *Secret of the Golden Flower*, and in 1933 in "The Relationship between the Ego and the Unconscious."[2] He found that a beneficial effect arises from attempting to objectivize contents of the unconscious in the awake state and relate with them consciously. This can be done through painting or sculpting—or, more rarely, through dancing—but principally through writing down inwardly observed phenomena. Conversations with inner figures play an especially prominent role here.

If one compares these written accounts of inner events and conversations with dream figures, one sees that the participation of consciousness often lends a significantly more coherent, more concentrated, and often also a more dramatic character to the same contents. In contrast to dreams, which represent a pure product of the unconscious, active imagination gives expression to the psychic factor that Jung called the transcendent function. (This is the function that brings about a synthesis between the conscious and unconscious personality.) Therefore, active imagination brings about something like an intensified and (compared with dream analysis alone) accelerated maturation of the personality.

Before going into greater detail regarding the general aspects of this theme, I would like to provide a few practical clarifications.

People who are not practicing active imagination, or not practicing it under the supervision of a teacher who understands it, can easily confuse it with so-called passive imagination, that is, with that "internal cinema" that nearly anyone with any gift for fantasy can cause to parade before his inner eye when in a relaxed state, such as before falling asleep. But also inner dialogue with a complex or an affect, or the kind of inner dialogue within an imagined situation that one so often carries on involuntarily with oneself, should by no means be confused with active imagination. In the mentioned forms of imagination, the party involved "knows" the whole time, as though in some other corner of his mind, that the whole thing is "only" fantasy. If he did not know this, we would have to regard him as being in a very dubious state. But the active imagination that Jung also called, with a grain of salt, "anticipated psychosis"[3] is distinguished from these forms of fantasizing in that the whole of the person consciously enters into the event.

Let me illustrate that with an example. An analysand recounted to Jung an imagination she had begun in the following terms: "I was on a beach by the sea, and a lion was coming toward me. He turned into a ship and was out on the sea—" Jung interrupted her: "Nonsense. When a lion comes toward you, you have a reaction. You don't just wait around and watch until the lion turns into a ship!" We might say that the fact that the analysand had no reaction—for example, fear, self-defense, amazement—shows that she did not take the image of the lion entirely seriously, but rather in some corner of her mind was thinking, "After all, it's only a fantasy lion."

Many beginners also think that when something goes wrong in the midst of fantasy events, one can just, as it were, roll back the film and run it again differently. In an imagination, for "hygienic" reasons an analysand had evacuated and burned down the house of her childhood, where she had found a sick child (her own infantility). But then she realized that this had been a mistake, because in this way the sick child had been too abruptly uprooted. So without further ado, she began imagining that the house was once again there and "played" the fantasy further with the child in the house. Here again we see an example of an imagination that is not a genuine active imagination. The course of events is not real, has not been taken seriously—because, as we well know, what really happens is irreversible.

Another kind of mistake that is often made occurs when the meditator appears in the inner events not really as himself but as some fictive personality.[4] Through this approach, of course, the inner happening is divested of any character of a genuine interplay and synthesis of the conscious and the unconscious. This mistake is often so subtle that it can often be detected only indirectly through reactions in dreams and through the absence of any effect whatever. When the imagination comes off very easily, this is often suspicious, since real active imagination is a considerable endeavor that in the beginning can rarely be kept up longer than ten to fifteen minutes. Also, there are often difficulties at the beginning, of which the following are the most common.

One difficulty is a kind of cramp of consciousness that makes it so that nothing comes to one's mind. Another typical difficulty expresses itself in lethargic resistance and insurmountable disgust or in a negative inner mood that is always saying, "This whole thing is not real, it's just being made up." Jung said:

> The art of letting things happen, action through non-action, letting go of oneself, as taught by Meister Eckhart, became for me the key opening the door to the way. We must be able to let things happen in the psyche. For us, this actually is an art of which few people know anything. Consciousness is forever interfering, helping, correcting, and negating, and never leaving the simple growth of the psychic processes in peace.[5]

While the first two difficulties mentioned can be overcome only with patience or with the courage to be objective, in my experience the best way to deal with the voice of the doubter is simply to let it talk and then answer it: "It's possible that this is not real, but for the time being, I'm going to go ahead." Usually then something happens that convinces one of the uncannily alive, independent reality of the conversation partner. One realizes, "I never could have consciously invented that myself." Whether an active imagination is genuine or not can be best told by the effect it has, for this is enormous and immediately perceivable, whether in a positive or a negative sense. That is why active imagination is such a dangerous instrument and should generally not be attempted without the supervision of an experienced person. It can, as Jung stressed, bring latent psychoses to the point of outbreak.[6] At such a point, patients may slip into a psychotic interval right in the midst of the imagination.

A further danger is the appearance of somatic symptoms. I remember the following example. The case was that of an artist who had undertaken analysis because of a tendency toward alcoholism and a general sense of disorientation. In his dreams there repeatedly appeared a particular shadow figure; let us call him Albert. This figure was a schizoid, highly intelligent, completely cynical, and amoral man who in reality had long since committed suicide. Since we were unable to come to terms with this "shadow," I advised the artist to try having it out with this inner Albert in a frank conversation. He undertook this with great courage and openness. But Albert very cleverly gave a negative twist to everything the artist said: he was only going through treatment because he was afraid of the consequences of alcoholism; he was a good-for-nothing, a coward who as a last resort was trying to save himself through psychology, and so forth. His arguments were so clever and incisive that at a certain point in the conversation, the artist felt beaten. He sadly admitted that Albert was right and broke off the conversation. Shortly thereafter, a psychogenic heart attack took place. The doctor who rushed to the scene concluded that there was no organic problem but that the artist's state was nonetheless rather disquieting.

It is significant that the heart, the symbolic seat of the feelings, revolted. I pointed out to the artist that though he had been intellectually defeated by Albert, there are such things as arguments of the heart that he, the artist, had not used against him. He then returned to his inner conversation. Albert immediately began to mock him: "So now your psychological governess has given you a piece of good advice; but it didn't come from you!" And so on. However, this time, the artist did not let himself be thrown, but kept his feet on the ground and got the upper hand with Albert. The following night he dreamed that Albert died, and starting from then, this inner figure, whom he had dreamed about until that point at least twice a week, appeared only once more in his dreams over the next few years, and then he was no longer quite the same old

Albert but had undergone a positive change. At the same time, a new and, in my view, more significant phase of artistic achievement for the artist began.

With this we come to what is perhaps the most important aspect of active imagination: it is a means of influencing the unconscious. It is true that the right understanding of a dream, if it is more than intellectual, brings about a change in the conscious personality, which in turn affects the unconscious; but the effect from active imagination is stronger out of all proportion. Moreover, a dream and the ability to understand it depends, as it were, on the grace of the Holy Ghost. By contrast, active imagination puts a key in our hand; at least within a modest framework, it enables us to constitute ourselves. For that reason, it is an invaluable means for the analysand in developing himself toward being less childishly dependent on his analyst. Beyond that, it is a liberating experience for all those whom fate—a marriage, a change of profession, a return to one's homeland, the death of the analyst—spatially separates from their analyst.

However, beyond that and far more important is that active imagination makes the autonomy of the analysand possible altogether. Indeed Jung referred to acceptance and practice of this form of meditation as the criteria of whether an analysand was willing to take responsibility for himself or would seek to continue forever living as a parasite on his analyst. Along the same lines as this liberating effect is the fact that active imagination makes possible extraordinarily direct work with affects that can provide a way out of the impasse of suppression or abreaction, of which the first is unhealthy and the second often impossible externally.

I am reminded of the example of a young girl who was suffering from a very pronounced negative mother complex with mild paranoid ideas. As the irony of fate would have it, she rented her student quarters in the house of an evil-tempered and totally paranoid old woman who was notorious in the whole neighborhood. This old woman immediately began to harass her unmercifully, which of course coincided in a very unfortunate way with the girl's subjective tendencies. It was part of the rental agreement that the girl was allowed to swim in the Rhine, which flowed right by the front of the house. But one day, the old woman, without any pressing reason, permanently forebade her this pleasure. The girl had enough self-control to accept this situation externally, but was so upset by her own rage that for two whole hours she could only curse away to herself and abreact internally, unable to return to her intellectual work. As we know, such affects are very unprofitable and exhausting, and the fact that one is "in the right" does not prevent one's own rage from wreaking havoc on oneself.

The girl then carried out the following active imagination. She saw the river with a sign in it surrounded by high waves saying "Swimming Prohibited." The "doubter" voice said: "That's no more than an image of your own emotions." Nonetheless she carried unwaveringly on with the fantasy. The waves separated, and from them emerged a froglike black gnome about two and a half feet tall. She thought, "Oh, that's just my personalized affect," but continued objectively watching to see what would happen next. The gnome padded on its frog feet toward the house, and she thought, full of horror, "Oh, God, surely he's going to murder the old woman, or maybe he'll explode all of a sudden like a bunch of dynamite!" A moral conflict began within her: "Should I let him into the house? But what if I refuse to and he gets angry at me?" She decided to let the gnome, who was ringing the doorbell, into the house and ask him what he wanted. He immediately indicated with gestures that he wanted to go up to where the old lady was. Once again, conflict arose on account of the murder problem. The girl decided at this juncture to go ahead and ring the bell of the old woman's apartment but to stay there with the gnome to prevent him from any misdeed. The old woman approached to open the door. At this point the girl was seized by the thought of what an infinitely funny and amazing impression it would make on the old woman to see her standing there with the black frog-footed dwarf, and she had to laugh. In fact the old woman in her amazement did make a preposterous face, but the girl said, "This gentleman would like to speak with you, Mrs. X." Embarrassed, the old woman invited the two of them into her best sitting room, which, by the way, in reality the girl had never been in before. (When much later she did have occasion to go in there, she discovered to her astonishment that in the active imagination she had imagined it as it actually was.) Now, when the two of them had seated themselves on the plush sofa across from the old woman, the dwarf began to tell the woman erotic jokes with double entendres in them, which made her so happy that she sent the girl away so she could be alone with the nice "gentleman."

When the girl emerged from this fantasy into consciousness, she was in a contented, detached mood and was able to devote herself to her intellectual work without any further problem. When toward evening she met the old landlady on the stairs, thinking of the imagined story, she had to smile. And now for a further unexpected result: the old woman was objectively as though transformed. Until her death, she never once troubled the girl again.

The liberating effect of this imagination is connected with an archetypal motif. That the "Great Mother," when absorbed in fury and grief, can be brought back to humanity through coarse jokes is something we know from the Demeter myth. Guides still point out today the well shaft in the ruins of Eleusis near which the resentful and mourning Demeter sat when the maid Baubo, with a coarse joke, stripped before Demeter and thus made the goddess smile again for the first time. But according to certain cultic inscriptions, Baubo, Demeter, and her daughter Kore are one and the same goddess!

That the Great Mother was accompanied from the most ancient times by phallic gnomes (Kabiri) who were her companions is surely known to many. Though this archetypal background was familiar to the girl in our example, it was not very present to her mind. We can also see in this example how the skeptically commenting consciousness makes false connections; for dwarfs, in contrast to giants, are personifications not of affects but of creative impulses. Thus the apparitions in the imagination had already taken on a constructive force, whereas consciousness with its "reasonable" static preconceptions suspected the presence of a destructive affect.

You might think that this imagination was not a very active one, and it is true that it unfolded relatively passively and cinematically. But it was genuine to the extent that in certain moments the girl participated in it fully and made ethical decisions: whether, on the one hand, to let the gnome in despite his being dangerous, or, on the other hand, to hinder him in attempting to murder the old woman. Naturally she could have behaved entirely differently. For example, she could have told the Kabirus that she would not let him in if he did not first confess what he wanted.

When I listen to the active imaginations of analysands, I often think at particular points, "I would not have behaved that way!" But this very reaction shows to what a great extent the imagination that comes about is a personally conditioned, unique series of events (the English would say, a "just-so story"), like the reality of the individual life itself. That the paranoid old woman also underwent a change is a bit surprising but not unusual. And this brings us to another danger inherent in active imagination, the danger of misusing it as a kind of black magic to achieve egoistic ends or to influence others.

A young female analysand once came to me with a dream that told her she had fallen under the power of a witch. As I was exploring her inner and outer activities of recent days, she reported that she had done an active imagination—at least that is what she called it—against (!) one of her acquaintances. This person had annoyed her, and she had indulged in a fantasy in which she had beheaded her, turned her on the rack, spat on her, and so on. In this way, as she put it, she wanted to "abreact her anger." Not I but her unconscious found the right name for what she had done—not active imagination, but witchery. Such a misuse of the imagination is very dangerous. Especially to people with schizoid tendencies, it may be very attractive. However, it by no means gets them out of their mess, but on the contrary makes them vulnerable to psychosis. Imagining as a form of "love sorcery" or in service of one's own delusions of grandeur (heroic fantasies) belongs to the same category. Wish-fulfillment fantasies have less than nothing to do with real active imagination. The girl whose case is described above had no intention whatever of influencing the old woman. She only wanted to get rid of the destructive influence of her own affect. This ethical purity of intention is one of the most important basic prerequisites for any active imagination.

The use of active imagination by analysands is not always

advisable. It is already limited by the fact that quite a few people simply cannot overcome their resistances to it and should not be forced to do so. Moreover, as mentioned, in cases of latent psychosis it is extremely dangerous. Also, in borderline cases of schizophrenia, ego weakness is often already so great that this meditative form is hardly advisable. (But here, too, there are exceptions; once in just such an exceptional case, I saw it have its liberating effect and greatly speed the healing process.) In general the use of active imagination is indicated either when there is heightened pressure from the unconscious—that is, when too many dreams and fantasies keep coming up—or, conversely, when dream life is blocked and does not "flow." In all cases where inner independence is sought, active imagination offers a unique opportunity to bring it about.

The element of rapid, efficacious self-liberation from obsessive affects and ideas makes active imagination an especially important instrument for the therapist himself. C. G. Jung even regards it as indispensable for the analyst to master this meditative form. As we know, strong emotions are very contagious, and it is difficult for the analyst, and often also not indicated, to withdraw from their contagion, because after all one needs *sym*-pathy and *com*-passion in order to be able to help. The same goes for having to listen to and watch the unfolding of perverse, morbid fantasies or images that, willy-nilly, destroy one's balance; for as Jung said, the impression of something ugly leaves something ugly behind in one's own psyche. And in relating to these "impressions," one cannot always wait around for a healing dream or until they fade away as a result of one's own healthy instincts. Especially when, on the same day, other analysands are coming in; after all, one cannot receive them in such a disturbed state, thus spreading the contagion still further. However, one can always fit in a short active imagination—in such cases, one rarely needs more than ten minutes—and free oneself by this means. When one does not even have time for that, sometimes just the sincere decision to deal with the disturbance through active imagination later on will help. After all, ultimately a psychotherapist is a person who can heal himself. According to Aelian, the dog is the animal associated with the god of healing, Asclepius, because he has the knowledge to eat grass in order to make himself vomit up harmful food, and because he licks his own wounds with his disinfectant saliva!

People from the polar regions distinguish the mentally ill from medicine men and shamans as follows: the mentally ill person is possessed by spirits and demons; the medicine man or shaman, however, is one who, though also possessed, is able to liberate himself again on his own.[7] Ugly affects and morbid, perverse ideas actually act like demons. They enter us and obsess us. The right active imagination, however, is a creative act of liberation carried out through symbols. It could be misunderstood as a dangerous tendency toward "self-salvation," but in fact this danger is precluded because the proper use of active imagination can only take place in a religious context, that is, in the presence of an awe-filled, conscientious regard for the numinous.

In addition to its protective quality referred to in the examples, active imagination is to even a higher degree the vehicle of what Jung called the individuation process, the complete and conscious self-realization of individual wholeness. Through this process the *imago dei* (God-image) is experienced in the individual and begins to actualize its influence beyond the level of the ego. The ego becomes a servant of its tendencies toward actualization, a servant without which the Self is incapable of incarnating itself in our dimension of space and time.

The small practical examples I have provided as an illustration of the nature of active imagination represent only a minor segment within such a process of individual development, and the archetype of the Self, the whole, does not even appear in them. However, when such a meditative procedure is undertaken for a longer period of time and in connection with essential problems of life, empirically almost always, this central content, that is, the Self, comes clearly to the fore, and in these more essential contexts a certain parallelism to various religious paths of meditation can be clearly seen. For this reason, Jung also made, in a series of lectures at the Zurich School of Technology, a detailed comparison between the unconscious as he conceived of it and Eastern forms of yoga, the exercises of Saint Ignatius Loyola, and the meditation practices of the alchemists. From this it emerges that this last is much more closely related to Jung's active imagination than the other two[8] for the following reason. In the Eastern yoga forms (perhaps with the exception of Zen Buddhist meditation, to which I will return later), the "guru" to a great extent takes over the lead, and certain instructions are also given in the texts which might guide the student to the experience of that which we call the Self. In the Christian exercises, the image of the Self is made visible in Christ, and here too the student is led to approach it inwardly in a certain way. In both cases, the student is warned about obstacles and is told how he should "dismiss them or shoo them off as temptations."[9]

In comparison with all these processes, Jungian active imagination is much less programmatic. There is no goal that must be attained (no "individuation training"), no model, image, or text as a guide on the path, no prescribed physical posture or breath control (and no couch, no participation in fantasies by the analyst). One simply begins with what presents itself from within, or with a relatively inconclusive-seeming dream situation or a momentary mood. If an obstacle arises, the meditator is free to see it as an obstacle or not; it is up to him how he should react to it. Thus each step becomes a unique, responsible individual choice and for that reason also a unique "just-so" synthesis of conscious and unconscious tendencies. Let us say an imaginer is struggling in a fantasy to reach the summit of a high mountain, and beautiful women come along and try to lure him into the depths. We do not say to him at that point: "That is an erotic fantasy, a temptation that is trying to keep you from achieving your lofty goal." We also do not say, "That is a part of life that you must integrate before you continue your climb!" We do not say anything. The imaginer must explore on his own what it is that he is encountering and what he should do about it — just the same way as in outer individual life.

It is this absolute freedom that differentiates the Jungian form of active imagination from almost all other known forms of meditation and what most makes it resemble the *imaginatio vera* of the alchemists. The alchemists were experimenting with the (for them) completely unknown nature of material reality and its psychic aspect. They also had no program, but were looking in the dark for nothing other than their own genuine experience of it. They had no views, or only vague intuitive ones, concerning what it was all about, and no externally adopted ethical guidelines of behavior — nothing but their own inner voice. They were seeking the "divine reality" in the here and now of material existence; they themselves, for the most part, knew nothing more than that. That is why their way and their experience of symbols so closely resemble those of many modern men and women.

In this freedom totally without a program, it is perhaps Zen Buddhism with its steps toward the *satori* experience that comes closest to the Jungian approach. Also here there is only the fact that a number of masters possess a real experience of the Self and live from it—everything else is unpreconceived and unpreconceivable. The only thing that distinguishes Zen from Jungian active imagination, as far as I can see, is the following. In Zen Buddhism—or so at least I was once assured in a conversation with Professor D. T. Suzuki—fantasy images and dreams that arise are not regarded as essential, but just the opposite, as relatively inessential elements that still cover up the "true nature." The master attempts to shake the student loose from them as from his other false ego attachments. By contrast, in Jung's active imagination, without judgment, we stoop to pick up every fragment of symbol that our psyche offers us and work with it, since to us it might seem to be an adumbration or a part of the Self—maybe an unrecognized part. In any case, there is no prescribed behavior. This greatest freedom is indeed the most difficult, but in my opinion the most valuable, aspect of the Jungian way inward.

That brings us to a certain problem that might possibly be a subject of controversy. Jung was part of that group of psychotherapists on the furthest left wing of those who unconditionally advocated the freedom of the individual. In meditation as represented, for example, by J. H. Schultz's autogenic training, we still find physical relaxation exercises prescribed. In Carl Happich's guide to meditation, themes like "childhood's meadow" or "the mountain" are suggested, and the psychotherapist "guides" the analysand within the fantasy toward them. As concerns René Desoille's *rêve éveillé* (waking dream), a method that owes a lot to Jung, a fundamental distinction is that the psychotherapist offers his own reaction to the symbolic inner events; for example, he suggests to the patient what the latter might or should do in the symbolic situation. Also, Desoille requires an experience of the collective unconscious and its archetypes and, at the same time, that these last be mastered. Thus, all too great an emphasis, for our taste, is placed on guidance by the psychotherapist and his reactions; this by no means fosters the moral and spiritual independence of the analysand.

As we see from this and the examples I have provided, in Jungian active imagination, the psychotherapist only takes a position on the question of whether a fantasy is genuine or ingenuine. His only further intervention is, when symptoms or dreams ensue by way of reaction, to interpret the significance of these dreams and symptoms in the way otherwise usual in analysis. As we may recall, it was a dream and not I that accused the female analysand referred to earlier of black magic; and it was a psychogenic heart attack that warned the artist not to forget the "heart."

These spontaneous reactions of the unconscious to active imagination occur frequently. They permit us to give analysands a free hand as described. For them it is a valuable experience that the "master" ultimately lives in his own psyche — a *medicus intimus*, as Professor Schmaltz so aptly called it. The Eastern meditative forms and the Christian ones are built upon age-old historical tradition and thus have the advantage of offering guidelines that have already been tried out and adapted by many people; but for this reason, they can become a straitjacket on the just-so-ness of the individual. As Jung repeatedly pointed out, modern human beings are already so heavily overloaded, both internally and externally, with precepts, demands, advice, slogans, collective suggestions, idealism, and other (also good) guidelines, that it is perhaps worth the effort to provide them with an opportunity to realize their own nature in an unforced and fully self-responsible fashion. This is the way, perhaps, that the divine influence makes its appearance in the psyche in its purest form—all by itself. And it is also likely that the individual best resists the destructive collective influences of his time when, all alone and through his own inner experience, he becomes rooted in his relationship to God.

NOTES

1. See C. G. Jung, "The Transcendent Function" in CW 8 (1960), pp. 67ff.
2. It is astonishing that Dr. Wolfgang Kretschmer in his essay "Die meditativen Verfahren in der Psychotherapie" (Meditative Procedures in Psychotherapy), *Zeitschrift für Psychotherapie und Medizinische Psychotherapie* 1, no. 3 (May 1951), in a detailed discussion of the various techniques of Schultz-Henke, Carl Happich, René Desoille, and Friedrich Mauz, among others, does not say a single word about the active imagination of Jung, which was developed and made known to the public considerably earlier than the work of the above-mentioned psychologists and had an indisputable influence on them.
3. C. G. Jung, *Mysterium Coniunctionis*, CW 14, para. 184, pp. 156–57.
4. Ibid., para. 184.
5. "Commentary on *The Secret of the Golden Flower*, 1929/1965, in Richard Wilhelm, *The Secret of the Golden Flower* (New York: Harcourt, Brace & World, 1962), 93.
6. *Mysterium Coniunctionis,* CW 14, p. 156.
7. See Mircea Eliade, *Schamanismus und archaische ekstasetechnik* (Zurich, 1957), 38ff. English translation: *Shamanism: Archaic Techniques of Ecstasy* (Princeton: Princeton University Press, 1964).
8. See especially CW 14, paras. 406ff.
9. As far as I know, the exception to this is a medieval text called "Hugo von St. Viktor's Conversation with His Soul" (*Soliloquim de arrha animae*). In this text the meditator seems to be so convinced that Christ is the true goal of his own soul that he brings it without force to that goal just through his loving conviction, even though it is attached to the world and vigorously resists conversion.

ON ACTIVE IMAGINATION

I would like to concentrate on a few points that make up the specific character of Jung's active imagination in contrast to the many other imagination techniques that are cropping up everywhere these days. Today we encounter a great number of people who have practiced some imagination technique or other before undertaking their Jungian analysis; and in my experience, in such cases it is very difficult to get people to move on to real active imagination. The latter can best be divided into four parts or phases.

1. As we know, first one must empty one's own ego consciousness, free oneself from the thought flow of the ego. This is already quite difficult for many people, who cannot stop the "mad mind," as the Zen Buddhists call it. It is easier in the case of painting and easier still in sandplay. However, the latter provides consciousness with already existing figures. Although it is true that this seems to make it possible to skip over the "barrenness," or absence of any ideas (which is frequently the first thing that occurs), it is apt to lead to difficulties later when the analysand has to go on to real active imagination. Most Eastern meditation techniques, such as Zen, certain yoga exercises, and Taoist meditation, bring us face to face with this first phase. In Zen meditation, one has to cut off not only all ego thinking, but also any fantasies that might well up from the unconscious. One either has to fend these off by means of a *koan* or let them pass by unheeded. The only objective of the

physical sitting posture is the symbolic stopping of all the activity.

2. At this point one must let a fantasy image arising from the unconscious flow into the field of inner perception. In contrast to the Eastern techniques mentioned above, here we welcome the image rather than chasing it away or ignoring it. On the contrary, we concentrate on it. Having reached this point, we have to be on guard against two mistakes: either concentrating too hard on the image that has arisen and literally "fixating" it, making it freeze, or not concentrating hard enough, with the result that the inner images begin to change too fast and a speedy "inner movie" begins to run. In my experience, it is primarily intuitive types who fall prey to the latter mistake. They write endless fantasy tales that have no focal point, or they do not enter into any personal relationship with the inner events. This is the level of passive imagination, of *imaginatio fantastica* in contrast to *imaginatio vera*, as the alchemists would call it. This strongly reminds us of H. Leuner's *katathyme Bilderleben* (catathymic image life). Leuner admitted to being inspired by Jung's active imagination but decided to simplify it—with, in my opinion, not very good results. I find it very difficult to help analysands who have done this form of imagination practice to change over to real active imagination. W. L. Furrer's *Objectivierung des Unbewussten* (objectification of the unconscious) also suffers from the same deficiencies, as does the older technique of *le rêve éveillé* (awakened dreaming) of René Desoille. These techniques also allow the presence and intervention of the analyst—a great mistake that I will discuss later.

3. Now comes the third phase. It consists of giving the innerly perceived fantasy image a form by writing it down, painting it, sculpting it, writing it as music, or dancing it (in which

case the movements of the dance must be noted down). In dancing the body gets to participate, which is sometimes essential, primarily when certain emotions and the inferior function are so unconscious that it is as though they were buried in the body.[1] Often it also seems helpful to invent a little concrete ritual, for example, lighting a candle or walking around in a circle. This brings in the participation of inorganic matter. Jung once told me that this is more effective than the ordinary way of doing active imagination, but he could not tell me why this was the case.

In my view this also casts light on a question that is much discussed these days—the role of the body in analysis. In fact the alchemical opus, according to Jung, is nothing other than an active imagination carried out with chemical substances, that is, by mixing them, heating them, and so on. The Eastern alchemists, especially the Chinese Taoists, did this for the most part by seeking to work with the materials in their own bodies, more rarely with those in their laboratory retorts. The Western alchemists worked with matter mostly outside the body, in the retort, affirming that "our soul imagines great things outside the body." Paracelsus and his pupil Gerhard Dorn, however, also undertook to work with the so-called inner firmament within the body, on which they hoped to bring external magical influences to bear. These they thought to have a synchronistic relationship *per analogiam* with the matter of the body. In this form, active imagination is essentially linked with the body via the symbolic meaning of its chemical components. I myself have frequently experienced strong positive and negative physical reactions to rightly or wrongly executed active imaginations. One analysand even suffered a serious psychogenic heart attack when he acted against his feelings in an active imagination. Strong affects and emotions are sometimes an obstacle to practicing active imagination. Jung himself, as he reports in his memoirs, sometimes had to resort to yoga exercises to gain control of his emotions before he was able to draw an image from them that he could relate to in an active imagination.

A certain kind of active imagination can be carried out as a conversation with inwardly envisaged parts of one's body, in which one also listens to what they say (as Odysseus sometimes did in the *Odyssey* with his heart or his "phrenes"). This technique is sometimes favorable in the case of a psychogenic physical symptom. Whenever matter comes into play, whether inside or outside the body, synchronistic phenomena can be expected, which shows that this form of active imagination is especially "energy-charged." In its negative aspect it borders on magic and its dangers, which I will come back to later.

In this third phase, two types of mistakes tend to occur, which Jung describes in his essay "The Transcendent Function."[2] One kind of mistake consists in placing too much emphasis on the esthetic elaboration of the fantasy content and making it too much into a work of art, with the result that one neglects its "message" or meaning. In my experience this happens most with painting and writing. Too much form kills the content, just as the art of certain historical periods "buried the gods in gold and marble." (Nowadays we often get more pleasure out of looking at a primitive fetish or the crude art of the Early Christians than at the decadent art of Rome.) The functions of sensation and feeling are the first to lead us astray here. We forget that what we are depicting or describing is only the likeness of an inner reality and that the objective is to come in contact with the reality not the likeness.

The other kind of mistake consists in doing the opposite. One does a haphazard job of sketching the content and immediately goes into the question of meaning. Intuitive and thinking types especially often fall into this error. This shows a lack of love and devotion. One can see it at once when a patient brings in a sloppy sketch or a negligently written description, already knowing "what it means." This third phase, in which one provides the unconscious with a means of expressing itself, often brings great relief, but it is not yet real active imagination.

4. The fourth phase is the key one, the one that is missing in most imagination techniques—moral confrontation with the material one has already produced. At this point Jung warns us of a mistake that is frequently made that jeopardizes the whole process. This is the mistake of entering into the inner events with a fictive ego rather than one's real ego.

I would like to illustrate this through an example. An analysand dreamed that he found a horse's hoof in the desert. It was somehow very dangerous and began to chase him. It was a kind of demon connected with the god Wotan. He tried to continue to fantasize this dream in an active imagination. He was now fleeing on horseback, but the demon was getting bigger and bigger and closer and closer. The analysand turned around and somehow managed to trample the demon into the ground. When he recounted this to me, I was struck by an odd discrepancy between the way he looked and the outcome of the story. He himself looked frightened and tormented. So I told him that somehow I did not believe in the happy ending but did not know why. A week later he confessed to me that when the horse-hoof demon reached him, he split in two. Only a part of his ego conquered the demon; the other stepped out of the action and just watched it from the outside. Thus he achieved his victory only with a fictive hero-ego; his real ego absconded, secretly thinking to itself: "After all, this is only a fantasy."

When an analysand's currently observable state fails in this way to harmonize with what happened in an active imagination, we can assume that this fictive-ego error has occurred. It is difficult to keep this out. Another analysand, in an active imagination, had a long romantic love affair with an anima figure. He never told her that he was recently married. When I asked him about this, he said that he would never do this in reality (conceal his marriage). Thus his ego in the active imagination was not the same as his everyday ego! The whole thing was clearly not entirely real for him; it was more like writing a novel than doing active imagination. This point is of enormous importance, because the entire effectiveness of active imagination depends on it. People with very fragmented characters or with latent psychoses cannot do active imagination at all, or they do it just with this fictive ego. For this reason Jung warned us against having borderline cases do active imagination. In point of fact, the analysand in my second example was not a sick person but an intellectual. The intellect is the greatest trickster; it misleads us into overlooking the moral aspect of the events and succumbing to the doubt that after all the whole thing is only fantasy and wishful thinking. A certain naiveté is required for active imagination.

Jung once remarked that the psychiatry of today has discovered this process up through the third step, but does not yet understand the fourth. Most of the current imagination techniques stop short of this point. There is another aspect that has not yet been understood. Most of the current creative or imagic techniques permit a certain participation on the part of the analyst or even require his intervention. He either proposes the theme (as in Happich's technique or in J. H. Schultz's advanced autogenic training) or intervenes when the analysand is stuck and makes suggestions. Jung himself, on the other hand, used to let his patients stay stuck in whatever hole they were in until they found a way out themselves. He recounted to us that he once had a female patient who in life was always falling into certain "traps." He recommended active imagination to her. She promptly saw herself in her imagination going across a field and coming to a wall. She knew she had to get to the other side, but how? Jung just said, "What would you do in reality?" She simply could not come up with anything. Finally, after a long time, she thought of walking along the wall to see if it came to an end somewhere. It did not. Then she looked for a door or an opening. Again she did not get anywhere, and Jung did not offer any help. At last she thought of going for a hammer and chisel and pounding a hole in the wall. This was the solution.

The fact that this woman took so long to find such a solution was a reflection of her inept behavior in outer reality. It is for this reason that it is so essential that we do not step in with a helping hand; if we do, the patient learns nothing, but remains just as infantile and passive as ever. When, on the other hand, he painfully learns his lessons in active imagination, then he also learns something for his outer life. Jung did not help a patient even if he remained hung up for weeks, but insisted that he continue trying to find a solution on his own.

With the controlled use of drugs, the fourth step is missing once again. The person supervising bears the entire responsibility rather than the person doing the imagination. I came across an interesting book by two brothers, Terence and Dennis McKenna, called *The Invisible Landscape*.[3] These two courageous young men went to Mexico and experimented on themselves with a hallucinogenic plant newly found there. According to their own account, they suffered from schizophrenic states of mind which led to a "broadening of their spiritual horizons." Unfortunately, they do not give a precise description of their experiences, only hints about going to other planets and receiving the support of an invisible helper who often appeared as a gigantic insect. The second part of the book gives us the insights arising from their "broadened spiritual horizons," and that is where the disappointment comes. They are in no way different from other highly intuitive modern speculations about mind, matter, synchronicity, and so on. They give us nothing creative and new, but only things that the well-read authors could just as easily have thought up consciously. The most important point comes at the end, when the book closes with the idea that all life on earth will be destroyed and for that reason we will either have to escape to another planet or escape inwardly, into the realm of cosmic mind.

I would like to compare this with a dream. It is the dream of a student, not in danger of psychosis, who is currently undergoing a Jungian analysis. I am grateful to him for his permission to recount his dream. Since I delivered this lecture, Edward Edinger has presented the same dream and given a very good interpretation of it.[4] The dream (in slightly shortened form) is as follows:

> I am walking along what are called the Palisades, from which one can look out over New York City. I am walking with an anima figure who is unknown to me; we are both being led by a man who is our guide. New York has been reduced to rubble — the whole world as we know it has been destroyed. Fires are burning everywhere; thousands of fleeing people are running aimlessly in all directions. The Hudson River has flooded large parts of the city. It is twilight. Fireballs in the sky whistle earthward. It is the end of the world.

The cause of this was that a race of giants had come from outer space. I saw two of them sitting in the midst of the rubble, nonchalantly scooping up one handful of people after the other, eating them as one would eat grapes. It was a horrible sight. . . . Our guide explained to us that these giants came from different planets where they lived in peace together. They had landed in flying saucers (those were the fireballs). The earth we knew had actually been devised by these giants. They had "cultivated" our civilization the way one raises vegetables in a greenhouse. Now they had come for the harvest. There was a special reason for this, which I only learned later.

I had been saved because I had slightly high blood pressure. If it had been normal or too high, I would have been eaten. Thus I was chosen to go through this ordeal by fire and, if I came through it successfully, to be permitted to save other souls as well. Then I saw before me a gigantic golden throne, radiant like the sun. On it sat the king and queen of the giants. They were the perpetrators of the destruction of our planet.

My ordeal, in addition to the torment of having to experience all this, consisted in having to climb the steps of the throne up to the point where I could look the king and queen in the face. This took place in stages. I began the ascent. It was long, but I knew that I had to do it, that the fate of the world and humanity depended on it. Then I woke up soaked in sweat. I realized afterward as I awoke that the destruction of the earth was a wedding feast for the king and queen.

This dream recalls the invasion of the earth by giants that we find described in the biblical Book of Enoch, which was interpreted by Jung as a "premature invasion [of consciousness] by the collective unconscious." This led to a generalized inflation. The angels who (according to Enoch) had fathered giants with human females instructed humanity in many new forms of knowledge, and this brought about the inflation. It is clear that the above dream reflects our similar modern situation, and the McKennas' book shows clearly, among other things, where a premature exploitation of the visions of the collective unconscious leads—that is, to a very precarious state of mind. At the same time, however, this dream very aptly shows the difference between drug hallucinations and an approach by the unconscious that has not been sought out. In the dream the dreamer is set a task: to reach the king and queen. According to the conclusions of the McKennas, on the other hand, all the individual can do is try to get away. It thus seems that a constructive aspect of the unconscious is only constellated when it is face to face with an individual ego as partner. That is the situation we are seeking to reach in active imagination, and this is why taking drugs—even under supervision—or practicing imagination techniques in which the analyst takes the lead, is not right, for then the ego as it is cannot confront itself with the unconscious.

The apocalyptic scenes in the McKennas' book and in our dream are related to our fear of an atomic war. But instead of fleeing into outer space, the dream sets the dreamer the task of seeing the wedding of the king and queen on a face-to-face level. It represents the union of opposites—father and mother, mind and matter, and so on. I am reminded of how Jung once told us, when we asked him whether a third world war was inevitable, that such a war could only be avoided if a sufficient number of individuals could hold the opposites together within themselves. Here also the entire collective burden rests on the shoulders of just one dreamer. The unconscious can only show us a way out of crisis if we as individuals remain conscious of the opposites.

An important motif in the dream is the guide, who instructs the dreamer. Such a figure only appears if the analyst does not take its place. Hermes, the soul guide of the alchemists, called himself "the friend of every solitary" (*cuiusque segregati*—each one who is separated from the herd). The most important result of active imagination according to Jung is getting the analysand to become independent of his analyst. For that reason, we ought not to interfere in it (with the exception of making corrections in the method). When an analysand reads me an active imagination, I often silently think: "I would never have done or said that!" This shows in what an individual way the reactions of the ego arise in relation to the unconscious in active imagination—and this is what determines what course the inner events will take.

A new (or rather age-old) approach to active imagination is described in the books of Carlos Castaneda. This is the method of the sorcerer and medicine man Don Juan, which he calls "dreaming." Behind this are the ancient traditions of the Mexican Indian medicine men. Rumor has it that a great deal of what is in these books was invented by Castaneda, though using genuine material of the medicine men. "Dreaming" is certainly part of this genuine material. It is exquisitely Indian and could never have been invented by a white man. "Dreaming" is achieved with the help of outer phenomena of nature. The teacher Don Juan takes Castaneda out into the solitary wilds of nature. In the half light of evening, Castaneda thinks he sees the dark shape of a dying animal. Frightened to death, he wants to run away, but then he looks more closely and sees that it is only a dead branch. Afterward, Don Juan says: "What you've done is no triumph. . . . You've wasted a beautiful power, a power that blew life into that dry twig. . . . That branch was a real animal and it was alive at the moment the power touched it. Since what kept it alive was power, the trick was, as in dreaming, to sustain the sight of it."[5]

What Don Juan calls power here is *mana*, *mulungu*, etc., in other words, the energy aspect of the collective unconscious. In devaluing his fantasy by looking at it rationally, Castaneda drove the power away and lost a chance to "stop the world." (That is Don Juan's expression for bringing ego thinking to a halt.) Don Juan also calls this dreaming "controlled insanity," which recalls Jung's remark that active imagination is a "voluntary psychosis."

This kind of active imagination with outer things in nature recalls the art of the alchemists, who carried out their active imagination with metals, plants, and stones, but with one difference: the alchemists always had a vessel. This vessel was their *imaginatio vera et non fantastica* or their *theoria*. With this they did not lose themselves but had a "grasp" on events in the literal sense, a kind of religious philosophy. Don Juan also has such a grasp, but he cannot convey it to Castaneda and therefore always has to assume leadership himself.

As we have already mentioned, rituals accompanying active imagination are particularly effective but also dangerous. This frequently constellates a great number of synchronistic events, which can easily be interpreted as magic. People who are in danger of becoming psychotic also often misinterpret such events in a very dangerous way. I remember the case of a man who at the beginning of a schizophrenic interval physically attacked his wife. She called both the village policeman and a psychiatrist for help. As these two, along with herself and the disturbed man, were standing in the hallway of the house, the single lightbulb illuminating the scene exploded into a thousand pieces, and they were left standing in the dark, covered with bits of broken glass. The disturbed man immediately thought that since the sun and moon had hidden their light at Christ's crucifixion, this event was a sign that he, the savior of the world, was being unjustly arrested. But, quite to the contrary, the synchronistic event was bringing a sane message—it was warning him against having a mental blackout (for an electric lightbulb signifies ego consciousness, in contrast to the sun, which is the Godhead). Here we are moving on dangerous ground. Although this event did not occur in connection with an active imagination, similar events often do occur during active imagination. This example shows us how we can go astray in this "voluntary psychosis." Thus the alchemist Zosimos rightly warns against demons who may throw the alchemical work into confusion. Here we touch upon the distinction between active imagination and magic, particularly black magic. As we know, Jung advises against doing active imagination involving living people. It can affect them magically, and all magic, including "white" magic, has a boomerang effect on the person performing it. Therefore, in the long run it is self-destructive. All the same, I recall a case in which Jung advised me to use it. I had an older female analysand who was totally possessed by her animus; she was no longer accessible and on the verge of a psychotic interval. Jung advised me to speak to her animus in an active imagination. This would help her but harm me; nonetheless I should try it as a last resort. And in fact it did have a beneficial effect, and Jung helped me afterward against the boomerang effect. However, I have never again dared to repeat this experiment.

The boundary between active imagination and magic is a subtle one. In the case of magic, there is always some wish or desire in play, in connection with either a good or a destructive intention. I have also observed that strong animus or anima possession prevents people from doing active imagination. It makes the required inner openness impossible. One should only practice active imagination in order to get at the truth about oneself and for this purpose alone. But in practice, often an ulterior desire sneaks in, and then one falls into *imaginatio fantastica*. I have observed a similar danger in connection with casting the *I Ching* oracle. If one fails to give up all desire for a specific result beforehand, one frequently misinterprets the oracle. There is also the opposite case of seeing or hearing "the right thing" in active imagination but then doubting that it is genuine. One is often freed from this by the active imagination suddenly taking so surprising a turn that one feels: "I couldn't possibly have invented that myself!"

Finally there is still the concluding phase — applying in daily life what one has learned in active imagination. I remember a man who in an active imagination promised his anima that he would devote ten minutes a day to her. He bungled this and got into a neurotic ill humor that lasted until he realized that he had failed to keep his promise. But of course this goes for all realizations in analysis. This is the "opening of the retort" in alchemy, something that is naturally produced when one comes to an understanding of the previous step. When someone fails to do this, it is simply a sign that he or she has not really accomplished the fourth step of moral confrontation.

NOTES

1. Cf. R. F. C. Hull, "Bibliographical Notes on Active Imagination," in *Spring* (1971); E. Humbert, "L'Imagination active d'après C. G. Jung," in *Cahiers de Psychologie Junghienne* (Paris, 1977); C. G. Jung, "The Transcendent Function," CW 8.
2. C. G. Jung, "The Transcendent Function," CW 8.
3. Terence and Dennis McKenna, *The Invisible Landscape* (New York: Seabury Press, 1975).
4. See Edward F. Edinger, "The Myth of Meaning," *Quadrant* 10 (1977): 34ff.
5. Carlos Castaneda, *Journey to Ixtlan* (New York: Simon and Schuster, 1972), pp. 132–33.

THE RELIGIOUS DIMENSION
OF ANALYSIS

"The main interest of my work," writes Jung, "is not concerned with the treatment of neuroses but rather with the approach to the numinous. But the fact is that the approach to the numinous is the real therapy and inasmuch as you attain to the numinous experiences, you are released from the curse of pathology. Even the very disease takes on a numinous character."[1] This citation says everything of essential importance about a Jungian analysis. If it is not possible to establish a relationship with the numinous, no cure is possible; the most one can hope for is an improvement in social adjustment. But then, what is left for the analyst to do? Jung expressed himself on this subject in a letter in the following terms:

> Since neurosis is a problem of attitude, and the attitude is dependent on or grounded in certain "dominants," that is, the ultimate and highest ideas and principles, the problem of attitude can be called a religious one.[2] This is supported by the fact that in dreams and fantasies religious motifs appear with the clear purpose of regulating the attitude and restoring the disturbed equilibrium. . . . I have observed, for example, that as a rule when "archetypal" contents arise spontaneously in dreams, etc., numinous and healing effects emanate from them. These are *primordial psychic experiences* that very often reopen a patient's access to religious truths that have been blocked. I have also had this experience myself. . . .

Just as through preconceived opinions I can hold back or actually stop the *influxus divinus* [divine influence], wherever it may come from, it is also possible for me through the suitable behavior to come nearer to it and, when it happens, to accept it. I cannot force anything; I can only make an effort to do everything that favors this and nothing that goes against it. . . . What can, but not necessarily will, then come about is the kind of spontaneous action arising form the unconscious that has been symbolized by the alchemists, Paracelsus, Böhme, and modern students of the unconscious as *lightning.*[3]

From this point of view, the work of the therapist can only consist in dismantling preconceptions and blockages to possible numinous experience. (This is connected with the old problem of theology—whether salvation comes from grace or human efforts; obviously both are necessary.)

Ways of avoiding the numinous are quite numerous. I would like here to present a few that I have encountered. One is a certain extraverted superficiality. An older woman, who had never had anything on her mind but love, clothes, travel, and the like, had the following dream: She was standing on a ladder and was about to dust a big crucifix. To her infinite horror, the Crucified One suddenly opened his eyes and said, "You could dust me a little more often!" The dreamer was Catholic and had been content up to this point with superficial fulfillment of the Church's external precepts. This dream set her thinking for the first time.

For the most part one encounters in modern people a collection of philosophical and rational-pseudoscientific prejudices from the nineteenth century that in fact have already been discredited by the leading scientists of our time. They got these ideas from their school days and from cheap journalistic accounts: dreams are meaningless, or are expressions of sexual desires; there is no such thing as ghosts; the unconscious has been heard of but is not really regarded as real; there is no effect without a rationally graspable cause; a person only has to be reasonable and everything will be fine; if society were straightened out, everything would be straightened out, etc., etc. Next to this assortment of prejudices, the worst and most pervasive one is overt or implicit statistical thinking: "What I do makes no difference; I'm just one grain of sand among millions; my existence is a meaningless accident." This mindset is direct and deadly poison for the soul.

The analyst has little hope of getting rid of such prejudices through argumentation. This job is taken care of far more effectively—sometimes quickly, sometimes gradually—by the patient's dreams. But it is essential that the analyst himself have a connection with the numinous and have a belief in it that is based on his own experience; otherwise he overlooks the element in dreams that is directed toward numinous experience and instead projects into them his own ideas of what the patient "should" be or do. He tends automatically to develop convictions such as: this analysand should get away from his parents, that analysand should be less intellectual, another analysand should be more disciplined—and still other convictions based on whatever opinions and preconceptions he has about normalcy. For this reason, the analyst must say to himself again and again, "I do not know what God wants from this person!" All he can do is help the patient hear better what the patient's own psyche is whispering to him.

When I had my first patient suffering from severe psychosis, she was drifting toward a schizophrenic episode as a result of an outward blow of fate, and I was struggling with her to prevent this. At this point, Jung, who was supervising the case, earnestly said to me, "How do you know so surely that this woman doesn't have to go through such an episode? Many patients are better off after an episode. You should not be trying to learn the secret of her destiny; that's just a power play. You don't know what God wants from her!" Frightened, I just let go and restricted myself to quietly interpreting her dreams as straightforwardly as possible. The analysand unexpectedly improved. When I told Jung about it, he laughed and said, "That was what I was hoping for, but I couldn't let you know that, otherwise you might have tried to force something again!" That cured me once and for all of excessive juvenile therapeutic enthusiasm.

In addition to intellectual preconceptions, in my experience another problem that can arise is for an analysand to have a highly numinous dream but somehow fail to be appropriately moved by it or even touched at all. Usually in such a case, it is a matter of a certain state of inferiority of the eros. It has often happened that I have been profoundly shaken by a patient's dream that he himself is recounting in a very cool and matter-of-fact way. I have learned in such cases not to hide my own feelings, not to hide how deeply touched I am emotionally, but to express it. In my experience this has always had a positive effect.

Jung himself always had strong emotional reactions to dreams. He reacted to the dreams people brought to him with laughter, outcries of fear, ill humor, or excitement, and often his reaction would trigger in a patient a realization of what the dream was really about. Behind the absence of reaction in an analysand, besides weakness of emotion, there often lurks the secret prejudice that in fact dreams have nothing real about them.

One of the most difficult situations in my experience is when the unconscious seemingly produces only banal dreams, nothing that is remotely numinous. However, it is very often possible to see behind the personal aspect of a dream the basic archetypal structure. It was a particular gift of Jung's to be able to recognize the deeper archetypal meaning of a dream that, from a superficial point of view, is banal. On the other hand, we must sometimes be more suspicious of mythical dreams, since they might be based merely on something the patient has read or have some other inauthentic basis.[4] Particularly beautiful and mythically structured dreams do not always betoken something of special significance for the dreamer. Instead they may reflect an intention on the part of the unconscious to attract the dreamer; that is, they indicate that for the next period of time, inner development is to take place through an encounter with the unconscious and dreams.[5]

Banal dreams, by contrast, show that also latent behind one's often disregarded personal everyday reality a deeper meaning is at work. Again and again people are taken in by the defensive reaction: "This is just an absurd, stupid little dream." Jung always used to say that there are no stupid dreams, only stupid people who do not understand them! The fact is, the Self seems also to care about the details of our personal lives. God warned Emanuel Swedenborg in a vision not to eat too much. Swedenborg was an intuitive person and therefore in things based on the sensation function—sexuality, eating, and so on—was primitively immoderate. It is thus rather typical for the Self to manifest in just this area.

An analysand of mine dreamed that a voice from above told her she needed a "breakfast girdle." Detailed questioning brought out that the whole morning she would lounge around sloppily in her bathrobe (she was an alcoholic before analysis) and only put on her girdle and began the day around noon.

We often laughed together about this dream, and I periodically used to ask her, "How is it going with the breakfast girdle?"

It is also especially difficult for the analyst to bring theologians and clergymen closer to the *influxus divinus*. Sometimes they are just not "called," and then analysis leads them away into the world. However, far more often, though they did actually originally choose their profession through a kind of constellation of destiny, they have lost their genuine faith along the way and replaced it with rote phrases and formulas.

A monk during his analysis had a formidable experience of God. I asked him whether his colleagues would be more frightened if they were to experience, as he did, the reality of God or if they were to discover that God did not exist. He answered, "They would be more frightened by the reality of God, for that He does not exist is what they almost all secretly believe." But even to this analysand I later sometimes had to say, "This damned God that you're always talking about, does He really exist for you, and if so, does He have something to say about your present problem or not?" He kept slipping back into his old intellectual pseudoreligiosity, where "God" was stored away in a drawer for the next sermon and the questions of his life were decided on only by the ego.

To my amazement I met a Japanese Buddhist with the same problem. He had had significant experiences of light from the time of his youth and had become a teacher of Buddhism. He was suffering from a stomach ulcer that seemingly no diet that was prescribed could help. So I said to him, "Ask the *dharma-kaya* [Buddha body] in yourself what you should eat and what else you should do to heal yourself." He stared at me entirely stupefied; nothing like this had ever occurred to him. Later he wrote me that he had tried it and been healed. He added, "I see that Jungian psychology adds a foundation of reality to religion that we have lost."

This loss of touch with the empirical basis in matters of religion is often the result of too much traditionalism. Therefore Jung points out that when we emphasize the historical development of Christianity too much, we overlook what is new in it.

> What we need is a new point of departure, and this cannot be found without the assignment of new meaning. The message is alive only if it creates new meaning. . . . That Christ is the self of [human beings] is implicit in the gospel, but the conclusion Christ = self has never been explicitly drawn. This is an assignment of new meaning, a further stage in the incarnation or actualization of Christ.[6]

This is the same thing that happened to the Buddhist mentioned above in the form of a conferral of new meaning to the *dharmakaya*. The religious dimension in analysis is nothing other than finding new meaning in just this way that sometimes brings already existing religious ideas back to life, and sometimes transforms them.[7]

This brings me to a further problem that comes up again and again in analysis. The unconscious is "religious"—that is, it is the matrix of all primal religious experience—but it is often not "orthodox." What many dreams and visions express sometimes contradicts this or that dogma or religious moral precept. For example, I have met a number of priests whose dreams seemed to go against maintaining celibacy. However, when later they left the priesthood, their dreams told them that they were still priests in some kind of invisible way. After all, celibacy is only a *regula moralis*, not a dogma, and therefore could sometime be changed. A balance should be maintained between innovation and maintenance of tradition. Jung wrote to the Dominican priest Victor White:

> If you try to be literal about the doctrine [of the Catholic Church], you are putting yourself aside until there is nobody left that would represent it but corpses. If, on the other hand, you truly assimilate the doctrine, you will alter it creatively by your individual understanding and thus give life to it. The life of most ideas consists in their controversial nature, i.e., you can disagree with them even if you recognize their importance for a majority. If you fully agreed with them you could replace yourself just as well by a gramophone record.[8]

That means that if the unconscious causes a churchgoing person to favor something that conflicts with the doctrine of his denomination, he should make this into a personal conflict, into a form of cross-bearing. Ultimately then, it will not be he who decides the conflict but the *vox dei* within him—once his ego, with all its opinions, pro and con, has died upon the cross. And as Jung points out: *extra ecclesiam nulla salus* (outside the Church there is no salvation), but the grace of God reaches even further.[9]

More difficult still, it seems to me, is to help orient a person toward the religious dimension when he has been so tormented by religious indoctrination that he throws out the baby with the bathwater and wants to have nothing more to do with religion at all and looks at everything purely in secular terms. Without his being aware of it, the numinous catches him from behind and possesses him with sexual fantasies or greed for money, with craving for power or drugs, with political fanaticism—that is, he becomes possessed by substitute gods. Thus Jung writes in *Psychology and Religion* that ultimately anything dominant and inescapable can be called God, unless, by an ethical decision freely chosen, one succeeds in building up against this natural phenomenon a position that is equally strong and invincible. . . . Man is free to decide whether "God" shall be a "spirit" or a natural phenomenon like the craving of a morphine addict, and hence whether "God" shall act as a beneficent or a destructive force.[10]

The substitute gods bring an absence of freedom—possession. Thus we must ultimately decide which lord we want to serve, such substitute gods or God as He reveals himself within us if we make an honest effort toward self-knowledge. "God has never spoken to man except in and through the psyche, and the psyche understands it and we experience it as something psychic. Anyone who calls that psychologism is denying the eye that beholds the sun."[11]

Nowadays from time to time we also have people coming for analysis who have been raised in that other "church," Marxism as it has been established east of the "Iron Curtain." Their difficulties are very similar to those of any followers of a religion that claims to represent the only truth. What has struck me most in these cases is the complete suppression of the feminine principle and thus of personal feeling—a nasty intellectual sense of detachment. With this the ability to be moved, to experience meaning or value, falls away. Also for these people all religious words, such as *God*, *soul*, and *conscience*, have been so stigmatized that it is best not to use them with them at all, but rather to try to convey whatever "new meaning" their psyche is trying to reveal through, and in terms of, their dream images. In a certain regard, these people also have an advantage: they can experience the religious dimension of the psyche with spontaneous freshness, unburdened by the past, without having an overweening sense of tradition that immediately relates their discoveries to material from the past.

It is my hope that sometime, in these very countries, a particularly bountiful crop will grow, as happens after a flood.

Just as most curative substances are also poisons, the encounter with the numinous has an extremely dangerous side. Indeed religions are not only something constructive — we have only to think of the burnings of heretics and witches, of the devastating invasion of Europe by the Turks reaching to the very gates of Vienna, of dubious missionary activities that have wiped out the indigenous religious and cultural forms of many peoples, leaving them without roots. Jung writes:

> Religions are not necessarily lovely or good. They are powerful manifestations of the spirit and we have no power to check the spirit. Surely great catastrophes such as earthquakes or fires are no longer convincing to the modern mind, but we don't need them. There are things much more gruesome, namely man's insanity, the great mental contagions from which we actually suffer most indubitably.[12]

In individual cases we can see the dangerous side of the *numinosum* at work in the phenomenon that, when an archetype comes to the threshold of consciousness, it develops a tendency to fascinate the conscious ego and push for its symbolic content to be concretely acted out. If the individual does not succeed in keeping his head and heart, then he becomes possessed and inflated. If a schizophrenic element is present, he might well act out the most dreadful things. Thus, for example, a schizophrenic who was working in the garden of a mental institution suddenly caught hold of the director's little daughter and cut her head off. He explained that the voice of the Holy Ghost had ordered him to do this. If he had understood this voice symbolically, its meaning would have been to sacrifice his own excessive childishness. The concrete acting out of compelling archetypal contents is the greatest danger accompanying numinous experience. In cases like this one, the demonic aspect of the numinous has triumphed. The chance of finding new meaning and effecting a cure are lost. Possession always also means fanaticism. One has and represents the only truth and feels justified in beating down everything else. Only understanding the psychological meaning can protect us from this danger. Theologians representing a religiously "militant" position regard this as an inappropriate relativization of the truth of their faith. However, this is not the case. When a primal religious experience has taken place, for the one who has had it, it is absolute. However, if at the same time he understands this experience as a personal discovery of meaning, he will admit that God, or the *numinosum*, might also reveal itself in a thousand other forms, for ultimately it is something unfathomable that only reveals itself through the filter of the human psyche, where it speaks to us in terms of images and mythical forms. What it is "in itself," however, we cannot know, at least not in this life. Therefore, such a person will never wish to preach his experience as the universally valid truth.

This is indeed the meaning of Jesus' parable in which a man found a treasure hidden in a field, hid it there again, then sold everything he had to acquire the field (Matt. 13:44). A person who has had a real religious experience keeps it hidden in his heart and does not shout it from the pulpit. Perhaps he might talk about it with other people who have experienced something similar, knowing that what he experienced is something God revealed to him but might have expressed to others as well in a completely different form or with different content. Thus there arises quite naturally a profound awe toward the *religio* of the other (if it is genuine) and a need not to attack this. Only a person who doubts himself feels compelled to win over as many admirers as possible so as to drown out his own doubt. Therefore Jung points out that religious experience brings its own evidence with it, even if at the same time the ego, despite that experience, never gives up doubting that it understood it correctly. "I for my part," said Jung, "prefer the precious gift of doubt, for the reason that it does not violate the virginity of things beyond our ken."[13] Such an attitude remains forever fresh and open to even more comprehensive inner experiences.

When a numinous, healing experience occurs during an analysis, it is the duty of the analyst to help avoid the possible negative consequences, possession and inflation. These usually take place when the ego or the moral capacity (feeling) of the analysand is weak. Dreams provide the needed basis for preventing these effects. Sometimes also the patient fails to understand the experience, but this is easier to remedy.

Because of the many possible concrete forms the deeply touching, numinous (i.e., religious) experience can take, it is difficult to generalize about it. For this reason Jung concentrated in his writings on delineating certain general tendencies that he had observed either in himself or in his many patients. It is mainly these "currents" in the collective unconscious that we are able to observe on the one hand, in the officially still Christian Western world and, on the other, in its areligious, rationalistic scientific theories. The compensatory "current" in the collective unconscious of our culture manifests especially often in mythical contents that resemble the symbolism of alchemy. Alchemical mythology seems to relate particularly to four problems: (1) elevating the status of the individual in relation to the uniformity of the mass; (2) heightening the valuation of the feminine principle or eros (in both women and men); (3) the problem of evil; (4) reconciling the opposites in the fundamental psychic structure of the human being.

The elevation of the status of the individual shows itself in experiences of being called upon directly by God; or in dreams, being in a position to determine the course of the world, or the like. An example is the following dream of a young American.

I am walking along what are called the Palisades, from which one can look out over New York City. I am walking with an anima figure who is unknown to me; we are both being led by a man who is our guide. New York has been reduced to rubble—the whole world as we know it has been destroyed. Fires are burning everywhere; thousands of fleeing people are running aimlessly in all directions. The Hudson River has flooded large parts of the city. It is twilight. Fireballs in the sky whistle earthward. It is the end of the world.

The cause of this was that a race of giants had come from outer space. I saw two of them sitting in the midst of the rubble, nonchalantly scooping up one handful of people after the other, eating them as one would eat grapes. It was a horrible sight. The giants were of different sizes and shapes. Our guide explained to us that these giants came from different planets where they lived in peace together. They had landed in flying saucers (those were the fireballs). The earth we knew had actually been devised by these giants. They had "cultivated" our civilization the way one raises vegetables in a greenhouse. Now they had come for the harvest. There was a special reason for this, which I only learned later.

I had been saved because I had slightly high blood pressure. If it had been normal or too high, I would have been eaten. Thus I was chosen to go through this ordeal by fire and, if I came through it successfully, to be permitted to save other souls as well. Then I saw before me a gigantic golden throne, radiant like the sun. On it sat the king and queen of the giants. They were the perpetrators of the destruction of our planet.

My ordeal, in addition to the torment of having to experience all this, consisted in having to climb the steps of the throne up to the point where I could look the king and queen in the face. This took place in stages. I began the ascent. It was long, but I knew that I had to do it, that the fate of the world and humanity depended on it. Then I woke up soaked in sweat. I realized afterward as I awoke that the destruction of the earth was a wedding feast for the king and queen.

The motif of an invasion of giants that destroy everything reminds us of the biblical Book of Enoch (c. 100 B.C.), where it is told that the angels fell in love with human women and begat on them a race of giants who threatened to destroy everything. At the same time, the angels taught humanity many new arts. As Jung has interpreted this, what we have here is a chaotic invasion of human consciousness by the contents of the collective unconscious.[14] The giants are embodiments of the resulting inflation, who raise the import of humanity to the level of the "gigantic" through an overspeedy development of technological knowledge. But this negative development has a secret positive background: it challenges the individual to make the difficult ascent to higher awareness, to individuation.

Such a dream could easily be misunderstood as an expression of delusions of grandeur, but this was not in fact the case with the dreamer. On the contrary, the ultimate function of the dream lies in helping the dreamer to realize that everything depends on him alone, that all outer efforts—for example, political or any other collective efforts—cannot rescue the world from the situation from which he, like all of us, is suffering. Also, the placement of higher value on the feminine principle and the union of opposites is clearly represented.

The union of the opposites of nature and mind, light and dark, is often represented in modern times by a strange alteration of the image of Christ in inner visions and dreams. For example, Christ appears with horns like ancient Pan or made of metal like Mercury, the savior figure of alchemy. Only by adding features like these can Christ function as a complete symbol of the Self for modern people. Such dream motifs also indicate that the unconscious seems to be interested not in destroying our Christian cultural tradition, but rather in creatively developing it further.

Alchemical literature is a chaos in which we find a great deal of nonsense and at the same time the most essential, infinitely individually varied religious symbols. Jung made it his life's task to pick out from this chaos, through painstaking detail work, the most essential and significant basic motifs and put them together like pieces of a puzzle. The best summary of what this was all about we find in his introduction to *Psychology and Alchemy*.[15] Here it is shown that the production of symbols in alchemy is related compensatorily to the teaching of Christianity with its one-sided patriarchal orientation.

> The historical shift in the world's consciousness towards the masculine is compensated by the chthonic femininity of the unconscious. In certain pre-Christian religions the male principle had already been differentiated in the father-son specification, a change which was to be of the utmost importance for Christianity. Were the unconscious merely complementary, this change of consciousness would have been accompanied by the production of a mother and daughter. . . . But as alchemy shows, the unconscious chose rather the Cybele-Attis type in the form of the *prima materia* and the *filius macrocosmi*. . . . This goes to show that the unconscious does not simply act *contrary* to the conscious mind but *modifies* it more in the manner of an opponent or partner. . . . Thus the higher, the spiritual, the masculine inclines to the lower, the earthly, the feminine; and accordingly, the mother, who was anterior to the world of the father, accom-

modates herself to the male principle and . . . produces a son—
not the antithesis of Christ but rather his chthonic counterpart,
not a divine man but a fabulous being conforming to the nature
of the primordial mother. . . .

This answer of the mother-world shows that the gulf between
it and the father-world is not unbridgeable, seeing that the unconscious holds the seed of *the unity of both*.[16] The essence of
the conscious mind is discrimination; it must, if it is to be aware
of things, separate the opposites, and it does this *contra naturam*.
In nature the opposites seek one another . . . and so it is in the
unconscious, and particularly in the archetype of unity, the self.
Here, as in deity, the opposites cancel out.

Alchemy ever and again provided the basis for the projection
of archetypes that could not smoothly be made a part of the
Christian process.[17]

Something that emerges as a fundamental trait of alchemical
symbolism is a heightened valuation of the feminine principle,
and this trait is found also in very many of the numinous
experiences of individuals in our modern Western culture.
Jung, as we know, was enthusiastic about Pope Pius XII's "Declaratio Assumptionis Mariae," which he called the most important event in the spiritual history of our times. Most people
cannot see this, despite the fact that the conflict over the celibacy of priests, the feminist movement, and the nature of
woman and the feminine have since become themes of the day.
They fail to see that the archetype of the goddess has been
activated. They shift the discussion to juristic, sociological, and
political questions and the like without perceiving the *numinosum* that is at work. In dreams, by contrast, the *numinosum*
often becomes quite clearly visible as a groundswell beneath
the ripples on the surface.

A Protestant woman who had read the newspaper article
about the Pope's *Declaratio solemnis* but had paid it no heed,

had the following dream: She is walking across a bridge in Zurich toward a public square where she sees a huge crowd of people. Someone explains to her that Mary's Ascension is about to take place here. She sees a wooden platform with a wonderfully beautiful naked black woman standing on it. The black woman raises her hand and floats slowly toward the heavens.

What seems to be unorthodox in this dream is the nakedness. Through this, the unconscious stresses what the *Declaratio* only hinted at, the importance of the body. The image does not contradict the new dogma but develops its consequences further.

A Catholic woman, who also did not place a great deal of importance on the *Declaratio*, dreamed that female priests were now allowed in the Church. In this case also, the unconscious "thought out" the further consequences of the *Declaratio*. According to the *Declaratio*, Mary enters a heavenly bridal chamber. This points to a further development, a holy wedding in the beyond.

Today we are confronted with a nearly, or perhaps completely, unsolvable problem regarding the question of how to relate with evil. In most non-Christian religions (with the exception of Buddhism), the gods (or the supreme deity) are destructive as well as good. The Greco-Roman world and late Judaism (in the wisdom books of the Old Testament) one-sidedly reinforced the tendency to see God as a *summum bonum* and to exclude evil from his realm. This culminated in the scholastic teaching that evil has no being of its own, but represents only a *privati boni*, an attenuation or absence of good. This kind of psychological one-sidedness cries out for a compensatory counterthrust. Christ himself foresaw this when he pointed to the coming of the Antichrist. As Jung describes, mainly in his works *Aion* and *Answer to Job*, from about the year 1000, in the period corresponding to the second fish of the Piscean age,[18] this countermovement has been in gradual progress, undermining the Christian teaching step by step. Nowadays, he says in his last writing on this subject in the "Late Thoughts" chapter of his memoirs:

> The old question posed by the Gnostics, "Whence comes evil?" has been given no answer by the Christian world, and Origen's cautious suggestion of a possible redemption of the devil was termed a heresy. Today we are compelled to meet that question; but we stand empty-handed, bewildered, and perplexed, and cannot even get it into our heads that no myth will come to our aid although we have such urgent need of one. As the result of the political situation and the frightful, not to say, diabolic, triumphs of science, we are shaken by secret shudders and dark forebodings; but we know no way out, and very few persons indeed draw the conclusion that this time the issue is the long-since-forgotten *soul of man*.[19]

Jung saw this present-day culmination of evil as typical of the historical catastrophes that tend to accompany the great transitions from one age to another, in our case the end of the Piscean age and the beginning of the Aquarian. In fact we are even menaced with a total eradication of life on our earth, either gradually, through the destruction of the environment, or through a global war. The increase in criminality, the occurrence of holocausts, and so on, are a first warning. Everyone is talking about these problems these days, and nobody knows what ought to be done. Appeals to reason seem to echo away unheard. As the above quotation shows, Jung also did not have a simple answer, but he was convinced that every individual who undertook to come to terms with the evil in himself would make a more effective contribution toward the salvation of the world than idealistic external machinations would. Here we are talking about more than just insight into one's personal shadow; we are speaking also of a struggle with the dark side of God (or the Self), which the human being cannot face but must, as Job did.

> The myth must ultimately take monotheism seriously and put aside its dualism, which, however much repudiated officially, has persisted until now and enthroned an eternal dark antagonist alongside the omnipotent Good. . . . Only thus can the One God be granted the wholeness and the synthesis of opposites which should be His. It is a fact that symbols, by their very nature, can so unite the opposites that these no longer diverge or clash, but mutually supplement one another and give meaningful shape to life. Once that has been experienced, the ambivalence in the image of a nature and creator God ceases to present difficulties. On the contrary, the myth of the necessary incarnation of God can then be understood as man's creative confrontation with the opposites and their synthesis in the self, the wholeness of his personality. In the experience of the self it is no longer the opposites "God" and "man" that are reconciled, as it was before, but rather the opposites within the God-image itself. That is the meaning of the divine service, of the service which man can render to God, that light may emerge from the darkness, that the Creator may become conscious of His creation, and man conscious of himself.[20]

Absolute evil is thus also a divine mystery, also a form of the experience of the *numinosum,* a mere glimpse of which leaves us speechless. When Jung's students once asked him if the third (and probably most horrendous) world war could be avoided, he answered that it depended on how many individuals could reconcile the opposites within themselves.

In analysis we frequently encounter dreams of global catastrophe (like the one described on pages 190–91); thus we should not reject out of hand the possibility that the unconscious, i.e., nature itself, is striving toward the destruction of humanity. Jung took this possibility into account, but his optimism made him hope that we might be able to just scrape by at the critical moment and avoid the total destruction of the earth.

In a letter he went so far as to say, "Deviation from the numen seems to be universally understood as being the worst and the most original sin."[21] However, he points out elsewhere in the same letter that there is nothing that at one time or another could not be called evil, that thus good and evil are only relative human value judgments. The decisive point is always whether or not one is conscious of one's conflict and endures it consciously; but one should not indulge in the illusion that even in this way the evil is eliminated. Jung points out that

> we do not know whether there is more good than evil or whether the good is stronger. We can only hope that the good will predominate. If good is identified with constructiveness, there is some probability that life will go on in a more or less endurable form; but if the destructive were to prevail, the world would surely have done itself to death long ago. . . . Hence the optimistic assumption of psychotherapy that conscious realization accentuates the good more than overshadowing evil. Becoming conscious reconciles the opposites and thus creates a higher third.[22]

Since evil is for the most part a deviation from the numen, that also means that repeated deviations of this sort are unavoidable, and the conflict between turning away from the numen and turning toward it is a long one, if not a life-long one. The image of the crucifixion is therefore an eternal truth, and therefore also analysis does not promise the patient happiness, but can only liberate him from the neurotic stagnation of his life, not from its authentic suffering.

I myself can say no more about this problem than Jung could, other than that in my work I have seen that at least in individual cases the problem of evil can sometimes (not always!), with God's help (that is, with God standing against God!), be resolved. When such a success occurs, it is a miracle and one of the most deeply moving experiences of the *numinosum*. In the religious image of the deity, that is, the Self, the opposites coexist; however, they are not consciously unified. That can only occur in conscious people in whom both sides of the Self, the good and the evil, are working toward incarnation. In the incarnated form both sides are diminished and humanized and thus, through the agency of human consciousness, are able to enter into connection. Self-knowledge, or the development of consciousness, is thus the key factor.

The fourth theme that comes up repeatedly in the dreams of modern people is the *coniunctio*. As is clear from our discussion up to this point, this is inextricably bound up with the three motifs already mentioned. It appears in the American's dream of having to bring forth the royal *coniunctio,* in the Pope's *Declaratio* (Mary enters the bridal chamber for the wedding with the Lamb), and as the answer to the problem of evil. The surface ripples over this ground swell in the depths of the unconscious take the form of the omnipresent discussion of sexuality and the relationship between man and woman. However, the productions of the unconscious are related to something that lies much deeper, a *unio mystica* with the Self, which is experienced as a unification of the cosmic opposites. This is connected with the relationship between man and woman insofar as all serious love relationships of the more profound sort ultimately serve mutual individuation, the process by which each partner becomes whole. That is also clearly the meaning of marriage taken as a sacrament. But this is something that is constellated not only in marriage but in any love relationship that is accepted as a commitment. The experience itself cannot be conveyed in dry words. Jung described the vision of this that he had as he was approaching death in his memoirs.[23] But one also finds it hinted at in Meister Eckhart and in the works of many mystics, often in the language of the Song of Solomon. This is an experience that liberates the human being into a cosmic expanse. In the symbolism of alchemy, it is the central motif of the *coniunctio solis et lunae* and of all other opposites.[24] Jung devoted the magnum opus of his old age to this symbol,[25] indicating orally that it had still far greater meaning that he was unable to articulate. Only a few people these days experience this level of individuation, but it is also the driving motive even behind all more short-termed superficial development of consciousness[26] and behind all analyses of the profounder sort, in which it first manifests as the problem of transference and countertransference.

Because many contemporary people as yet have no understanding of this experience, Jung has been disparagingly described as a mystic, a prophet, as the founder of a religion, all with the connotation of "unscientific" confusion. If this connotation were not there, I would even partially agree with the first two descriptions, because the great mystics of the Christian tradition (but also many Taoist and Zen masters in the East and saints in Islam) speak as he does of primordial personal experience of the numinous. And the prophets (without the negative connotation) were people who received insight into the archetypal background situation of their time in a primordial experience, which caused them to be able to foresee future spiritual developments and to warn against the mis-understandings of their time. The third, the founder of a religion, Jung never was and never wanted to be. When his students, under pressure from the outside world (mainly from the laws regulating professions), organized a professional asso-ciation, Jung consented to it only reluctantly. For him it was an absolute that the mind must be free to follow its inspira-tions, which cannot be bottled or canned. If we are looking for historical parallels, Jungian psychology could most readily be compared to the original Taoism of China, a wisdom that embraced the whole of human life. The Taoists, too, later came together in organized communities, but in so doing lost to a great extent the meaning of the Way (the Tao) as indicated by Lao-tzu or Chuang-tzu. In the affinity of the Taoists with al-chemy, we find another similarity between the two worlds.

Because of their interest in natural science, the Taoists were not rejected by Maoism, and there, too, is a parallel of a sort. The point here is that it is not at all true that Jungian psy-chology is "not scientific," as one so often hears said. Many aspects of it, such as the archetypes and their influence, the dream theory, and the understanding of complexes, definitely stand up to an examination by the "hard" methods of natural science. It is only the healing experience of meaning, the en-counter with the numinous, that because of its evolving and creative uniqueness cannot be grasped through statistical methods. It can only be proven by exposing oneself directly to it. And, moreover, as Jung points out, even then, although something *might* happen, it will not happen necessarily. Other-wise the action of the divine principle would not be free; it would be bound by the laws of nature. But, in view of its essentially creative nature, this seems not to be the case. Jung goes so far as to say that the creative imagination is "the only primordial phenomenon accessible to us, the real Ground of the psyche, the only immediate reality."[27] It is the divine principle itself. And this symbol of the creative spontaneity of the unconscious ultimately stands behind the creation of any religion.

> In the formation of the great religions, first there is a collective disorientation that constellates everywhere an overwhelming ordering principle in the unconscious (a collective longing for salvation). The prophet, out of the critical need of the time, recognizes through inner vision the helpful pattern in the collective unconscious and expresses it in the symbol. . . . When the situation changes, a new "truth" is needed; therefore truth is always relative to a particular situation. . . . As long as a symbol is the true and thus liberating answer to a situation that corresponds to it, it is true and valid, indeed, "absolute." If the situation changes and the symbol is simply perpetuated, it becomes no more than an idol with an impoverishing and stultifying effect, since it simply makes us unconscious without providing any clarification or enlightenment. . . . Symbol is teaching, idol is delusion. . . .
>
> The symbol needs man for its evolution, but it grows beyond him, therefore it is called "God," because it expresses a psychic state of affairs or factor that is stronger than the ego.

The Self then takes over the lead and this provides the ego with release from its feeling of impotence. It becomes clear from these factors, only roughly sketched here, that for Jung the *numinosum*, the symbolic experience, is everything, the only significant dimension of the analytical process.

NOTES

1. C. G. Jung, letter to P. W. Martin, 20 August 1945, *Letters*, vol. 1, p. 377; cf. also vol. 1, p. 118.

2. See Jung, *Psychology and Religion*, CW 11, para. 523, p. 341: "Healing may be called a religious problem."

3. Jung, letter to Vera von Lier-Schmidt Ernsthausen, 25 April 1952, *Letters*, vol. 2, pp. 56–57.

4. Jung, *Letters*, vol. 2, p. 225.

5. Jung, letter to Hermann Keyserling, 21 May 1927, *Letters*, vol. 1, p. 46.

6. Jung, letter to Dorothee Hoch, 23 September 1952, *Letters*, vol. 2, p. 84.

7. Cf. Jung, CW 11, para. 148: "To gain an understanding of religious matters, probably all that is left us today is the psychological approach. That is why I take these thought-forms that have become historically fixed, try to melt them down again and pour them into moulds of immediate experience."

8. Jung, letter to Father Victor White, 10 April 1954, *Letters*, vol. 2, p. 169.

9. See also Jung, CW 12, para. 96.

10. Jung, CW 11, paras. 142ff.

11. Cited in Jung, letter to Pastor Damour, 15 August 1932, *Letters*, vol. 1, p. 98.

12. Jung, letter to Leslie Hollingsworth, 21 April 1934, *Letters*, vol. 1, p. 159.

13. Jung, CW 12, para. 8.

14. Jung, "Answer to Job," CW 11, para. 669f.

15. Jung, CW 12, paras. 26–30.

16. Emphasis mine.

17. Jung, CW 12, paras. 26–30.

18. A a notion from the astrological tradition to which Jung occasionally alluded is that of a Piscean age comprised of two periods of a thousand years each. The astrological symbol for Pisces is composed of two fish, each of which is said to stand for one of the two millennia. — Translator

19. Jung, *Memories, Dreams, Reflections* (New York: Vintage Books, 1965), pp. 333–34.

20. Ibid., p. 338.

21. Jung, letter to Rev. H. L. Philp, 11 June 1957, *Letters*, vol. 2, p. 370.

22. Jung, letter to Hélène Kiener, 14 May 1955, *Letters*, vol. 2, pp. 253–54.

23. Jung, *Memories, Dreams, Reflections*, p. 294f.

24. An excellent example is in the *Aurora Consurgens*, III, in *Mysterium Coniunctionis*, CW 14.

25. Jung, CW 14.

26. Cf. Jung, "Psychology of the Transference," in CW 16.

27. Jung, letter to Kurt Plachte, 10 January 1929, *Letters*, vol. 1, p. 60.

THE RELIGIOUS OR MAGICAL ATTITUDE TOWARD THE UNCONSCIOUS

Within this restricted framework, it is not possible to describe the course of even a short analysis in such a way as to present all the subtleties of dreams, of processes of transformation, and of their mutual relationship. I will therefore confine myself to singling out just one problem that played an essential role in the analysis of a dreamer and therefore around which her most important dreams revolved. This problem could be described as the opposition of the "religious" and "magical" attitudes toward the unconscious. C. G. Jung writes:

> Religion appears to me to be a peculiar attitude of mind which could be formulated in accordance with the original use of the word *religio*, which means a careful consideration and observation of certain dynamic factors that are conceived as "powers": spirits, daemons, gods, laws, ideas, ideals, or whatever name man has given to such factors in his world as he has found powerful, dangerous, or helpful enough to be taken into careful consideration, or grand, beautiful, and meaningful enough to be devoutly worshipped and loved.[1]

This kind of careful consideration presupposes a certain humble, honest, and simple attitude of consciousness vis-à-vis the *numinosum*, an attitude, however, that for many people will require a great deal of effort. In the absence of this, one often finds in its place a driven and unconscious attitude of the ego toward the *numinosum* from which arises an attitude vis-à-vis the unconscious that could be described as "magical." I should like to attempt to convey a more precise impression of what is involved in this through the dreams presented in this essay.

Again and again one encounters people in all levels of society in whom the unconscious is fatefully strongly constellated to an extraordinary degree and wells up in an abundance of affect-laden archetypal images. The peril of being overwhelmed by the unconscious in such cases is always looming, but this can often be warded off through creative structuring of the onrushing contents. The dreams of such people often themselves clearly insist on this structuring possibility, and one is frequently reminded of the many old traditions that tell of a god, demon, or spirit demanding that an individual perform certain quite specific labors in its service. This demand is often accompanied by the threat of punishment through physical or mental illness or even death, should the person fail to obey.

But why is it that a person is often unable to complete such a task? Why is every psychological development, every forward step of consciousness, always conditioned by an ethical decision that has to be made on the razor's edge? It is easy to condemn people, but there are imponderable factors involved here that we may not all be aware of. In individual cases, dreams often give us indirect indications of what is the matter.

The following dreams are those of a forty-three-year-old unmarried grammar school teacher from Styria in Austria. She had begun an analysis in her hometown, which had failed due to the local analyst's lack of mythological knowledge, since the dreams contained almost exclusively archetypal material. Ongoing migraine headaches that were not physically caused and a peculiar symptom had brought her to undertake this first analysis. The peculiar symptom was that whenever her pupils annoyed her beyond a certain point, she would emit a horrendous animal-like shriek, which did indeed immediately silence the children, but having something so dark and savage come out of her all by itself also profoundly frightened her. When she sought me out during her vacation, she was in an extreme state of exhaustion, and at the same time she was being harried by visions and dreams, which threatened to entirely overwhelm her. Really the need for physical recuperation should have been looked after first, but the hard-driving unconscious could no longer be held back. I only hoped that the dreams themselves would show the way out of what was, almost from the beginning, an impossible situation. The initial dream was as follows.

Angel's Birth [2]

I am imprisoned in a big fortress, in part formed from the living rock. We are completely to the rear of the fortress; the front part seems to be a churchlike area, since our imprisonment has something to do with religion. With me are my grandfather and my sister Agathe. The rock-walled room where we are is in the upper part of the fortress. It is nighttime. In front of me an opening in the rock takes shape. All the way at the back of this, a powerful spring with lots of water flows, forming itself into a broad waterfall. I am glad about this sight, which has a freeing effect on me.

I look for a place to sleep. The rock is too hard and uneven. There is a rock staircase that goes far down below. I go down a few steps so I can lie down there. It is completely dark, the stone is cold and damp, and I'm freezing cold.

I get up and go a bit further forward. There, there is a second staircase made of wood that goes to an inner room where my sister and grandfather are. We have to go down, Agathe and I, to answer a call of nature. I ask our grandfather to keep us company so he can protect us. I am wearing a dark red brown house robe, the fabric of which has begun to ball up on the back. Since I'm freezing, I ask Grandfather if he needs the other robe; if not, I would put that one over me too. I ask this with tenderness and warmest concern for him. He replies that I should definitely take the robe; he doesn't need it.

We walk through a big, empty room. Then we come into my mother's bedroom. Behind a curtain is a chamber pot. Grandfather accompanies Agathe over to it so that nothing will happen to her. Then they come back, and I go over.

In the pot, a used sanitary napkin of my grandfather's is hanging. He hadn't removed it so it could be seen that he needs sanitary napkins too. Then it's as if the sanitary napkin belongs to me. The most embarrassing part for me is that I have to clean it up, but I'm willing to do it in the same spirit of love in which I'd offered him the robe before.

Since the time I myself have been behind the curtain, a big, beautiful woman has been present.

I come out. In the place where the chamber pot was, the woman is now in the bed that I used to sleep in as a child (in the same room of my mother's). Of the woman I now see only a wonderful angel's face, surrounded by a fragrant, very soft veil. It is like an apparition. She says she doesn't understand how it works (this accomplishment or transformation). At her side, quite small, appears the figure of a saint, and behind it, an angel that leads and guides her. Both figures are colorful and composed of many parts like the figures in church windows. I look at the apparition and I realize! I say, I know it. (Background thought: through the guidance of the angel!)

At this moment, my grandfather is overcome by nausea. It is as though he has risen out of my mother's bed. He sits in front of it, leaning on the nightstand. Crying, he says he has to die, and adds: I never thought this would be our last walk together. I approach with great tenderness and send Agathe to call a doctor. What I would most like to do is kneel down and put my arms around him. I stroke his face and kiss him on his red-lipsticked mouth.

The dreamer was from a peasant background and was orphaned at the age of six. Her father died in a tragic way in the war, and her mother died soon after. The little girl was taken in by relatives but had no one she was close to. Her only feelings were toward a female dog, which she often cuddled up with for warmth. Her sisters, too, had been taken in somewhere else. The sister Agathe who appears in this dream had long ago died of a carcinoma. The grandfather who appears in the dream had also died long ago, so that in effect the dreamer here, led by two spirits of the dead, is descending to a *nekyia* into the depths of the unconscious. It is not difficult to recognize in these "spirits" the shadow and the animus in the sense of Jungian psychology; that is, the sister represents the dark, unknown side of the ego and the grandfather an unconscious spiritual attitude toward the unconscious.

The fortress or the religiously significant cavity in the rock is a known archetypal symbol expressing the inescapability of becoming oneself, the torment of absolute introversion, which has now obviously become necessary. This motif recalls the incubation chambers of Asclepius and other gods of healing or the *katoche* of antiquity, that "imprisonment" which was also regarded as possession, that is, thralldom to a chthonic god. Individuals entered into this imprisonment in order to be initiated into the mystery cult of the god through their dreams.[3]

The spring is part of this image. As C. A. Meier shows in his book *Der Traum als Medizin* (Dream as Medicine),[4] springs or artificial streams were found in or near all places of healing. He says:

> Water plays an altogether powerful role in the Asclepian process. These springs and pools were never mineral or thermal waters. Rather they simply belonged to Asclepius as a chthonic god,

exactly like his serpent, and the spring became a *hagiasma* (healing spring) simply through its connection with the god. All the
dii chthonii have near the place sacred to them a *pege*, a spring;
. . . even the Christian successors of the ancient gods of healing,
the saints who worked miracles of healing, almost all have a
spring in their churches.[5]

Bathing in these springs was tantamount to a lustration and
even had the baptismal quality of an inner rebirth and a *coniunctio*, that is, an inner attainment of oneness and wholeness.[6]

Psychologically the image of the spring signifies that in the
depths of the unconscious the stream of life can be rediscovered. Whether one is really alive or languishing like a dead
person is after all a matter of a subjective psychic feeling that
depends on whether one is moving in the flow of unconscious
psychic energy or is cut off from it.

The dreamer is freezing. She is inadequately clothed in her
worn house robe. Her attitude toward the unconscious is neg-
ligent, not "warm" enough, thus inadequate. Therefore she
borrows her grandfather's robe; that is, she tries to adopt his
attitude toward the unconscious. This grandfather is the long-
dead father of her mother, of whom she only knew that he
used to do "black magic" and that people used to gather in
his house by night to conjure the devil: "The people often
heard the devil rattling a chain." The dreamer herself had a
strong interest in such things. She had read the works of Eli-
phas Levi and had obviously been deeply affected by them.
However—and this was the dangerous thing about it—she was
not willing to talk about it much. The grandfather clearly personified this "impure" attitude toward the powers in the
depths that had to be purified. He appears as a hermaphrodite,
as a symbol of wholeness, yet with something monstrous about
him,[7] for in him two elements are unified into wholeness be-

fore they have been properly polarized apart — it is a case of opposites still clinging together rather than of a new *coniunctio oppositorum*.

The grandfather figure contains in essence the principal problem of the dreamer: consciousness and the unconscious, the ego and "the other" are in contact in the wrong way within her, in a way that could be described as magic rather than *religio*. The former involves a partial possession by the unconscious, which is portrayed in the dream by the fact that the magician-grandfather has assimilated an aspect of femininity that actually belonged to the ego. By getting this femininity on his side, the animus as unconscious magician spirit has achieved the upper hand, and as a result not only does he dominate the dreamer's ego, but in such cases a woman can no longer sense whether it is herself or her animus that feels or believes something — the opinions of the animus have exactly the same inner feeling to them as her own. In addition, feminine feeling and masculine secret calculation and planning are improperly blended.

By having a piece of her ego assimilated by the unconscious, there arises a kind of unclear identification with the latter, which in the case of the dreamer manifested as a considerable degree of clairvoyance and pronounced mediumistic capacities. Through this, however, there then readily develops a covertly arrogant, mysteriously concocted pseudosuperiority and false "knowledge" concerning the unconscious. This knowledge is based on the possession, that is, based on the impersonal "knowledge" of the unconscious, on its vague luminosity. As Jung proved, the unconscious does possess a certain diffuse quality of consciousness,[8] and in the case of possession by an unconscious complex, this naturally becomes partially available to the ego. This does indeed bring about a certain clairvoyance, but only at the expense of a clear delimitation of the field of consciousness or a deficient clarity of feeling. In our case, it is the latter of the two. The dreamer was strangely uncertain in her feelings and inconstant as well—her heart fell ever and again under the domination of cold, mistrustful calculation, that is, of the magician-grandfather. Correspondingly, in her outer life, she repeatedly fell in with cold, calculating men who abused her capacity for love and did not give her what she needed most after her unhappy childhood—genuine warmth and feeling.

The befoulings of the toilet in her mother's bedroom point to just such unrewarding sexual experiences. However, there the Self is also born—*in stercore invenitur!*[9] The mother's bedroom, where the dreamer came into the world and first lived, symbolizes the inner place of origin and the realm of the feminine instinct. When the dreamer resolves to create a state of cleanliness there, the "big, beautiful woman" appears, an image of the Self, as Jung put it, that is, a personification of the higher, more encompassing personality and of inner wholeness. This "beautiful woman" comes into being in the place where the dreamer herself came into the world—the place pervaded by the mystery of the coming into being of a human individual.

But this great inner figure knows nothing of its own coming into being; it has as much need of the ego in order to experience itself as the ego has of it in order to become conscious of itself. The ego is like the eye of the Self, and only it can see and experience how the Self came into being. It sees this in the next image of the dream in the two joined figures: the angel leading a saint.

The figure of the saint repeats the motif of the "beautiful, big woman," representing again the individuated religious personality that the dreamer could become if she were to give herself over to the guidance of the angel. The angel—a messenger of the divine—was clarified through a later dream, in which a lofty figure ceremonially proclaimed: "The unconscious clothes itself in the form of an angel." Thus the angel is the mystery of the unconscious itself, the divine mystery of the primordial ground of the soul or psyche. The dreamer should let herself be led by him.

That these figures have the appearance of a pieced-together glass window points to the motif of the "conglomerate soul," the Self as a multifaceted unity, the oneness of many outer and inner elements.[10] In this moment it becomes clear that the dream now demands of the dreamer a humble religious attitude, and therefore it is just at this moment that the spirit of the magician in her becomes deathly nauseous, for the two attitudes are incompatible. The magician possesses and uses the unconscious and behaves as though, through his knowledge, he has complete control over it, whereas in fact at best, like the rest of us, he is able to glimpse a few intuitively grasped symbolic connections.

In the meantime, the dreamer's situation as a whole remained very disquieting. Her exhaustion made it difficult for her to arouse hope, and even writing down the rushing flood of dream images was often too much for her. However, after a number of more personal dreams came a dream that seemed to be giving me a sign about how to proceed further.

One often hears in psychological circles the comment that when there is danger that the unconscious will flood over, the analyst should take suppressive measures or measures that do not stimulate the unconscious. In my experience, this is not always necessary, for the unconscious itself often shows us a way of bringing it under control—that is, if one correctly understands the subtle meaning of the dreams; and a way suggested by the unconscious itself is for the most part more convincing to the analysand than anything the analyst might undertake just on his own hook. In our case, the following dream arose.

The Spring

I'm standing in the desert. They're digging for water. A man is digging with a shovel. He seems very knowing and superior, a kind of "professor." Another one seems to be working up from below. Suddenly the two collide and end up lying with the face of one on top of the face of the other. This looks quite funny. The one from below has a kind of iron face or mask, and above and below seem to change places. Suddenly the situation is completely different—the overabundance of water has to be bailed feverishly to prevent a flood and at the same time to direct the water to the city of Rome. Lots of blacks are working under the direction of the professor. My girlfriend Alberta arrives with a pretty green container, and we help to bail. The professor is driving us on and hits me once in fun on the bottom with a stick. But then the professor sends me away—I'm supposed to lie down on a bed for a while and rest. In the meantime, the others are going to continue to work for me.

This dream at once gave me a helpful practical signal. I advised the dreamer, just as indicated in the dream, simply to lie in bed all the time and just get up briefly for analysis sessions. As for the rest, I simply continued to interpret her dreams according to the usual principles. This solution proved favorable; the flood of dreams came to an end without the dreamer's collapsing or getting out of touch. Her long hours in bed provided a good rest and put her in a peaceful, meditative mood. As I only found out later, driven by her tyrannically dutiful animus, she tended continually to bully herself into excessive efforts; thus this bed rest was also unexpectedly very helpful in providing relief from this strain caused by the animus.

In addition, the dream seems to me to be an impressive, nearly classic representation of the mysterious process that occurs when an aspect of the unconscious is made conscious.

The point is that we "explain" the unconscious with the aid of symbols and concepts which themselves are derived from the same primordial ground—*ignotum per ignotius*,[11] as the alchemists say and as Jung repeatedly points out. The symbolic images that arise out of the unconscious by their very nature refer to material that is essentially unconscious,[12] and therefore "every interpretation remains an as-if."[13] Each interpertation is only an "approximate description and characterization of an unconscious kernel of meaning,"[14] and thus is itself a "new costuming of the myth." But this process must be carried through in order to keep the cultural consciousness in contact with the instinctual ground of the unconscious.[15] The "professor" obviously represents an intellectual approach that is attempting to assimilate the contents of the unconscious (whereas the man in the iron mask personifies the myth-generating spirit of the depths itself). The temporary switching of the roles on the one hand shows the natural affinity of the two but, on the other, is also to be interpreted in terms of the danger of magic. If the spirit of the unconscious assimilates the interpreting spirit, the result will be an arrogant-mystical pseudointerpretation and the intuitively suggestive "proclamation" of a "new" myth. This sort of thing has of late been much held in esteem by many students of mythology as well as by half-mystical "movements" that neglect the conscious human approach and the conscious human way of looking at things. The difference between the professor and the spirit lies precisely in the fact that one of them is human and the other partially inhuman.

Even in academic mythological research today, a tendency is developing once again to let symbols speak in and of themselves, proliferating more symbols without any reference to the fundamental parameters of depth psychology. I am thinking of such studies as those in *Symbolon* or the journal *Antaios* by Mircea Eliade, J. Schwabe, and others. These studies run the risk of losing themselves in unbounded amplification, in which ultimately everything is everything else and at the same time nothing whatever. What is missing is a concrete framework and the Archimedean point outside of the symbolic system itself. This framework can only be the human individual, for it is from his or her psyche that the symbols arise. Therefore it seems to me that research into symbols that disregards the psychology of the unconscious is a meaningless undertaking. It necessarily results in the researcher's being possessed by the symbols and ends up cold and shapeless, since it is missing the individual human being as the "fundamental structuring element" in the material.

In addition, today new Rosicrucian, Anthroposophical, and "magical" movements are seeking to bring back the viability of our relationship with the symbol without taking into account depth psychology—which they reject—because this allows them to play intuitively and intellectually with these contents without having to draw any personal consequences.

The dreamer sympathized with such approaches to symbols, because in this way she could flee from the misery of her actual life into a mythical world of magic where no ethical decisions, or any other kind of decisions for that matter, had to be made. She related only lukewarmly to my attempts to refers all dream interpretations to the current state of her own life, and the temporary predominance gained by the man with the iron face shows that she sometimes let herself indulge in her affects and images. But thank heavens, in her dream the mixup was only temporary and the "professor" was again able to gain the upper hand.

However, we then have the threat of a flooding over of the unconscious, the contents of which, as the dream account tells us, are to be directed to "the city of Rome," that is, to a religious inner center.[16] It is not the ego that is meant to enjoy the rapture of this wealth welling up from the depths; rather it is an inner center, the Self, that is to be vivified by it.

The dreamer had the association about the blacks, "working like a nigger," which is what the blacks in the dream indeed do. They obey the professor and embody once more that simple humble devotion toward the inner world that is always brought about by conscientious, serious work on oneself in which one seeks not only to get an intuitive whiff of the contents of the unconscious but to assimilate them in their essential nature.

But the most important symbol in this set of relationships is the pretty green container that the dreamer's girlfriend Alberta uses for bailing water. The dreamer is an introverted intuitive type,[17] and her sensation, that is, her reality function, was—as often happens in such cases—primitively intense, but it was only partial and it was insular and functioned autonomously. Thus she had a good relationship, almost too good, with matters of money and clothing, but neglected her body when it came to eating and sleeping, and she never set up her living quarters comfortably. As laboriously and dubiously as the inferior function usually works in relating to the outside, it is especially valuable in relating to the unconscious, because it still possesses that primitive spontaneity that is helpful in grasping the contents of the unconscious. The person who carries the container, Alberta, also indicates this direction, being, according to the dreamer, a simple, "realistic" woman. Among other things, the container recalls the symbolism of the Grail[18] and represents the Self in its function of a supreme feminine symbol, which is that element in the psyche that is capable of comprehending the divine principle. Thus it was clearly indicated for the dreamer to bring her ego to a state of meditative calm and then to let something simple and natural in her spontaneously convey to her the contents of the unconscious.

The man with the iron mask or the iron face is definitely deserving of closer examination. He is an archetypal motif that is to be found in alchemy as well as in the Grimm's fairy tale "Iron Hans." As a man of iron, he appears in alchemy as a personification of Mars or Ares, and was conceived of by the Paracelsian Adam von Bodenstein as the *natura prima rerum* (the primal nature of things), whereas Rulandus likened him to Paracelsus' Archeus, who, as Jung showed, is a personification of the unconscious.[19] According to Rulandus, Ares is the shaper of the individual, that is, as Jung says, the *principium individuationis sensu strictiori*.[20] Paracelsus describes him in his *De vita longa* in the following terms:

> He emanates from the forehead, from the *corpora supracoelestia*; for such are the properties and nature of the supracelestial bodies that right out of nothingness they produce a corporeal fantasy image (*imaginationem corpoream*) that is such that one takes it for a solid body. Of this nature is Ares: that when one thinks of a wolf, it also appears. The world is similar to the creatures produced by the four elements. Out of the elements arises that which in no wise resembles its origin, but nonetheless Ares bears everything within him.

Thus Ares appears (Jung says in interpreting this passage) as a preconscious creative shaping force. Johannes Braceschius von Brixen, an approximate contemporary of Paracelsus, likens Ares to the Demogorgon, said to be the progenitor of all the heathen gods. "He is the god of the earth, a horrible god, and also iron." Astrologically, Mars stands for the natural drives and affectivity of human beings.[21] Their taming and transformation in the philosopher's stone is the aim of the alchemical work.

In the case of the dreamer as well, strong emotions and affects were constellated beneath a shy, mild surface. These were not least of all, as we shall see in connection with the following dreams, a problem related to creation. The powerful imaginative force of her "Ares" was connected with magic, just as we find it clearly expressed in the citation from Paracelsus.

In "Iron Hans," we find a similar figure. There he is a "wild man," or demon hidden in a pond who in actual fact is an old king bound by a spell and waiting to be saved. In the forest, he possesses a spring that colors everything gold that is dipped into it. As an "old king," he represents a spiritual principle that formerly ruled but in one way or another was dethroned and downgraded to the level of an evil nature spirit. This shows a connection not only with alchemy but also with the pre-Christian Germanic religious tradition and particularly with Wotan. As the guardian of the golden spring, however, Iron Hans is also a magical nature spirit in the sense of the alchemical philosophy of nature, a *deus absconditus* of matter.[22] In his unredeemed state as an iron demon, however, he also stands for untamed barbaric aggression and affectivity; therefore, it is not surprising that during World War II, the dreamer developed National Socialist tendencies, which, however, she did not actualize externally—thank heavens, at least it went no further than mild sympathy.

This demon is evidently linked with the dreamer's shrieking symptom, which was indeed an autonomous outbreak of wildness. After I had discussed these relationships with her and elevated them into consciousness, there came a dream in which a boar in the yard behind the school let out a great thunderous bellow. A hunter appeared and shot the boar, and the dreamer then saw that the dead beast's belly was giving off a strange golden shimmer. One is reminded of Wotan's boar Gullinborsti. From the fact that the shrieking symptom never recurred after the dreamer returned home, one must assume that this dream represents the defeat of the autonomous affective outbreak after the spiritual-religious aspect of the man in the iron mask and the other related contents had been brought to the dreamer's consciousness. Such dream motifs also show, however, that magic, pagan religion, and false political doctrines of the modern era are in a hidden way directly connected with nonintegrated religious contents, and that the old Wotan, as hunter, iron man, boar, and so on, still haunts the psychic background of people of Germanic derivation.

The green vessel, which through its color is connected with the sensation function,[23] indicates that it was necessary for the dreamer to integrate the onrushing flood of unconscious material through practical, real measures—something that went quite against her grain, for she would have preferred to misuse it for rapturous, intuitive flights of the mind. She had a pronounced contempt for all modest, simple problems of life and always wanted to behave like the hedgehog in the well-known North German tale who ran a race with a hare. The hedgehog stationed his wife at the finish line, and when the hare breathlessly arrived, she mockingly called out, "I'm already there!"

This is the way the intuitive type likes to behave—he splits himself in two, and with one part of himself, his intuition, he is already at the finish, forgetting that his other half is still squatting in the dust at the starting line or is just a few yards along the course!

This problem was illustrated by a subsequent dream, which because of its complexity and length I have abridged in parts 1 and 3.

> 1. First the dreamer sees many animals being tortured by being tied to a heavy war machine and being forced to drag it. Then she tries with one of her sisters, who represents her realistic shadow, to save a ham sandwich from a cat. She takes both the sandwich and the cat into the kitchen, where an unknown woman, her sister, herself, and the cat take their places at a table. Later she wonders if her dream shouldn't perhaps be published.

This part of the dream first shows how much the dreamer bullies her natural instincts, then gives the solution to the problem: forming a group of four as a symbol of the wholeness of her personality. Three further parts of the dream followed the same night.

> 2. I'm on a ship—very friendly ship's crew. We're sailing a curve around a cliff. People who came too late are following on a raft. We stop on land to take them aboard. We have to wait a bit to do this. Then we continue sailing on dry land in a completely normal way—the ship has been equipped for this. . . . Then we go down into the water again.
>
> We glide over the water. It is night. Then we see on a cliff on our right something strange and mysterious: the cliff wall has a shelf about halfway up. There are birds standing on it, divided into two groups of three or four each. They are of human size,

stand upright like humans, and are wearing human masks and wigs. White wigs and white faces in one group, black on the other side. On their bodies can be seen the bird features: wings and so on. On one side, they also have white in the wings, otherwise they're black. . . . We look at them, amazed. A mood of mystery pervades the scene. The birds are making faces, gossiping, and singing to each other as though with human voices and are making corresponding eager gestures and faces. It looks unearthly, like a mystery play. I say to my neighbor (a woman): "Now it no longer surprises me that people invented the theater; they learned it from the animals (from nature)!"

My neighbor (much darker than I am) suddenly goes, "Gssh!" The birds perk up and notice, then instantly turn themselves into natural birds and fly away over us, unearthly, with broad beats of their wings. They don't want to be watched at this game. This "gssh!" was offensive.

3. After a session of analysis in which the dreamer tried to trivialize a mistake, a slip of the tongue she had made, she has to get to a certain ship, and now follows the typical tormenting dream in which she rushes and rushes and is delayed again and again. First she is delayed by a woman ironing, who, however, wondrously renews her wash by magic, then by a heap of clothes that she has to walk around; then the female analyst who is accompanying her amiably greets a simple woman whom this makes very happy, while the dreamer herself is upset about the waste of time. Then the dreamer greets a servant girl, whom the analyst finds unpleasant, and finally, following the advice of this girl, the dreamer gets lost in a labyrinth of train tracks.

The whole time she knows that this evening she really has to go to a party—that's what the rush is all about. In the train station, she comes onto a "tilted level" and slides off it into snow and ice and wanders further among tracks and stairways. The dreamer's narrative continues:

All the way in back I come to a door in the rock. I open it, and I am looking into a rock cave in the back of which peculiar, significant water is flowing from a powerful spring that is beyond my field of vision. It is a kind of wonder of nature. The cave is guarded by a woman. She thinks I am coming to look at the cave, but I say I have no time, I have to go on the ship. She accompanies me to show me the way. We still have a considerable way to climb; then we're standing on the ship dock. A ferryman is standing there giving information: the river is frozen, but the ice is broken. I ask if the ship to O——[24] has gone. He says yes and explains that the ice was broken in order to make the departure possible. I ask if another one is sailing. He says the next one doesn't go until eight o'clock,[25] that it's a police ship,[26] but that he thinks they could take me along. But I would only be able to ride as far as T—— and would have to walk up to O——; then I would arrive too late, and at night it's closed. It's getting close to midnight, and people say that after twelve o'clock it's strictly prohibited to be on the street.[27] So I have no other choice but to phone O——, tell them that I'm not coming, and then look for a place to stay here. It is Christmas Eve and I have to spend the night in "Darmstadt!"

4. My brother has finished off a little handicraft project that represents something meaningful—a symbolic project. A woman is holding it in her hand and giving explanations about it. There are little floors or levels, and on each there is a particular exhibition. As part of her explanations she says a sentence in Italian, then continues in solemn tones: "The unconscious then takes on the form of an angel. . . ." On the level below there is a big knife with a wrapped handle fastened in the middle. The woman goes on: "The unconscious, that refuge, one does not slit or slice!"[28]

The end of the first part of the dream, which brings up the idea of publishing the dreams, seems to me to represent an attempt on the part of the unconscious to suggest the idea of the dreamer's making use of her rich source of inner images as an author. This theme is then further developed in the second part with the play-acting birds. This image speaks for itself and shows particularly well how our artistic inspirations ultimately arise from our unconscious nature, not from our ego, as we often imagine. The ship is a veritable Dionysian "Thespian car," and in this artistic sphere of life, the use of intuition, which can sail through all obstacles posed by reality, is in its right place. On the other hand, the people on the raft who have to be waited for are the "retarded" elements of the dreamer's personality, the hedgehog still sitting at the starting line. This inferior realistic side disturbs the birds with its vulgar "gssh." It is the embodiment of such considerations as "Writing doesn't pay," "It's so tiring," "Nobody will read it," "It's a waste of time," and so on. This is the sort of thing with which the dreamer repeatedly throttled her creative impulses. All the same, she had been quite suuccessful with various short Christmas plays that she had written for her pupils—but the creative activity always had to be accomplished *religiosē*,[29] with no regard for success or monetary gain—as "the birds of the heavens" do it—and a small-minded shadow element repeatedly obstructed her in this.

That is why this "realistic" shadow element constitutes the theme of the third part of the dream and appears there partially in a positive form, as a woman ironing and a simple woman, but also in a destructive form as the servant girl who sent the dreamer into the chaos of the tracks and the "tilted level" and undermined her confidence in the analyst. However, this is also how she finds the way to the spring in the depths, which is guarded by a personification of the Self. But she does not want to stay there and looks for a place for the "party"[30]—landing after many detours back in her own depths, for with the word "Darmstadt," the dreamer associated "guts" and "city," hence the "city of guts."[31] So Christmas, the sacred holiday of God's birth, is taking place in the body's dark cave, the seat of the emotions, in her own innards.[32] Then the creative handicraftsman crops up, and then another venerable feminine figure, an image of the Self, who warns the dreamer not to dissect the unconscious intellectually but to give it form *religiosē* in a naive and humble fashion (as the handicraftsman does).

The creative problem, which she always evaded with the excuse of lack of time or fatigue, was expressed even more blatantly when in a later dream the dreamer found the author Karl M. asleep in the toilet. The toilet is a place of "creative" production, and the whole symbolism of excrement often points in dreams to creative problems. It plays an especially major role with schizophrenics, for after all, as Jung often pointed out, a case of schizophrenia can only be cured insofar as it is possible to bring the patient to a creative structuring of the contents that are oppressing him. We cannot be pushed to this kind of creativity through ambition and craving for material success. One can only be creative in this way "for God's sake."

René Gardi describes in his lovely book *Sepik* how the natives of that region finish off the construction of a house. First the "profane" builders go to work, and the future owners are no longer allowed to enter the house. Then it is the turn of the artists, who comprise a kind of priestly class, and they fashion totem poles with the images of spirits and gods in the center of the house, whereupon, lastly, the house is consecrated by other priests who perform rituals. Only in the fourth phase does the owner enter the house. Here it becomes clear that art as a primordial psychic phenomenon fulfills a religious task and represents an aspect of that "careful taking account of transcendental powers" that parallels the chants, prayers, and rituals of the priests. Giving form to the spirits is a "sacred" task, and they have to be formed for their own (the spirit's) sake, not according to the taste or mood of the artist.[33]

This is also the art of creativity that the unconscious demands from consciousness in many such cases; the unconscious demands that the work be done for its sake, even if the world is never to see the finished product. But this presumes a generous attitude, not the social ambition of an uncertain servant girl, but the selfless love of a handicraftsman. This also does not work without acceptance of what I have called "creative disappointment." Even the most talented person must repeatedly come to terms with the experience that, when compared with what he has seen with the inner eye, the finished product, in spite of all of the love and devotion that may have gone into its fashioning, is a sadly imperfect representation. Many people, however, cannot accept this disappointment. They are not willing to sacrifice the brilliance of their inner vision. They are unwilling to wean themselves from this, and so they do not come to the humility that is naively able to get on with creating. In my experience, this is connected with a secret inflation that hinders creativity in a way similar to that in which the "magical" posture blocks the *religio* — in fact ultimately it is the same problem. The ego has been overblown and the Self has been blown apart, and therefore the ego cannot serve the unconscious as a positive counterpole. Basically we do not want to accept being as stupid, naive, and helpless as we in fact actually are vis-à-vis the phenomenon of the unconscious, and we are not willing to begin where everything does begin, with the *religio* — with the careful taking into account of the numinous for its own sake.

The following dream now expressed this in a blatant fashion.

Witch's Kitchen

1. Lake Zurich, very beautiful and colorful—big city grouped around the north shore—in same, a strange, fairy-tale castle rises—the image immediately falls away again.

2. Two young people who are engaged and want to get married wander about. . . . The young man asked me to write the letter to his lover's father asking for permission to marry her. I have accepted this charge and composed the letter, but since I am unsure about it because he strikes me as awkward and because the task is also embarrassing, I read the letter to two young girls to get their view. They are somewhat contemptuous, smile to each other about me, and are of the opinion that this is really none of my business. The letter is acceptable, but I also say that the young man could have written it himself. I add that we often used to make fun of love letters, that there are people who try to get their hands on such letters just for the fun of it.

3. In a room at the Arons'. A rite of black magic is to take place. In addition to myself, present are Mrs. Aron, Mrs. Meier (a mildly neurotic woman, long a friend of the Aron family), and one of the young girls (from part 2). Mrs. Aron is going to perform the rite. I am sitting on the sofa with the young girl; we're to take part as spectators.

There is a kind of oven there that is brightly lit inside, probably by an invisible fire. Mrs. Aron gets all kinds of things ready near the oven and begins working with them. Mrs. Meier is assisting her. She says, "You [I'm the one she means] are going to experience that Mary too is only a witch's phantom!" In other words, the aim of the proceedings is to conjure Mary down into the prepared magical substance. Mrs. Meier leaves after these words.

I have three books of Masereel of different sizes on my lap that I'm supposed to look through while the substance is brewing. Mrs. Aron says to me I should open the biggest one, the one with the inscription: Masereel . . . ? (a sharp-sounding word with *st*: twist? master?).[34] I open the book. There are colorful, very peculiar pictures inside. They project themselves on the wall enlarged (or is there an enlarging mirror there?). They depict ghostlike black and gray figures who are fighting in the midst of the fire of war; it's a hell that the enemy has prepared for them. The colors are fire, blue green, and black. I am thinking that Masereel is presenting here the inhumanity of the enemy, of the others, only the one side, but that these people whose side he is on have done the same things to the first people. Still other chaotic images are presented.

In the meantime Mrs. Aron has gone to the fireplace in the other corner of the kitchen in order to complete the conjuring. The flame burns and lights up the whole corner. The magic substance is in a round container that is submerged in a water bath,[35] that is, in another big round container. It is mainly composed of egg (mixed with something) and looks like the makings for an instant pudding. The water bath is hanging over the fire—above it a wide chimney opens out. Everything is brilliantly lit by the firelight. Mrs. Aron is standing in front of it, stirring the substance and loudly singing the conjuring incantation.

I have moved to behind her. I am feeling strange and frightened. I try to calm myself by saying that after all it is Mrs. Aron who is conjuring and I am only watching. I nevertheless question whether I might not be harmed anyway. It is also only Mary who is being conjured, not God Himself. Then I realize that Mary is the mother of God, and therefore includes God, or God as the son. I think of the black mass. Mary is certainly not the holiest figure, but she is part of the Godhead. I am getting frightened. I want to get away.

Mr. Robert appears (the head of the school where I had my first job; doesn't believe in magic). The substance is already beginning to gel; it will soon be ready. It seems that the whole thing can only succeed if the magic ring is in it (a gold ring). I think, to comfort myself, that it isn't in there, but Mr. Robert answers, "The ring is in."

It's high time—I go out with Mr. Robert. We are discussing black magic together. He has doubted all these things. I tell him that magic is very dangerous. He replies, "Luckily nothing has ever happened to you!" I answer, "It has happened already!" I am thinking of two powerful glimpses of the invisible world that I had while dreaming. Robert explains that by my nature I'm very vulnerable. I confirm this. Yes, I am very exposed. Some people don't perceive these things, others, however, if they make the slightest mistake, if their awareness slips only slightly, immediately get a shock (strong emotion as though caused by electric current). Then I tell him that every misuse of the unconscious is already black magic.

We are approaching a large closed iron gate, through which we are to pass on our way to a gathering or a conference with lots of other people.

4. On the road in the car with my friend Mrs. Lindner. (She's married, has a good sense for the practical side of life, has a deeply religious nature, is interested in all philosophical and religious problems, is a churchgoer with pietistic tendencies.) There is a fork with a sharp curve (three directions). Cars are coming from two directions. They manage to get by each other. We're just at the fork. A big car is coming. Mrs. Lindner gets out of its way by backing up onto the little area next to the curve and then describes a circle with the car.

The dreamer's association for Lake Zurich was her present analysis, which had indeed brought her to a lake, and the first part with the appearance of the castle is like an auspicious visionary intimation of the Self. Among other things, the castle is a known symbol of Mary and as such also constitutes a link to the third part of the dream.

The second part of the dream depicts a pair of lovers trying to get together—thus, the inner *coniunctio* or the unification of opposites—and how the dreamer is supposed to take an active part in bringing about this unification, but is obstructed in this by shadow figures of the giggling teenager type. She obviously is unable to serve the god Eros *religiosē*: here too a frivolous egoistic element enters, something infantile that prevents her from taking the experience of love, and therefore herself as a woman, entirely seriously.

This lapse leads to the eerie image of the third part of the dream, the witch's kitchen. Mrs. Aron was an acquaintance of the dreamer's who was a fanatical devotee of Communism. Mrs. Meier, as she tells us, was a neurotic woman who was friends with the Arons. Here the dream tells us that Communism belongs, from a spiritual point of view, in the witch's kitchen. The production of Mary in the form of a "witch's phantom" shows the entire distortion of the *religio* in the shadow realm: a human takes it upon herself to control the divine figures as though they were objects, whereas in fact they were present as archetypes long before her ego was there and originally provided it with all its ideas about their nature.

During the conjuring the dreamer is supposed to look at the works of Franz Masereel. The scenes in the dream remind us most of his well-known "Dance of Death." This, according to the dream, is the hell which the enemies of certain people have prepared, and here is woven in the reflection that these latter people had probably done the same to the first. This hell shows what happens when an ideological conflict is not withdrawn from its projection onto the outside—it leads to the hell of negative affects, to injustice and revenge in an endless back-and-forth, in an individual as well as in the lives of peoples.

The penetrating sudden or distorted sound recalls the disturbing "gssh" in the previous dream and also the later remark of the woman that one does not "slit or slice" the unconscious. These clearly have to do with the danger of a sudden autonomous affect explosion. Patients sometimes describe the moment of outbreak of schizophrenia as being like a pistol shot sounding in their heads or like something ripping. The idea of someone's mind "snapping" is also connected with this kind of affective event. It is the excessiveness of the affect that causes matters to take a hopelessly irreversible bad turn in the form of an aggressive or otherwise insane action or fatal decision. In the life of the collectivity this corresponds to a declaration of war or a military attack.

In the witch's kitchen, negative projections are not processed but fed, and the religious symbols of the psyche are presented as no more than a human-controlled illusion.

The magical procedure described is an interesting one, for the vessel is very clearly a *bain-marie*, the *balneum Mariae* of the Jewish prophetess, the great woman alchemist.[36] Also the egg and the golden ring, the two most important ingredients, are known alchemical symbols and represent the Self as *prima materia*, "which contains in itself everything it has need of," and as the perfect golden mandala.[37] But the Communist Mrs. Aron, who is cooking these substances, is only trying to show in this way that Mary is a witch's phantom, that is, an illusion created by human beings, as indeed the Communists actually say about religious symbols and as the dreamer at one time was also inclined to believe. For if this is true, the ego need not place itself at the service of the inner process, but by making an illusory gesture of power can pretend that it is in control of all situations and can do with them what it likes. Because in this kind of magic there is something dishonest and unclean, it provokes the arising of rational skepticism as a counterpole, which is embodied in Mr. Robert. The Communist "Enlightenment," for example, is also such a posture. As long as the reality of the psyche remains unaccepted, one can only either insist on the crude material reality of psychic phenomena as magic does (and in this a latent intellectualism plays a certain part), or on their purely subjective-mental reality, as the schools of thought of the Enlightenment do (and in this a philosophical materialism furtively enters).

Thus in the psyche of the dreamer, witch's magic and dull skepticism stand at loggerheads, but then as a kind of liberating factor in the dream, the dreamer's friend Mrs. Lindner appears, who clearly embodies the attitude that is the right one for the dreamer. The two cars whose collision has to be avoided might well have to do with the two psychological attitudes that are on a collision course with each other, the magical and the rational-skeptic. Belief and knowledge are two modes of technical progress (= car) which also are repeatedly driving head-on at each other in the collective life of our time, although from a Jungian point of view, this is a pseudoconflict. The dreamer's friend Mrs. Lindner avoids the possible collision and backs up; that is, she distances herself from the question and then instead describes a circle with her car.

The drawing of the protective circle is in fact the oldest religious gesture of man, with which from time immemorial he has protected himself against influences that threaten the psyche with dissolution, such as affects, false ideals, and other "evil spirits." This is no "black magic" circle, because the person who draws it in the dream is not a witch but a religious woman. The witch's work, by contrast, is distinctly inflated — as in fact is Robert's skepticism, for how can he affirm with such certainty that the irrational does not exist? Therefore Mrs. Lindner stops, an act of humility: the truth is that we are not so terribly "advanced" that we are capable of making judgments on the ultimate reality of such things. We have to go back to the only thing that we can really directly experience, the psyche, and *religiosē* circumambulate its contents. Only in this way can the meaningless conflict between superstition and rationalism be avoided.

Her Protestant churchgoer friend Mrs. Lindner (the dreamer belongs to the group of Protestant peasants of Styria that migrated there from Germany) seems possibly to be a suggestion that a return to the Protestant church is called for. However, the next dream provides a different nuance in this regard.

The Greenhouse Bath

1. I am in a Catholic church, and with two or three other people I am walking by the place where the sacred rite is in progress. I receive communion in some way, but this is a special priestly ritual in which I am included. I have a strong inner experience like a fulfillment experience, an experience of renewal, and am very happy about it—that is what I was looking for. I have to realize that clearly. A kind of church servant or second-class priest writes down for me the verse or the words that express the secret of the experience. In front of him the little book in which the words are written lies open, and I read them (but can't remember them when I wake up).

2. I go to the toilet. Karl M. (the Styrian "author," my former teacher and present friend) is sitting on the board sleeping. I lift the lid, and the excrement is piled up to the brim. It stinks terribly. I say to Karl M. that he shouldn't be sleeping there in that stench. He looks at me strangely with his sleepy and furtive eyes and then goes back to sleep sitting up. I am astounded that he can even sleep in that foul place.

3. The school. School activities are beginning again. I come and explain to the woman head of the school that I still am on leave for health reasons. I am very happy about this leave, because it will mean gaining my health, and beyond that, a development that will free me for a higher level of achievement. Schulz (the materialistic school head) is standing there leaning against the wall with a very disgruntled look on his face. I ask him how he is. He replies, "Not well!" Not well healthwise and put out because of my leave. I go for the treatment that is supposed to help me. I am supposed to be bathed by Eberhard

Müller (a simple laborer who often does odd jobs around our house). The bath is in a greenhouse. I go in. The tub is built in, in a beautiful modern way, and the water is streaming into it. It is almost full. . . . Eberhard Müller will also be naked for the bath. This is quite natural and will provide an opportunity for me to get to know him.

Toward the rear, the bath area has been spaciously extended. There are other tubs there among plants and rocks. It looks rather like a park setup. The water is flowing in all over. I walk around in the bath area (or park) with my friend Lisbeth (married teacher, also a good housewife, artistic, generally balanced and even-tempered). . . . We are standing further over to the side where the springs that feed the baths are. We see three of them, pouring out their foaming waters among the plants and rocks. I say to Lisbeth that that's the most beautiful part of this installation.

We go a bit further up to the bath. Lisbeth has projectiles in her body. They are small and large silver needles that are moving about in a dangerous way in her body (bright metal needles that shine like silver). A part of them are presently moving toward her breast, into the breast, which is very dangerous. For that reason she cannot yet be bathed.

Other people have come, among them also Frieda (a very religiously oriented colleague who also has a lot of practical sense). All of them want to be bathed here. The tubs are going to be occupied. I climb down to where a woman has a toilet and lavatory setup, but furthest in the back, there is a bath compartment, and I call to her to ask if I could be bathed there. There is still hot water for me, and the woman immediately sets it running into the deeply inset basin.

4. I am in a boardinghouse or in a hotel and awake in my very spacious room. The watch and time question. Next to me a second bed is prepared. The double door opens, and a young woman enters, holding a child. She is dressed up and wants to go to church. She puts the child down on the edge of my bed and gets it ready too, because it is supposed to go along to

church. She excuses herself for going through my room, which is not customary, but she had to go through.

In the first part of the dream, a Catholic church is the site of a major experience, but later Lisbeth and Frieda appear as positive figures, neither of whom are Catholic. Therefore it seems to me that for the unconscious the important point is not so much a particular denomination as a genuine religious attitude, no matter what framework it is experienced in.

The first part is concerned with the writing down of an inner experience with a sense of service that makes it seem like a religious task. The person writing it down is a second-class priest or a servant, which suggests a humble attitude of service. The ego must take a second-class position before the Self. Then comes the scene we interpreted earlier with the author Karl M., who represents the opposite of the priest-servant who wrote down the experience. He is an ambitious journalist and therefore can have nothing to do with the activity of giving creative form to the religious experience.

Then follows the alchemical bath of healing and baptism. The man who is supposed to perform this has a first name containing the word *Eber* (German, "boar"), and is a simple laborer. The great savage emotionality that the boar embodied in the earlier dream has now become a laborer, that is, become work energy to serve the inner labor! The materialist Schulz in the dreamer, on the other hand, is not well when she turns to her inner work.

But also the extremely positive figure of her friend Lisbeth is full of silver needles and therefore cannot get into the bath. This is an old motif of magic, the evil spirit needles or "icicles," which, for example, the Siberian shamans send to afflict their rivals. Psychologically, these needles symbolize negative projections, which have to be made conscious for the first time. At whatever point we are still unconscious and projecting our own shadow elements, we are at the same time especially sensitive to the "barbs" of our dear fellow men and women, and this can even go as far as the development of persecution ideas. The witch shadow of women often excels in sending and receiving these "barbs"! Finally at least the dreamer herself can get into the renewing bath and thus be born again out of the waters of the unconscious. The reborn child, however, as the next part of the dream shows, is not her ego, but the Self (represented by the unknown child that the unknown woman puts on her bed), and the child is to go to church, that is, to a religious service. The woman who is carrying it to church is unknown, betokening that her own appropriate religious attitude is still unknown to the dreamer, but this attitude has at least already been aroused within the unconscious and is present.

The further development of matters was not so felicitous as this last motif perhaps might have led us to expect. An acquaintance of the dreamer's came to join her, half to share her new experience and half to destroy it out of jealousy. She succeeded in sowing mistrust in the analysis, and thus the analysand did not return during her subsequent vacations to continue analysis, which she partly excused by saying it was too expensive for her. The dreamer, it is true, was in a better state. She had been healed of her symptoms, the migraines and the shriek. However, the religious-creative development portended in her dreams proceeded no further. The negative-realistic shadow, in projected form, intervened. As a result the analysand got involved with a spiritual movement that advocated symbolic-intuitive teachings. In this way, the magician-grandfather, from whom the dreamer did not want to separate at the end of the initial dream, partially regained possession of her. The end of the initial dream does indeed often "prophesy" the course of a treatment—nonetheless it still remains to be seen whether the "magician" might not possibly die later.

A human life lasts longer than the analysis of two short summer vacations, and we cannot know if and when the appropriate *religio* will prevail in the psyche of the dreamer over the magician, the skeptic, the sleeping author, the witch, and the frivolous girls. All the same these dreams seem to me to illuminate with vivid clarity the individuation process as a primal religious phenomenon. They also show what attitudes within the psyche most hinder this process. These many obstructing influences, which are partly represented by shadow figures and partly by animus personifications, are seen in remarkably clear form in these dreams, contrasting with the sublime but vague and unknown forms of the Self. This shows that the tendency toward individuation had as yet been only very slightly realized in the dreamer. Only such positive figures as Lisbeth and Frieda are more sharply outlined. Thus the dreamer, in order to make progress, should have begun with them, that is, should have attempted to adopt within herself their attitudes toward life. Though these women were members of different denominations, according to the dreamer, they were all simultaneously religious and rooted in practical life. They properly bring together the two sides of life that in her case were too widely separate, and thus are used by the unconscious as models of a right attitude.

Moreover, in my view, these few dreams (and they represent only a tiny selection from a flood of similar archetypal dreams) show us something that could perhaps be termed a fundamental religious tendency of the psyche, a tendency that is inextricably bound up with the process of individuation and also encompasses all creative potentialities of the personality.

NOTES

1. C. G. Jung, *Psychology and Religion*, CW 11, p. 8.
2. The dreamer herself, unprompted, gave her dreams titles when she wrote them up for me.
3. On this, see also my discussion in *The Passion of Perpetua* (Dallas: Spring Publications, 1980), pp. 16ff.
4. C. A. Meier, *Der Traum als Medizin* (Zurich: Daimon, 1985). Published in English as *Healing Dream and Ritual: Ancient Incubation and Modern Psychotherapy* (Evanston, Ill.: Northwestern University Press, 1967).
5. Meier, *Der Traum als Medizin*, p. 78.
6. Ibid., p. 84.
7. Cf. Jung, "Psychology of the Transference," CW 16, pp. 307ff. The major role played by the hermaphrodite in the symbolism of alchemy is connected with the "impure" mixing together of matter and the unconscious psyche, something the alchemists were not aware of.
8. Jung, CW 8, pp. 189ff.
9. *In stercore invenitur*: "discovered amid excrement." — Translator
10. Cf. Jung, "The Spirit Mercurius," CW 13.
11. *Ignotum per ignotius*: "the unknown by the more unknown." — Translator
12. Cf. C. G. Jung and C. Kerényi, *Einführung in das Wesen der Mythologie* (Zurich: Rhein-Verlag, 1951), p. 113. Published in English as *Essays on a Science of Mythology* (Princeton: Princeton University Press, Bollingen Series, 1973).
13. Ibid.
14. Ibid., p. 114.
15. Ibid., p. 115.
16. According to the dreamer's associations, this is what Rome meant for her. She had never actually been in Rome herself.
17. I am here presuming familiarity with Jungian typology; the reader is referred to Jung's *Psychological Types*, CW 6.
18. Cf. Emma Jung and Marie-Louise von Franz, *The Grail Legend* (Boston: Sigo Press, 1986).
19. Cf. Jung, "Paracelsus as a Spiritual Phenomenon," CW 13, para. 176, p. 140.

20. The principle of individuation in the strict sense.—Translator

21. Jung, CW 13, para. 176.

22. See H. von Beit, *Symbolik des Märchens* (Symbolism of Fairy Tales) (Bern, 1952–1957), vol. 2, pp. 380ff.

23. The color green, as the color of the earth's surface, is usually connected with the sensation function.

24. The place where the dreamer lived during the analysis.

25. Eight is a number that indicates wholeness.

26. Police ship = moral supervision!

27. Midnight, as the "witching hour," is in fact dangerous here.

28. The dreamer's account here contains words that do not actually exist in the German language but still convey some meaning. These words, *zickt* and *zermessert*, have been rendered "silly" and "slice." It should be noted that both German pseudowords begin with the sharp *ts* sound of the German *z*.—Translator

29. This is the adverbial form of the Latin *religio*, meaning "conscientiousness, scrupulousness, exactness." This was a key term for Jung. Two short quotations may serve to define and give a sense of the flavor the term had for him: ". . . the original meaning of the world *religio*—a careful observation and taking account of . . . the numinous." And again: "But fortunately the man had *religio*, that is he 'carefully took account of' his experience." CW 11, pp. 596, 43.—Translator

30. The association of the dreamer for "party" was Christmas.

31. The name of this major German town could be literally translated "gut city," though this is not the actual derivation of the name.—Translator's note

32. In tantra yoga, this corresponds to the fire center, *manipura*.

33. The Naskapi Indians of the Labrador Peninsula have a similar conception.

34. Here the German gives partial words based on incomplete memory of certain sounds, which a translation can only render by analogy. The dreamer remembered a sharp-sounding word with *err* in it and guessed it contained either *zerr* or *herrsch*. These can be taken as the radicals of verbs meaning "distort" and "master." It should be noted that one has the sharp-sounding *ts* of the German *z* and the other a sharp *shh* sound.—Translator

35. This somewhat antiquated term (*Wasserbad* in German) refers to a large pot of water in which the contents of a smaller pot partly immersed in it can be heated—in effect, the larger lower part of a double boiler. As will be helpful to know later, this piece of cooking or (formerly) chem-

ical apparatus is also known in German as a *Marienbad*, literally meaning "bath of Mary." This is analogous to the French term *bain-marie*,
also used in English. The source of these terms is the Latin *balneum
Mariae*. — Translator

36. Cf. Jung, CW 12, p. 225. [This alchemist is more usually known as Maria
    Prophetissa. — Translator]

37. Jung, CW 12, p. 173f.

SOME ASPECTS OF
THE TRANSFERENCE

I was asked to speak about some of the more profound aspects of the transference problem, and I agreed, perhaps a bit precipitously; for I must openly admit that I do not feel qualified for this task. When Jung had finished *Mysterium Coniunctionis*, he himself said, "I believe I have not said everything about this subject here; there is a lot more to it still, but I have presented it as far as I was able." So what can be added by someone like myself? Thus I will only speak about a few aspects of the problem regarding which I have had at least glimpses of understanding.

It seems to me that it is helpful at the outset to divide the problem into four main aspects: (1) archaic identity, (2) mutual projections, (3) personal relationship, (4) fated togetherness in "eternity."

In practice it is not the first aspect that most clearly appears at the beginning, but rather the second. Here we are dealing with the fact, already seen by Freud, that many projections arising from familial relationships enter into the transference—transference of father and mother images and of brother and sister images—and this creates an unrealistic erotic attraction darkened by infantile demands and prejudices. As Hans Dieckmann has confirmed in his experiments, these projections also constellate in the analyst all parallel images that have not yet been processed consciously, and as a result an enmeshing of the problems of both parties becomes manifest almost immediately. An analysand's negative mother complex, for example, evokes similar negative images in the memory of the analyst. On the positive side, this forms the basis for the analyst's empathy and understanding; but there is also the negative side, a common unconsciousness, which, among other things, may necessitate guidance from the analyst's colleagues.

The first aspect: When we speak of "projections" at this stage of events, we must remember that Jung, in his definition of this concept,[1] says that we can only speak of projections when there is a disturbance or an unconscious doubt that makes the prevailing view about the partner no longer seem to fit; before this point there is the archaic identity (which is why I have designated this the first phase). I believe that we often make a mistake regarding this in our practical work: we speak to the analysand about a "projection" because we ourselves see it as such (that is, we doubt), even at a point where there has still been no indication—for example, in dreams—that could make this doubt clear to the analysand. This then arouses justified and unnecessary resistance in the analysand. I believe that it is right in connection with this first phase simply to behave with the analysand in accordance with the way one actually feels, but without any verbal confrontations. For example, one could react to a demand for mothering simply by stressing one's own lack of time or desire for this, without accusing the other of projecting the mother onto oneself. With time, this alone brings about the aforementioned disturbance or doubt in the other, which is reflected for the most part in dreams. Only at that point, in my view, has the right moment come to speak openly of a projection. This is because the foregoing stage has a vital function that should not be prematurely disrupted, since it often constitutes the effective vehicle for the beginning of the treatment. This is also the reason that group experiments are of such dubious value—because, as is generally known, through them the phenomenon of the transference is held in check.

The same thing holds true for the analyst: he must let the archaic identity in himself live on as well. I have noticed in my own case that I have sometimes experienced relatively intense countertransference fascinations with analysands who from my conscious point of view did not seem particularly likable, and in these cases it regularly turned out that a severe problem or a threat of death was present that I had failed to see. Once the condition of the analysand improved, the whole fascination would disappear as if by magic. Especially an unrecognized imminence of death had this effect. It seems to me that in this way nature, that is, the unconscious, was simply trying to force the necessary emotional participation and effort of understanding upon me, since my conscious approach was inadequate. If in these cases I had tried prematurely to dismiss this fascination as a "projection," it would not have been able to function positively on the analysand's behalf. It therefore seems to me that, as uncomfortable as it might be, one must let the first phase of archaic identification run its course; and if I understand Jung aright, he himself did this as well. In fact, when we look at the first pictures from the alchemical *Rosarium Philosophorum* series,[2] where the king and queen meet each other, we find that a lovely, positive love relationship is taking place, a touching of the *left* hands of the two. Only following that do the bath, the nigredo, and death occur, i.e., those disturbances that require us to undertake the work of bringing about conscious recognition of projections.

The second aspect: Bringing about conscious recognition of

projections is, it seems to me, first and foremost a moral problem. I have often seen analysts tending intellectually and prematurely to dismiss as a projection the romantic fascination of an analysand that they had no desire to become involved in, without any consideration for whether or not the time for this had come as indicated by the inner life of the analysand. Conversely, many do not interpret their own love fantasies as projections but rather as necessary relationships "destined" by life or the Self just because this is really their own secret desire. In this way one is simply taken over by an unconscious lust or rejection tendency, with negative results for both parties involved.

As I have already said, it seems to me more appropriate if, for example, a mother transference is present, to the extent that one feels it, actually to be motherly until the projection has become ripe for talking about. I have been particularly struck by the fact that often almost compulsively vehement transference phenomena appear in cases where the analysand has had to be forced to relate to the inner process, because otherwise he or she, out of resistance or superficiality, would have run away from it. To continually "discuss the transference," as the Jungians of the Society of Analytical Psychology in London do, I consider to be outright harmful in such situations. The painful, sticky, unresolved quality of the situation must simply be endured by both sides. In fact, Jung writes in a letter that people become entangled in unanswered love when it is important for them to avoid an erotic experience because such an experience could divert them from the goal of individuation, that is, from the striving toward greater consciousness.[3]

I have also sometimes observed a male analyst not make himself available to the "justified" emotional demand of a female analysand and thus bring about an unnecessary loss of time and energy and cause the patient unnecessary tears. In these cases, after a while the transference rebounds onto another partner with whom the potential for relationship is better.

The third aspect, which should be part of the analysis from the very beginning but often by its nature can develop only gradually, is personal relationship or even friendship. Naturally this cannot come about with all analysands, and especially the closeness or remoteness of such a relationship varies according to incalculable and imponderable factors. Thus Jung writes in a letter to an analyst:

> One of the most important and difficult tasks in the individuation process is to bridge the distance between people. There is always a danger that the distance will be broken down by one party only, and this invariably gives rise to a feeling of violation followed by resentment. Every relationship has its optimal distance, which of course has to be found by trial and error. The problem is a particularly delicate one with women, where sexuality is apt to rear its ugly head. Scrupulous attention must be paid to *resistances*. They can hardly be taken seriously enough, since one is only too prone to self-deception.[4]

While many a love-struck analysand may seek to force themselves on us by reducing the distance too much, there are others who do not want a personal relationship. They want us to remain for them like a mechanic who mends a car, no more than an impersonal psychic repair shop. And between these extremes there are a thousand nuances. Even in the analyst both extremes exist. There is either a tendency to enter into a loving, familiar relationship and adopt the analysand as a partner, son, daughter, or the like, thus reducing the distance too much; or to take the approach of a cynically aloof stuffed shirt who "flushes the inner process into the sewers," as Jung once formulated it, that is, denying all need for human contact. And in between once again there are all the thousand nuances that are so tricky to pin down and among which the optimal middle ground is so difficult to find.

Especially in the realm of the first and second aspects, archaic identification and conscious recognition of projections, it is of course the power shadow that plays the role of the great destroyer, against which Adolf Guggenbühl-Craig has warned us in his book *Power in the Helping Professions*. "Where love is absent, power occupies the vacancy," Jung says. As part of the power shadow we not only find the urge on both sides to compete and dominate; there is also the analyst's urge to heal, which is not the least component here.

I recall in this connection my first analysis with a seriously disturbed analysand, a borderline case. I tried desperately with all the forces at my command to prevent her from slipping into a psychotic episode. At that point Jung had me come to see him. He listened to the whole story and then said very seriously, "What makes you so sure that the analysand doesn't have to go through an episode? Many people improve after such an episode. What makes you think you know her destiny so precisely? Perhaps you are hindering the very thing that according to God's will should happen." I was flabbergasted, and then I saw for the first time that my urge to produce an improvement was a power play. When I let go of my misguided pushing, the analysand got better rather than slipping into an episode. Later I was deeply impressed to find the following in a medieval exorcism guide for priests: The priest should first attempt to discover inwardly through silent prayer whether God wants to free the afflicted person from the tormenting demon, or in his mysterious wisdom wants him to keep his suffering and labor with it. Only when the former seems to be the case should the priest prepare for a healing ceremony. Too much Christian helping spirit is, as Jung once wrote, "an invasion of the will of the other. One should behave like someone who is offering an opportunity that can either be grasped or turned aside. Otherwise one gets into difficulties. This is so, because the human being is not totally good, but is nearly half a devil.[5]

However, Jung also rejected the cynical detachment that leaves everything to God or to fate just as much as the urge to do too much. Keeping to a medium between these extremes seems to me a very difficult task indeed, because it varies from person to person and from moment to moment. I do not believe it is possible to manage this just on the basis of thought or feeling alone. The only thing that can help is to be in the Tao, so that what one should or should not do here and in this moment can come to one instinctively from one's own Self. But of course we are all by no means always in the Tao, in right inward contact with the Self, or at least I am not.

The situation from the very beginning, but with increasing intensity in the third phase, is such that one can no longer function at all by using rules and conceptual insights or personal feelings; from the third phase on, everything of crucial importance in the work depends on oneself and how far one has developed; for here all general reference points fall away, and it becomes a matter of a unique human encounter with its own unique timing. Situations repeatedly arise in an analytic dialogue in which one must react immediately, with lightning speed. At that point it is not only what one thinks or says or feels that is decisive, but the sinking tone in one's voice, an involuntary movement, a hesitation—everything becomes crucial. Thus at this moment what counts is only what one is and how far one has come in one's own development, by no means any consciously learned "behavior," as well meant as it might be.

This brings us to the fourth aspect, which I have called a "fated togetherness in eternity," the real *mysterium coniunctionis*. This stage has to do with the experience of the Self, the inner wholeness that cannot be understood intellectually, but only through love. Jung writes: "This love is not transference and it is no ordinary friendship or sympathy. It is more primitive, more primeval and more spiritual than anything we can describe."[6] In this realm, it is no longer two individuals relating with each other on the personal level, but the "many, including yourself and anybody whose heart you touch."[7] There, "there is no distance, but immediate presence. It is an eternal secret. . . ."[8] In a certain sense, in the manifestation of this fourth aspect a return to the first aspect takes place, but on a higher, more conscious level. For that reason an inkling of this highest stage is already present in the first and brings about the depth of passion with which many try to cling to the stage of *participation mystique* and to fight off a conscious coming to terms with, and recognition of, the limited human reality. Jung said in the letter cited above that this aspect of love is more primitive and more spiritual than transference, friendship, and sympathy in the usual sense of the word. This is the reason for the outlandish paradoxes through which the *coniunctio* symbolism of alchemy attempts to represent this kind of relationship. I would like to try to illustrate it through the dream of a young woman. It was dreamed during the last world war at a moment at which the dreamer was resolving to accept her transference. The dream is as follows.

I am in Munich at an administrative building that I know Hitler is inside of. To my astonishment, it is not guarded. Curious, I go in and immediately find myself face to face with Hitler. I am holding a pistol in my hand and am suddenly struck by the thought that this is a unique opportunity. I shoot Hitler and run away. [There follows a long chase sequence.] Finally I find myself on foot on a dirt track over the fields toward the Swiss border on my way back home. I see in front of me a white rooster with a host of hens walking in the same direction. The rooster asks me if I would take him and his hens into Switzerland with me. I agree, but on the condition that on the way there should be no sexual intercourse. The rooster agrees, and a voice says: "And so along they went, like a prince abbot with his nuns." As we go on, I see a handsome human couple who are also on their way to the border. They are wearing golden crowns on their heads. It is a king and his queen. Since they seem to be very much strangers to the world, I invite them to come along with us, and they gratefully accept. In the night we manage to cross the border. The Swiss border guards put us in quarantine, where we are supposed to remain for four weeks. They demand that the eggs laid by the hens during this time should belong to the Swiss state.

The shooting of Hitler signifies getting rid of the power animus that is standing in the way of the individuation process. Then comes the flight to Switzerland, back home, that is, to the inner place that one belongs in and to the land of freedom. The primitive, primordial aspect of the *coniunctio*, as Jung called it, is represented by the rooster and his hens, an image that also occurs in alchemical symbolism. Thus the Arabic alchemist Senior describes how the lunar substance says to the sun, "Oh sun, I need you, just as the rooster needs the hen."[9] In other texts it is a wolf and a dog, a deer and a unicorn, or other animals that represent this aspect. The eggs that come into play at the end of the dream are a well-known image for the initial material of the individuation process. In the dream this host of chickens has a spiritual discipline imposed upon it, so that their animal nature will not pose an obstacle on their path to inner freedom. According to the above quotation from Senior, the rooster and the hen actually represent the sun and the moon, just as the king and queen do in alchemical symbolism. Thus the royal couple that appears later in the dream actually signifies the other aspect of the same thing.

This recalls a remark of Jung's that this form of *coniunctio*, the *hierosgamos*, is both more primitive and more spiritual than anything we are capable of describing. The king and queen, as well as the animals, represent something completely transpersonal, like something that exists in the divine realm, beyond space and time. That is why the dream tells us that the royal couple are "strangers to the world." The human ego has to help them to move in this concrete sphere. The dream beautifully depicts the intermediate position of the ego, which on the one hand imposes a certain spiritual discipline on the animals and on the other has to provide the royal couple with an element of earthly reality.

Feeling for this middle point constellates endless painstaking care, but as Jung pointed out, it is of vital importance not only for the individual but also for the moral and spiritual progress of humanity. Thus if the psychotherapist labors over this, he is working not only for these individual patients but also for his own soul, and as small as his achievement might be, it is accomplished at a place to which the *numen* has currently migrated, that is, a place to which mankind's problems have shifted.[10] That is also the reason that in this dream a bit of possible world history, the killing of Hitler, appears as a reaction to the fact that the dreamer had decided to take her transference seriously. That is why the unconscious often uses

such very cosmic and elevated images to express the transference problem, that is, to express that something significant is
happening.

Thus an analysand once dreamed after she had seen the film
Hiroshima, Mon Amour that either the lovers would be able to
be together properly or the atom bomb would explode. In this
way the unconscious was saying that something ultimate and
crucial was happening.

Just how significant the love problem is considered by the
unconscious may also be illustrated by the following dream. It
was dreamed by a woman of middle age who had experienced
a deep love for a married man, which he had reciprocated; but
she had in part continued to struggle against this love for conventional and rational reasons. Here is the dream.

I heard the mighty, deep sound of a bronze bell, an extraordinary ringing, such as I had never heard or imagined, a sound
from beyond, of extraordinary beauty, irresistible! Fascinated, I
got up, for I somehow had to get to the source of this sound,
which could only be a divine one. Since the sound seemed sacred to me, I thought it could come from a church, and instantly I was in a church of the purest Gothic style, of white
stone, and I was getting ready to climb the bell tower to find
the bell, the source of this grave, rhythmic ringing, which I
could still hear. But everything changed. The church became a
broad vault, like the nave of a cathedral made of a transparent
living red-orange material, bathed in a reddish light and sup-
ported by a forest of pillars that reminded me of stalactites in a
cave that I had once seen in Spain. For a moment I saw myself
as standing tiny and alone in this immense hall, dazzled with the
sense that I had a whole world to explore there. It was my heart.
I was standing in the interior of my own heart, and I realized at
this moment that the wonderful bell sound, which I could still
hear, was nothing other than the beat of my own heart, or that

this external sound and my heartbeat were one and the same. They were beating in the same rhythm. Macrocosm and microcosm were synchronized; the rhythm of the world's heart and my own heart were identical.

I think this dream requires no interpretation. It speaks for itself and shows how Eros and the individual are inextricably bound up together.

I would like to refer at this point once more to the dream of a married man that I have discussed briefly in another lecture.[11] He was in love with a married woman, Alberta, and had a sexual relationship with her. At the time of the dream, both parties were thinking about divorce.

I was with my teacher, an invisible presence, at the edge of a sphere that he had described as "the ultimate reality," something timeless and spaceless, indescribable. Only those who have seen it can understand this experience as an "everything-nothing," an "everywhere-nowhere," an "everyone–no one," as "the word that has not yet been uttered." Somehow the teacher helped me to pick two beings or somethings out of this ultimate reality. I didn't see them, but I knew of them. In order to make them visible, the teacher helped me to extract a silver-gray mist-like matter from the space we were floating in, and with that we coated the two beings and a third something that separated the two. When I saw them coated, I was struck with a profound amazement. "These are angels!" I called out. "Yes," he replied, "that is you." I saw the gray curtain that separated the two angels, and the teacher explained, "That is the veil of illusion." It had lots of holes. I was deeply moved and shouted, "Oh, it's falling away, it's falling away," and I had the feeling that thousands of years that had been lived through in the half-conscious hope that it could be broken through were now fulfilled. I went to the angel who was "me" and saw a silver string reaching down from him into a very tiny creature that was also "me" in the realm of illusion. Another string reached down into a woman down there. It was Alberta. The two angels seemed identical and sexless, and they could "think together" in a kind of identicalness (that sometimes happened to me with Alberta in reality "down there"). And we thought, "Such a small part of our consciousness lives in these little creatures, and they worry about such little things. Poor little creatures!" And we saw that their union could not come about properly if the two little creatures did not fulfill their obligations to those near them rather than following their egoistic desires. And at the same time it was clear to us that it would be a sin against that "ultimate reality" (a sin against the Holy Ghost?) if we did not go on with the process of mutual striving for consciousness.

Here the alchemical royal couple is replaced by two angels, messengers of God. However, they represent the same consciousness-transcending deeper aspect of the love relationship, which in this phase of development had slipped too much onto the concrete sexual level. As Jung points out, it can be as misguided to affect elevated spirituality as a way of evading concrete obligations as to let the relationship degenerate onto an atavistic-primitive level. These two represent a Scylla and Charybdis through which one has to steer one's way. In this phase, the second danger had been constellated, which is why the dream emphasizes the spiritual side so strongly. Previously though, the same dreamer had had a dream in which he had to accept a dangerous, significant round copper object around which serpents were coiled in wavy lines. In that phase of his life, he had illegitimately wanted to pull away from the physical side of the love problem. This round object reminded him in the dream of Christ's crown of thorns, and he knew it meant "blood and tears." And indeed the transference always does lead to a crucifixion, that is, to the death of the natural — that is, unconscious — person one has hitherto been.[12] We are the crossing point for conflicting forces, first for the manifestation of our own shadow in the form of jealousy, territoriality, sexual passions, and so on; and second for the fact that the partner is not as we would have him or her; and third for the contents of the collective unconscious, which through the transference come to the surface and begin to have a shaping influence on our destiny. All this leads to a death of the ego, and if everything goes right, to the birth of the Self. The principal task in this phase, as we know, is coming to terms with the animus and anima.

I would like to repeat here a description of the anima taken from an unpublished seminar of Jung's on children's dreams. The anima is a kind of desire or a system of expectations that a man has in relation to a woman, an erotic-relationship fantasy. If outer expectations like ordinary sensual desire or schemes regarding money, power, and so on, get mixed up with it, everything is lost. Thus conscious recognition of the anima means loving the other for herself and for love's sake. "When I follow my love, then my love is fulfilled." Only for a man who pursues the anima for her own sake does she become Beatrice. For such a man she becomes a bridge to the transcendental realms. "Meditating, I followed the path of love," as Dante expresses it. But the anima is initially also to be found in a man's ambition, and thus she entangles him in guilt and error if he does not consciously recognize his lust for power. If a man is incapable of this, he finally ends up completely isolated in a state of possession.

We could also apply this description to the animus, which is really a system of understanding.

For the animus what counts is insight or truth for truth's sake over and against any admixture of sensuality or power craving. Only a woman who loves the truth for its own sake can integrate the animus, and then he becomes, like the anima, a bridge to the Self, that is, to the knowlege of the Self. And when two people in a relationship with each other are on the path of a reciprocal individuation process, then the motif of the *coniunctio* of a suprapersonal couple is constellated. Jung pointed out in the citation given at the beginning that in the *hierosgamos*, it is not two egos that are face to face, but rather "everyone whose heart we touch." This strange multiplicity is very difficult to understand. It is as though in the "beyond" there exists only one divine couple, Shiva and Shakti, who are in eternal embrace, and the earthly human being participates in their *coniunctio* only as a "guest at the feast," as Andreae portrays it in his book *The Chemical Wedding*. This multiple unity can be illustrated by the following dream, dreamed by a young girl. She had lost her beloved fiancé through a tragic accident. After about two years another young man, now her current husband, approached her, whom she was quite fond of; but something in her was against accepting him, because she saw this as disloyalty to the first fiancé. Nevertheless, she became engaged to the second one, and he gave her a beautiful ring. But then she underwent a further bout of doubt. In a dream she had at this point, the dead fiancé appeared and said, "But it was *me* who gave you this ring" (and indicated the ring given by the second fiancé). This made it possible for her to accept the new relationship.

I do not pretend to really understand this dream, but it seems to me to that it points to the mystery of the single couple in the beyond, in whose union the many "whose hearts we touch" are included. In the symbolism of alchemy this is represented by the image of the so-called *multiplicatio*. When the philosopher's stone has been made, it multiplies itself a thousandfold as though by itself, by turning all nearby stones and metals to gold. When this event is highlighted in the background of a human encounter, when the god and goddess are present, than a feeling of eternity arises, as though the moment of the earthly encounter were now and always at the same time, as Jung expressed it, an "immediate presence." Thus Jung wrote in his memoirs that "emotional ties . . . still contain projections, and it is essential to withdraw these projections in order to attain to oneself and to objectivity. . . . Objective cognition lies hidden behind the attraction of the emotional relationship; it seems to be the central secret. Only through objective cognition is the real *coniunctio* possible."[13] And elsewhere, "In our relationships to other men, too, the crucial question is whether an element of boundlessness is expressed in the relationship."[14] This infinite seems to me to be the motif of the god and goddess manifesting in the background.

The problem of the multiple unity also seems to me to be hinted at in the Chinese Taoist view of life after death. According to this conception, the soul of the deceased breaks down into a masculine, spiritual part that escapes upward and a feminine, earthy part that sinks down to the earth. Then both migrate, the first to the east, the second to the west, and from there to a mysterious cosmic center, the origin, the "yellow springs." There the two celebrate their wedding, "the dark union," as the Lord of the East and the Lady of the West, as the one divine couple that every dead person always embodies.

When a relationship approaches real depth, then this *coniunctio mysterium* somehow lights up out of the timeless realm and shines through all the desires, resistances, projections, and ideas appearing on the surface. For the most part this happens only in certain moments and fades away the next moment. We will never be able to grasp it, but it seems to me important at least to have an inkling of the existence of this mystery, so that one does not on the basis of rational preconceptions shut the door on the god and goddess when they want to come in.

The motif of the *hierosgamos* is, as Jung expressed it another time, the mystery of mutual individuation, "for nothing can be completed without love, because love puts us in a state of mind in which we are are ready to risk everything without holding back anything of importance."[15] Only in this way is an encounter with the Self possible. This is why Jung called the figure of the Self that he painted in Bollingen, Philemon, "the loving one."

The urge to become whole is the strongest drive in a human being, and that is what is really hidden behind the deeper passion in the transference. At the end of his life, Jung admitted:

> I falter before the task of finding language which might adequately express the incalculable paradoxes of love. Eros is a *kosmogonos*, a creator and father-mother of all . . . consciousness. . . . Here is the greatest and smallest, the remotest and nearest, the highest and lowest, and we cannot discuss one side of it without discussing the other. . . . If he [man] possesses a grain of wisdom, he will lay down his arms and name the unknown by the more unknown, *ignotum per ignotius* — that is, by the name of God.[16]

And once in a conversation, he said, "The problem of love is so difficult that a person has to be happy if at the end of his life he can say that no one has been destroyed on his account."

NOTES

1. C. G. Jung, *Psychological Types*, CW 6, the "Definitions" section under "projection."
2. Jung, "Psychology of the Transference," CW 16.

3. Jung, letter to Elined Kotschnig, 23 July 1934, *Letters*, vol. 1, p. 170.
4. Jung, letter to Oskar A. H. Schmitz, 20 September 1928, *Letters*, vol. 1, pp. 53–54.
5. Jung, letter to Katherine C. Briggs, 4 July 1931, *Letters*, vol. 1, p. 84.
6. Jung, letter to Mary Mellon, 18 April 1941, *Letters*, vol. 1, p. 298.
7. Ibid.
8. Ibid.
9. Senior, *De Chemia* (1566), p. 8.
10. Jung, "Psychology of the Transference," CW 16, para. 449, p. 235.
11. In W. Bitter (ed.), *Lebenskrisen* (Crisis of Life) (Stuttgart: Klett Verlag, 1970), p. 82.
12. Cf. Jung, "Psychology of the Transference," CW 16, para. 470, p. 262. This is the reason for the crossed branches in the alchemical depiction of the royal couple.
13. Jung, *Memories, Dreams, Reflections*, pp. 296–97.
14. Ibid., p. 325.
15. M. de Serrano, *C. G. Jung and Hermann Hesse* (London: Routledge and Kegan Paul, 1966), p. 60.
16. Jung, *Memories, Dreams, Reflections*, pp. 353–54.

PROJECTION
Its Relationship to Illness and Psychic Maturation

DEFINITION OF PROJECTION

The depth psychologies of Sigmund Freud and of C. G. Jung have in common the use of the expression *projection*, but each uses it with a different meaning. In Freud's view, projection is a matter of a neurotic person's ridding himself of an emotional conflict by shifting it onto something else as the intended object. For example, a daughter transfers her incestuous desire to sleep with her father onto a father figure like a doctor or minister. In Jung's view, however, this is only one of many possibilities. According to Jung, all psychic contents of which we are not yet conscious appear in projected form as the supposed properties of outer objects. Projection, from this point of view, is a displacement, occurring unintentionally and unconsciously, that is, without being noticed, of a subjective psychic content onto an outer object.[1] In this process, the unconscious of the projector does not as a rule pick just any object at all but rather one that has some or even a great deal of the character of the projected property. Jung speaks of a "hook" in the object on which the projector hangs his projection like a coat.

Quite often—here Freud and Jung are in agreement—projections contain unprocessed false characterizations stemming from early childhood. Sons or daughters who have experienced their father as authoritarian (whether he really was or not) exhibit the tendency to project on all fatherly authorities— such as a teacher, a minister, a doctor, a boss, the state, and indeed even the God image—the negative property "authoritarian" and to react to them in a correspondingly defensive fashion. That which is projected, however, when examined more closely, is not at all merely a memory image of the father but represents the authoritarian tendency of the son himself or the daughter herself. They themselves unconsciously behave tyrannically without noticing it, but are self-righteously convinced that they are constantly encountering tyrants in the outer world; someone they are relating with has only to provide them with a trace of self-assertiveness or of a domineering quality to use as a hook. Such projections, which are based on the first childhood experiences of father and mother, are particularly stubborn. Male doctors, for example, always have to reckon with a negative or positive father complex in their patients. Female doctors, on the other hand, have to deal with projections of the mother image. Social workers, teachers, and psychotherapists experience this play of projections every day. It is not only one's own negative properties that are projected (although this occurs more frequently, since one is less likely to acknowledge one's negative properties than one's good ones); the positive in us that remains unconscious can also be projected. This brings about love in the form of unrealistic, intoxicated fascination that completely overlooks the reality of the partner.

PROJECTION AS AN ADJUSTMENTAL DISTURBANCE

It is essentially impossible to determine what, of everything we feel, sense, think, and perceive concerning outer objects and people, is "objectively" there and what is not. From the Eastern point of view, the whole of the external world is ultimately *maya*, a world of projections manufactured by our unconscious vital energy (*shakti*). Western science is beginning to realize more and more that it is unable to grasp reality "in itself" at all, but can only develop mental models of it. In this sense, the whole world is actually a projection. But on the practical level of everyday life, it is best to speak of projections only after a person's mentally represented image or judgment regarding an object of the external world clearly and obtrusively disturbs his adjustment. This is a signal that the person in question should reflect and perceive that that which so confusingly fascinates him on the outside, either in a positive or a negative fashion, is within himself. In everyday life the disturbance generally expresses itself as an excessively strong affect or an exaggerated emotion (love, hate, rapture, fanaticism, etc.) or as an illusion or false assertion regularly noticed by other people that is not susceptible to simply being corrected like an ordinary mistake. But what is an "excessively strong" affect? Italians, for example, intentionally cultivate dramatic emotions. The English and Buddhists suppress even the affectivity that seems normal to others. Who is to decide what is exaggerated and what is not? In our case what usually decides in practice is so-called good common sense. However, ultimately it is a problem of evaluation, for which until now there have been no objective scientific criteria. For this reason, one should be very careful in one's application of the concept of projection.

THE ARCHAIC IDENTIFICATION

In reality we are just beginning today to wake up in relation to this problem. From the historical point of view, the original condition was one in which the inner and outer worlds were not sharply distinguished, that is, subject and object were to a great extent identified with each other. Jung calls this the archaic identity. The primitive consciousness, like that of children, initially lives in a stream of events in which events in the environment and the inner world are not distinguished, or only unclearly distinguished.[2] This is also our normal state, which is interrupted only from time to time when our conscious ego reflects. In our case as well, the continuity of ego consciousness is quite relative. Who, for example, goes so far as to reflect over whether the image that he or she has of a spouse is accurate, unless he or she is forced to by some disturbance in the relationship? Basically we are still bound to our environment by a whole system of projections; in fact, the projections even serve as the actual bridge between the individual and the external world and other people. The projections bring about the play of unconscious sympathy and antipathy, participation or rejection, through which our whole life is shaped. Only when our psychic energy for some reason withdraws from these projections, for example, when our love changes to rejection or our hate begins to seem ludicrous even to ourselves—only at that point is the time ripe, and the opportunity for reflection given, for us to acknowledge the hitherto unconscious projection.

Here it is of crucial importance not merely to think that we have deceived ourselves but in addition to search until we have found in ourselves, very concretely and in terms of its actual practical effects, the element that has hitherto fascinated us in the outer world. For example, we hate someone because of his lying. It is not enough to think, "I myself lie sometimes"; rather we have to note that "on such and such occasions, I have lied in exactly the same style as the detested Mr. X!"

When we acknowledge something like this, not only "academically" but in a real way, it generally causes a shock that brings in its wake a positive change in our personality, a movement toward maturation. Acknowledgement of negative projections as in the above example brings moral differentiation, for now the person in question must come to terms with his lying problem. Acknowledgment of positive projections usually means further responsibility for us: instead of boundlessly admiring Mr. X for his intelligence, I will now have to work my own brain a bit harder! Or instead of always vainly expecting warmth from other people outside me, I will have to learn to express more emotional warmth to myself. It is understandable that most people do not willingly acknowledge their projections.

The most blatant manifestation of projections is in self-righteous political convictions—"isms"—and in passionately advocated theories, such as scientific preconceptions. As soon as tolerance and humor disappear, we can presume that projections have entered the picture. When we notice that someone is reacting with disproportionate affectivity in a discussion and begins to give in to the temptation to discredit his opponent, there are grounds for suspecting that he is projecting something on the opponent or his theory. If we have the useful habit of paying attention to our dreams, we will see that we often dream about such opponents. This gives us the signal: "Something about this opponent lies within myself." Even if only others are projecting, it is difficult not to be drawn in ourselves. Since affects and emotions are extremely contagious, it requires tremendous courage not to lose our level-headedness in group situations, as every group moderator or discussion-group leader knows.

THE RELATIONSHIP BETWEEN
PROJECTION AND ILLNESS

The Sender

In every process of projection, there is a sender, that is, the one who projects something onto someone else, and a receiver, the one on whom something is projected. Interestingly enough, these two show up as two highly important factors in the history of medicine. Sending is found in the conception widespread among native peoples of sickness projectiles, a magic arrow or some other, usually pointed missile that makes the person it hits sick.[3] A god, demon, or an evil person shoots such magic "points" at people. Extracting the projectile causes the victim to be healed. In the Old Testament, God himself shoots such arrows (Job 6:4): "For the arrows of the Almighty are within me, the poison whereof drinketh up my spirit: the terrors of God do set themselves in array against me." Or there are invisible demonic powers (Psalm 91): "Thou shalt not be afraid for the terror by night; nor for the arrow that flieth by day; nor for the pestilence that walketh in darkness; nor for the destruction that wasteth at noonday." Among ordinary people, it is usually venomous slander that is experienced as such arrows. (Cf. Jeremiah 9:3,8; Psalm 64:4.) We might also note the relationship of the German word *Krankheit*, meaning "illness," and *kränken*, meaning "to wound emotionally." We still speak today of "barbs" and "pointed remarks." In India the word *salya* means "arrowhead," "thorn," or "splinter," and of the doctor who removes such arrows from the bodies of sick people, it is said that he functions "like a judge who removes the thorn of injustice from a trial." The thorn is obviously something like a bad affect that has created a legal uncertainty. Psychiatrists and psychologists know that pointed or sharp forms in patients' drawings and paintings represent destructive impulses.

The positive projection, too, is a kind of arrow, which is why, for example, the god Amor and the Hindu god of love, Kama, carry bows and arrows. Buddha described the desire of love as "an arrow that digs savagely into the flesh."

That it is more rarely evil people and more often gods or demons who send these arrows of illness is in agreement with the observations of modern psychologists that projections are not enacted by us, but happen unconsciously; that is, that they emanate from complexes or archetypes of the unconscious. (Demons = complexes; gods = archetypal images.) The Greek philosopher Democritus believed that the whole atmosphere was full of *eidola* (images) or *dianoetikai phantasiai* (imagined ideas), which hover about us in dreams but also affect us during the day. "Only a subtle mind can distinguish them; ordinary people confuse them with objects of the external world."[4]

Projection of one's own not consciously realized psychic contents brings about in the sender a "loss of soul," one of the most feared illnesses among native peoples. This makes one apathetic, depressive, or susceptible to the compulsive thrall of people outside one.

The Receiver

The person onto whom someone else projects something is also affected—in the primitive view, he is hit by an arrow. If the receiver has a weak ego consciousness (as children do, for example), he will be easily influenced to act out what has been projected onto him. In the primitive view, this means that he is possessed. We feel compelled to relate to someone else's infatuation toward us, or we involuntarily do the evil thing to the enemy that he is expecting from us on the basis of his projection. Children often act out the unconscious shadow side of their parents—that which is hidden in them but is not consciously realized. That explains the known phenomenon that children of especially well-behaved parents often do particularly devilish things. "Preacher's children and miller's cow, seldom flourish anyhow," as the proverb says.

WITHDRAWAL OF THE PROJECTION

C. G. Jung distinguished five stages in the withdrawal of a projection:

1. The initial situation is the archaic identification. An inner psychic content is experienced completely as the behavior of an outer object; for example, one might believe one has been bewitched by a stone.
2. The stone itself is distinguished from the bewitching element, and the latter is described as an evil "spirit" in the stone.
3. A judgment is made as to whether this spirit is good or evil.
4. The spirit is declared to be an illusion.
5. One asks the question "What could have led to this illusion?" and recognizes it, not as something outwardly real, yet as an inner psychic reality, and one attempts to integrate this.

Many problems in the comparative history of religions and in the formation of academic hypotheses can be cleared up through seeing things as ordered in these stages:[5] archaic identification, animism, moral evaluation of a culture's own gods (as in the case of the ancient Greeks), enlightenment, recognition of a psychic reality.

People seem to experience strong resistance against any and

all progress within these five stages, but especially against progress in the last, the fifth stage. This is based on the fact that any withdrawal of a projection lays a burden on the reflecting person. He becomes responsible for a piece of his psyche that he has hitherto regarded in an unburdened fashion as not being part of him. A psychotherapist must therefore painstakingly weigh how much he can ask a patient or partner to acknowledge. The ego consciousness is like a fisherman in a small or large boat; it can only accommodate as many fish (unconscious contents) on its boat as will not make it sink. Sometimes one is compelled to permit the analysand to continue to believe in evil spirits or people who are persecuting him, because the acknowledgment that he has this devil within himself would literally kill him.

But even people with the greatest capacity for acknowledgment have their limits. So-called archetypal complexes (pictured as God or gods) cannot be integrated at all, because otherwise they would overexpand the personality in a way tantamount to an inflation (conceit, delusions of grandeur). It is wiser to understand such archetypal contents as psychically real collective powers with which one cannot identify oneself, but which one should attempt to render favorable through relating with them carefully (acts of respect, offering, speech = prayer). From this point of view, the various religions of the world were and are all psychotherapeutic systems that make it possible for people to relate with these archetypal psychic powers in projected form more or less with impunity. This is the ultimate basis of the connection between religion and medicine.

THE CONSEQUENCES

In spite of the resistance mentioned above, a tendency toward the development in man of an ever broader state of consciousness seems to emerge, which at the same time means an expansion of his psychic realm through the withdrawal of projections. The significance and positive consequences of this are easy to perceive. The more a person knows of himself and the less, therefore, of himself he projects onto others, the more objectively, illusionlessly, and genuinely he can relate to himself and to truly other people. Here ultimately lies the distinction between sympathy or infatuation and real love, or between hate and objective rejection and detachment. All progress in mutual understanding and improvement in relations between people depends on the withdrawal of projections. For such progress, however, a price must be paid: the cozy "stall warmth" in which we can let ourselves go ceases to be possible; gossip and the pleasure of a temper tantrum with the triumphant "I told you so!" cease to be possible. For this reason in my view it would even be sad if all people were suddenly to become "wise" and acknowledge their projections. The game of divine folly must after all continue. But wherever projections lead to death and murder or to severe hardship, it is advisable to reflect. This, however, is such an unpopular act that generally it is only done in circumstances of utmost emergency. Today, however, the overpopulation problem and the crowding of people that it has brought about has actually created an acute state of need, which in my view makes it absolutely necessary for us to consciously realize more of our true nature instead of continuing to burden others with our projections in an infantile manner.

NOTES

1. Cf. C. G. Jung, "Concerning the Archetypes, with Special Reference to the Anima Concept," in CW 9/i, pp. 54–74.
2. Cf. Jung, letter to Marie Ramondt, 10 March 1950, *Letters*, vol. 1, p. 549.

3. Cf. E. H. Ackerknecht, "Primitive Medicine and Culture Pattern," *Bulletin of the History of Medicine* 12 (April 1942), and "Natural Diseases and Rational Treatment in Primitive Medicine," *Bulletin of the History of Medicine* 19 (May 1946).

4. H. Diels, *Die Fragmente der Vorsokratiker* (Fragments of the Presocratics), 6th ed. (Berlin, 1952), vol. 2, p. 102.

5. For a more detailed discussion, see Marie-Louise von Franz, *Projection and Re-collection in Jungian Psychology: Reflections of the Soul* (LaSalle, Ill. & London: Open Court Publishing Co., 1985).

PROFESSION AND VOCATION

One of the most difficult questions in the training of future analysts is that concerning their suitability for this profession. Even the most comprehensive training program that is limited to purveyance of the indispensable knowledge, as necessary as this doubtless is, cannot convey to people that "something" which creates in a person a healing emanation. It is true that moral integrity and the will to help are indispensable, but they alone cannot produce the result in question. In my experience, every person who has devoted effort over a long period of time in his analysis to the conscious recognition of his own problems has become attractive to the people around him. The others sense that he possesses something that draws them to him. They begin to present their own dreams and problems to the person in question outside the professional environment. Nevertheless, it seems to me that even this is not always sufficient evidence of the person's suitability. Perhaps such a person has other duties of his own to fulfill for which he has a greater vocation than for passing along the relatively higher state of consciousness that he has achieved. I remember a woman who was in this situation. Although the necessary prerequisites had been fulfilled, her dreams did not seem to support her undertaking analytic work. Only after her two children had left home did she dream: "A voice said to me that now I could build a public pool in the forecourt of my house and work there as a pool attendant." This obviously meant that now she could make it possible for others to enter the waters of the unconscious and make sure that they learned to swim in them and not drown. She became a gifted analyst. Evidently before this her family needed her too much for her to be able to expend her energy on others outside it.

A difficult problem is presented by those prospective trainees who are possessed by the healer archetype. The archetypal image of the healer is related to that of the *puer aeternus*, the creative son-god of the Great Mother. A considerable number of young people who have a mother complex tend to identify with this archetype. They themselves manifest a "motherly" quality toward all who are helpless or suffering and often also have a gift for teaching.[1] From this point of view, they would be not unsuited for the profession of analyst; however, because of their identification with the archetype, these young people suffer from an inflation. In these cases it is helpful to compel them to undertake serious study, even possibly medical studies. For a person who is inflated does not like to work; he already knows everything better and more deeply than others. Hard work, then, together with the necessary clarifications through analysis, often makes it possible to overcome the inflation. For such people it is important to realize that it is the unconscious that ultimately brings about and directs the healing process and that the analyst is only a helper and supporter of this process, not its author. I would like to illustrate this through the vocational dream of a young colleague, who dreamed it on the night before his first analysis session. The evening before the dream he had been pondering over what "proper" dream interpretation and analysis in the Jungian sense really were. Then he dreamed:

> I'm sitting in an open, rectangular square in an old city. I am joined by a young man clad only in a pair of trousers, who sits

down in front of me with his legs crossed. His torso is powerful and full of vitality and strength. The sun shines through his blond hair. He recounts his dreams to me and wants me to interpret them for him. The dreams are like a kind of fabric that he is spreading out before me as he tells them to me. Each time he recounts a dream, a stone falls from the sky that strikes the dream a blow. This sets pieces of the dream flying off. As I take them in my hand, it becomes clear that they are made out of bread. As the pieces of the dream fly off, they lay bare an inner structure that resembles an abstract modern sculpture. With each dream that is recounted, a further stone falls on it, and thus more and more of this skeleton begins to appear, which is made of nuts and bolts. I tell the youth that this shows how to expose the meaning of a dream—down to the nuts and bolts. Then it further emerges that dream interpretation is the art of knowing what to throw away and what to keep, which is the way it is in life as well.

Then the dream scene changes. The youth and I are now sitting facing each other on the bank of a wonderfully beautiful broad river. He is still telling me his dreams, but the structure built up by the dreams has taken on a different shape. They do not form a pyramid made of nuts and bolts but a pyramid made of thousands of little squares and triangles. It is like a Cubist painting by Braque, but it is three-dimensional and alive. The colors and shadings of the little squares and triangles are constantly changing. I explain that it is essential for a person to maintain the balance of the whole composition by always immediately countering a color change with a corresponding compensatory change on the other side. This business of balancing out the colors is incredibly complex, because the whole object is three-dimensional and in constant movement. Then I look at the peak of the dream pyramid. There, there is nothingness. That is indeed the only point where the whole structure holds together, but at that point there is empty space. As I look at it, this space begins to radiate white light.

Once more the dream scene changes. The pyramid remains there, but now it is made out of solidified shit. The peak is still radiating. I suddenly realize that the invisible peak is as though made visible by the shit and that conversely the shit is also made visible by the peak. I look deep into the shit and recognize that I am looking at the hand of God. In an instant of enlightenment, I understand why the peak is invisible: it is the countenance of God.

Again the dream changes. Miss von Franz and I are taking a walk along the river. She laughingly says, "I'm sixty-one years old, not sixteen, but both numbers add up to seven."

I wake up abruptly with the feeling that someone has knocked loudly on the door. To my amazement, the apartment is completely quiet and empty.

In the language of primitive peoples, this is a "big" dream; in Jung's language, an archetypal dream, which is of suprapersonal, universal human significance. Since I have already interpreted it in "Self-Realization in the Individual Therapy of C. G. Jung," beginning on page 1, I refer the reader to that discussion. In the present context, what is important is only the fact that in the dream the unconscious comes to the fore as the main point of treatment, that the hand of God is seen in the "human, all-too-human," and that work on one's own development continues. That seems to be what is crucial here.

This big dream leads far away from the dreamer's fears and answers his questions with a philosophy of life, at the center of which lies the question of self-realization. The whole situation is presented as a happening that illuminates the dreamer. This should not, however, mislead us into thinking that analysis does not also require an effort on the part of the ego. We know from experience that analysis is hard work and requires lots of knowledge. This dream, which presents work as a mere happening, amounts to a compensation, for the dreamer in his broodings of the previous day took his ego and the role of the therapist too seriously. The actual patients who had been assigned to him, two young women, do not appear in the dream at all, but instead the patient, the "sufferer," is an inner figure in the dreamer himself, a piece of his Self.

The dream shows that the main part of the inner development of the analyst is something that is purely between his ego and the Self (or in old-fashioned language, the God image within him). The dream also clearly means that for the dreamer, it is important to see the "hand of God" that governs human destiny, rather than wanting to "do something" himself.

Every psychological truth can be, and even must be, reversed: no analyst should be without a solid fund of knowledge, as comprehensive as possible. It has often rightly been pointed out that psychologists without medical training easily overlook psychosomatic conditions. Although I am in favor of non-medically-trained psychologists, I would like to stress this point. It is of indubitable importance for the nonphysician thoroughly to learn the symptomology of psychosomatic illnesses, so as to be able to refer patients who require physical treatment to a doctor. But there are also other areas of which thorough knowledge seems to me indispensable. Here I am reminded of a Mexican student who was in his training analysis. I had the feeling that I did not really understand him, and he also seemed unable to make much out of what I had to say. The cause of this was completely mysterious to me, for I liked him a great deal. Then he came to me with the following dream:

He saw in the fork of the branches of a tree a big obsidian stone. As he came toward it, the stone leaped down from the tree and began to follow him. He sensed that it was very dangerous. As he was fleeing, he came upon some workers who had dug a quadrangular hole in the ground. They indicated to him with signs that he should climb into this hole and stand still in the middle of it. When he did this, the obsidian stone following him became smaller and smaller and finally lay down at his feet as a tame little pebble.

When I had heard this dream, I exclaimed, "What have you got to do with the god Tetzcatlipoca?" Then he came out with it. He told me that he was three-quarters Aztec. He had not mentioned this in his anamnesis, because in Mexico, it seems, racial prejudice is still quite prevalent. Suddenly I understood him. Inwardly, without knowing it, he lived in the spiritual tradition of the Aztecs but had denied this within himself. With this dream his individuation began and also his intellectual creativity. Tetzcatlipoca, the supreme Aztec deity, became his inner guru in active imagination.

But what would have happened to this analysis if I had not known that obsidian was a symbol of the god Tetzcatlipoca? Naturally an experienced analyst cannot be acquainted with all the mythological motifs there are, which number in the hundreds of thousands. Therefore it is important to educate the prospective analyst so that he does not interpret dreams off the cuff but continually takes the trouble to look things up in the specialist literature on symbols, and he must be trained so that he knows where to look. Afer all, a doctor also has manuals in which he can look up details about medicaments and symptoms. In a Jungian analysis, mythological knowledge is significantly more important than in the analysis of other schools. Other schools usually base their approach on an existing theory of dreams that suggests certain interpretations right from the beginning. According to the Jungian approach, it is a principle that every dream expresses something still unknown, something new for the patient. As long as one is deal-ing with dream images from the personal unconscious, painstakingly recording the dreamer's associations will often be enough. But with archetypal images, people often have very little to say by way of association. In this case what is necessary is to seek out objectively comparable mythological material.

Whereas this problem mostly concerns intellectual training and the knowledge of a prospective analyst, we must also not forget feeling, that is, the heart. As intelligent as a heartless analyst might be, I have never seen anyone of this type heal anyone! And "heart" cannot be instilled. Someone who does not have one, in my view, is the very least suited to this pro-fession. However, there are also people who really have feeling and the capacity for compassion but do not dare to express it. These people can be helped through training to become good analysts.

In fact, ideally speaking, an analyst must have trained all four functions of consciousness. He needs the sensation func-tion, because he has to be realistic and be able to see inner and outer facts in order to function. It should never happen (though I have witnessed it) that an analyst knows nothing of a patient's financial situation, or overlooks the fact that the patient is not eating enough. Intuition is also, of course, indis-pensable, because without it, it is impossible to grasp the pro-spective and prognostic function of dreams and also to guess all the things that the analysand has not told, which is gener-ally of particular importance.

Of course it is hardly possible in practical terms for all an-alysts to be so well rounded and complete as to have integrated all four of their consciousness functions. One must frequently be content with making the future analyst aware of what his undeveloped functions are, so that he knows his weaknesses and is on the alert for them and, in cases of uncertainty, when there are grounds for suspecting that something in the analysis is not going right, will call in a colleague for consultation.

The problems of knowledge and of the development of the consciousness functions are related to the state of normalcy of the prospective therapist, to his adjustment to the outer world and society. But the word *vocation* is related to something still deeper and more essential—the connection to God or the gods, that is, to the powers that manifest within the psyche. If we look at this historically, we see that in the Middle Ages it was not particularly the "normal" person who was considered to have a vocation as helper for the psyche or soul (although he had to be relatively normal too), but rather the priest; or people even sought help at the graves of the martyrs or saints, thinking that the supernatural influence of their personalities might heal the psychologically disturbed. If we look back even further in history, the specifically Christian split between religion and medicine comes into view. Then, still further back, we come to the figure of the physician-priest, who worked, for example, in the places sacred to Asclepius (Kos, Epidaurus, etc.).[2] What vocation meant in those days, we learn, for example, from Apuleius, who as a *katochos* (voluntary internee)[3] lived in the service of the goddess Isis.

The priest-healer of late antiquity is an archetypal variant of the type of medicine man or shaman found throughout the world. For him vocation remains what was originally meant by this word: a call from the gods or spirits to become a healer. Shamans (as well as many medicine men and women of other peoples) go through a specific period of training and development. They are called by clan spirits or other spirits, often against their will. "Before a shaman makes his appearance, the soul of the person destined for this function is taken by spirits and drawn into the underworld or the upper world."[4] The souls of shamans-to-be are then put in nests on different levels of the branches of a big tree and usually incubated and reared by an animal mother in the form of a raven or some other bird or by a winged elk or deer, etc. This animal mother is his alter ego, his double, his protecting spirit, and his vital principle. Sometimes she devours the shaman and gives birth to him anew, or she sits on him while he is in the egg. Beyond that, the shamanic initiation generally consists also, as we know, in the candidate's being mutilated and reduced to a skeleton. The skeleton stands for the imperishable basic substance from which the renewed shaman can be remade. Not always is the new shaman in control of his new form; sometimes he meets it only in crucial moments, during initiation or at the time of death, but it is through this inner alter ego that he accomplishes his healing.[5]

From the standpoint of modern depth psychology, this shamanic experience amounts to undergoing an invasion of the collective unconscious and dealing with it successfully. When the training analysis of a future analyst remains hung up in discussion of personal problems, in my experience, that person never turns out to be an effective analyst later on. Only when he has experienced the infinite in his own life, as Jung formulated it, has his life found a meaning. Otherwise it loses itself in superficialities.[6] And, we might add, then such a person can only offer others something superficial: good advice, intellectual interpretations, well-meaning recommendations for normalization. It is important that the analyst dwell inwardly in what is essential; then he can lead the analysand to his own inner center. A shaman said aptly to a piece of wood which he wanted to turn into a drum: "Make your mind free from quarrelsomeness and discord, larch, you're going to become a drum."[7]

The symbols of the animal-mother spirit, of the drum, of the tree, and many others, all of which I cannot go into here, are, in Jungian terms, all symbols of the Self. In the shamanic tradition, the future healer must not only have experienced an invasion of the collective unconscious, but he must also have penetrated through to its core, to that which Jung termed the Self. Oddly enough, the Self often first confronts a person in a hostile manner, as something explosive that might even cause madness.[8] The Siberian Tungus are aware of this. They even say that before a person can become a shaman, he must suffer the harassment of the spirits for a period of years. These are the souls of dead shamans who are causing him to have delusions. They are often the ones who mutilate him during the initiation.[9]

For example, there was a Buryat who was sick for fifteen years. He ran around naked in the winter and "behaved like a fool."[10] Then he found his helping spirit, who said to him: "Why are you carrying on like that? Don't you know us? Be a shaman. Depend on us, your *utcha* [ancestors = helping spirits]. Do you agree?" He consented, went through the initiation rites, and began to act as a shaman: "Everywhere he does good and heals." It is strictly forbidden to act as a shaman until the initiation time is over and the initiate has been healed from his initiatory illness.[11]

Everything we have said here about the shamanism of circumpolar peoples is surprisingly applicable to the vocational problematic of modern therapists. Someone who has not acceded to the depths of the unconscious and seen there "the ways of all spirits of sickness" can hardly possess enough real empathy for the serious psychic suffering of his fellow human beings. He will only treat them by the textbook, without ever being able to empathize with them, and this is often the key factor for patients. Also someone beginning prematurely to act as a shaman, before he has overcome his initiatory illness, is an all too familiar sight. Many enthusiastic young people want to begin treating others from the very beginning of their training analysis, before they have come to terms with their own problems and unconscious contents. In doing this, in *participation mystique* with a patient, they usually end up in the latter's blind spot. The result of this is a *folie à deux* and not a cure; or else the patient is smart enough to detect that his would-be "doctor" is on none too certain ground himself. "That fellow is more depressed than I am," I was once told by an analysand on whom a not yet fully fledged "healer" was trying himself out.

It has been asserted that shamans and medicine men have a great deal in common with the mentally ill, or at least with the psychologically unstable, but Eliade has pointed out, for example, that the Eskimos can clearly distinguish between a "shamanic" illness and an ordinary case of mental disorder.[12] In the course of the shamanic initiatory illness, the initiate succeeds in finding his own cure, which is precisely what the ordinary mentally ill person cannot do. Moreover, the shamans are the creative individuals, the poets and artists, of their communities. This touches upon a question that is also significant for modern therapists — popular humor is quite familiar with the figure of the psychiatrist who is crazy himself.[13] In this connection, I would like to associate myself with the view of the Eskimos: The person who is able to heal himself is not the sick one but the one who can help others. For such a person is intact in his innermost core and possesses ego strength, two indispensable prerequisites for the profession of therapist. He undergoes his initiatory illness not out of weakness, but rather in order to become acquainted with "all the ways of sickness," to know from his own experience what possession, depression, schizoid dissociation, and so on, mean.

Nor is his initiatory dismemberment schizophrenia. In accordance with the mythological description, it is a reduction to the skeleton. But what this means according to the peoples who made these myths is the indestructible, the eternal in the human being, and also that which is perpetuated through the continuity of the generations. Transposed into modern language, this means that the initiate undergoes an "analysis" in the sense of a dissolution of all his inauthentic—e.g., conventional or infantile—traits in order to win his way through to that which he is in his true being. In Jungian language this means he becomes individuated, becomes a solid personality who is no longer a football of inner affects and projections or of external societal trends and fashions.

In the ethnological context, however, the healer also has a specific shadow; that is, this vocation also has a dark counter-aspect. This is the figure of the demonic shaman or medicine man. The most superficial form of this is the therapist who is ruled by a power complex. It is of course evident that in this profession, in which one is one's own lord and master and in which others often cling to one in a childishly naive fashion, the abuse of power represents a great temptation. For example, one might be tempted to take over the role of the parent or of the wise man, the one who knows what is right. As repugnant as this is, it is, in my opinion, not all that dangerous, since such therapists are usually duly plagued by equally power-possessed patients, or punished through the fact that they tend to assemble about them a tedious kindergarten of patients who badger them with demands.

The "demonic" healer is something on a greater scale, something more dangerous. The Yakuts, for example, believe that at the time of his initiation a shaman has the choice of being initiated by the spirits of the "source of ruination and death" or by the spirits "of healing and salvation."[14] The confusing thing here is that someone initiated by the evil spirits may also be considered a great shaman.[15] But for such a person to become a shaman, many people (often from his clan) have to die,[16] whereas the clan of a shaman from the side of the light flourishes.[17] Therefore, the first kind of shaman is called "bloodthirsty." From a psychological point of view, the dark shamans are those who have found the access to the unconscious and shown themselves strong enough not to be overthrown by it, but who, as it were, intentionally yield to the dark impulses of the unconscious.

Jung described the "demonic," which could also be called "black magic," in the following terms.[18] Whereas "white magic" strives to drive out the forces of disorder in the unconscious, "black magic exalts the destructive impulses as the only valid truth in opposition to the order hitherto prevailing, and moreover bends them to the service of the individual as opposed to that of the whole community. The means used for this are primitive, fascinating or frightful ideas, images, utterances incomprehensible to the ordinary understanding, strange words," and so on. "The demonic . . . is based on the fact that there are unconscious powers of negation and destruction and that evil is real." A person who exercises such forces of black magic is usually himself possessed by an unconscious content. Jung mentions here the example of Hitler as negative savior or destroyer. In the sphere of shamanic tradition, dangerous shamans of this sort, of whom everyone is profoundly frightened, are known. Mircea Eliade gives many examples of the arrogance of shamans, which is often seen as the real source of evil and is believed to explain the current deteriorated state of shamanism.[19] In my opinion, this arrogance also exists among modern therapists, and therapists marked by it are, in my view, more dangerous than those with inadequate professional training. I suppose there is no organizational or rational means for keeping such individuals out of the profession of analysis. One can only hope that the general public has enough instinct to avoid them.

Reflecting on the points presented here so far, we see that the profession of analyst makes outstandingly high demands, demands that hardly anyone can entirely satisfy. Thank heavens the native peoples are also aware that it is not only the rare great shamans, but also the lesser and minor shamans who nevertheless can help people. The greatness or importance of a shaman depends on how often and how deeply he has penetrated into the unconscious and how much suffering he has taken upon himself in so doing. That is why, in my opinion, what is absolutely necessary is not to become a great healer but rather to know one's own limits. For it can happen—and it is not at all that rare—that a patient grows beyond one, that is, progresses further in the inner process than one has gone oneself.

The instinctive tendency of the analyst is then to try to bring the patient back down in reductive fashion to his own level of consciousness. Only when he is conscious of his own limits can he avoid this danger and not demean the meaningful and growing element in others through a "nothing-more-than" style of interpretation. When the analyst remains conscious of his own limits, he can sometimes even help a patient who is beyond him by being honest and contenting himself with contributing strictly what help he is capable of, and by entrusting the rest to the patient. Where he has weak points, he must admit this to the patient and, turning the tables, ask him for understanding. At this point, the process is no longer a "treatment" but becomes a relationship of mutual give and take. This of course should be taken into account in the financial arrangements.

A special problem in the profession of analysis is creativity. The best analysts are without a doubt those who, alongside their profession, are involved in some creative activity. It is not for nothing that in primitive societies the medicine men are also the poets, painters, and the like, of their peoples. The creative and the healing elements are very close. "The uprushing chaos," Jung explains, "seeks new symbolic ideas which will embrace and express not only the previous order but also the essential contents of the disorder. Such ideas would have a magical effect by holding the destructive forces of disorder spellbound, as has been the case in Christianity and in all other religions."[20]

What Jung is expressing here in connection with the general collective level is applicable also to smaller groups and to the individual. In all contexts it remains a matter of finding in one's own depths the ordering influence of the Self and expressing it in symbols, in art, in deeds. If the analyst, in addition to his consultations, is not working on this task as well, he falls prey, as Jung pointed out, to routine, and with time becomes a drab analyst. I have noticed that in this difficult work, sourness and a certain contempt toward one's fellow beings easily tends to creep in. Only continuing to work on one's own inner creative task can prevent this deterioration. And here it is not enough once to have experienced a sense of vocation; the right to practice this profession must be earned again and again within oneself.

NOTES

1. See Jung, "Psychological Aspects of the Mother Archetype," in CW 9 / i.

2. See C. A. Meier, *Der Traum als Medizin* (The Dream as Medicine) (Einsiedeln, Switzerland: Daimon Verlag, 1985).

3. Cf. G. Preusschen, *Mönchtum und Serapiskult* (Monasticism and the Serapis Cult) (Giessen, 1903), passim.

4. Cited in A. Friedrich and L. G. Budruss, *Schamanengeschichten aus Siberien* (Siberian Shaman Stories) (Munich, 1955), p. 45.

5. Ibid., p. 48.

6. Jung, *Memories, Dreams, Reflections*, p. 325.

7. Friedrich and Budruss, *Schamanengeschichten*, p. 80.

8. See Jung, "The Philosophical Tree," in CW 13.

9. Cf. Friedrich and Budruss, *Schamanengeschichten*, pp. 212–13.

10. Ibid., p. 209.

11. Ibid., p. 159.

12. See Mircea Eliade, *Shamanism: Archaic Techniques of Ecstasy* (Princeton: Princeton University Press, Bollingen Series, 1964), pp. 23ff.

13. More or less as in the following joke: What is the difference between a mentally disturbed person and the psychiatrist? Answer: The psychiatrist is the one who has the key to the office.

14. Friedrich and Budruss, *Schamanengeschichten*, p. 171.

15. Cf. ibid., p. 158.

16. Ibid., p. 154.

17. Ibid., pp. 150, 147.

18. Jung, letter to Horst Scharschuch, 1 September 1952, *Letters*, vol. 2, pp. 81–82.

19. Eliade, *Shamanism*, p. 72.

20. Jung, *Letters*, vol. 2, p. 81.

ON GROUP PSYCHOLOGY

In modern sociological literature, one generally makes a distinction among: (1) a *group*, i.e., a collection of people who are intellectually and on a feeling level related to each other and in which everybody fulfills a certain role; (2) a *crowd*, i.e., a random accumulation of people; and (3) a *mass*, i.e., a big crowd which is emotionally and instinctively unified and generally follows a leader.

According to most modern sociological theories the chaotic mass and the well-ordered group were originally closer to each other than they are today. This seems to me not quite accurate. They were not closer, they contrasted even more clearly, but they tended to topple over from one into another more easily; primitive groups easily get out of control, just as groups of young people or of mentally unstable individuals do, but as phenomena in themselves, they are more rigid on a primitive level (taboos!), and chaotic mass phenomena tend to be wilder and more hysterical. Even on the higher level of early civilizations, in the Samurai culture in Japan, for instance, or in the feudal societies in medieval Europe, we see a strong tendency at work toward formal rigidity, because under its cover the emotions and affects are still so powerful that they have to be domesticated by force. However, the more really civilized man becomes, the more his social rules of behavior become more flexible, and instead of a black and white contrast we find a many-colored spectrum of behavioral nuances.

Gustave le Bon and Sigmund Freud assumed that the mass represents the original form of human relationship (*Urhorde*), but this has proved to be wrong, for even in the most primitive societies which we know today, we find well-ordered social groups; mostly big families and clans seem to form the basis of social order, and sociologists have therefore rashly concluded that the interests of the "we" basically come first, before the interests of the "I."[1] *These theories leave out the problem of the unconscious, on its personal as well as its collective level*, and therefore suffer from terrible oversimplification. They ignore the role of the archetypes as patterns of mental and emotional behavior and thus overlook certain facts which should be considered more closely.

Following Pierre Janet, Jung distinguishes between a *partie superieure* and a *partie inferieure* of all psychological functions including the archetypes. The *partie inferieure* of an archetype is a pattern of instinctive behavior in the zoological sense of the word; it has more the aspect of an emotional drive and is more compulsive (all-or-none reaction). The *partie superieure* contains more possibilities of conscious inner realization and is more flexible. Jung compared the psyche to a spectrum, the infrared end of which would be the psychosomatic behavioral impulses, the ultraviolet end the symbolic realizations of meaning or the experience of *idées fixes*, collective norms, religious inspirations, etc. A group with its social order would be placed closer to the ultraviolet end, the mass with its compulsive emotional reactions would be closer to the infrared end of the color scale. In sociological literature, the group is generally evaluated positively, the mass negatively. This seems to me quite arbitrary, because often in history the fight of a nation, for instance, for its freedom (displaying all the emotional features of a mass phenomenon) has generally been evaluated positively (for instance, the Swiss liberation from Austria). Conversely, reasonably organized groups which stand for a political ideology can dominate a nation so inflexibly that they suffocate all emotional life with its charm and warmth. Thus both ends of the spectrum can be either positive or negative, according to different viewpoints. To me it seems that a middle position between the two poles represents an optimal situation. Sliding toward the infrared end (mass phenomena) produces explosions of too large an emotional and affect content. Aberrations towards the ultraviolet end produce ideological fanatacism and states of religious or political possession. There is no freedom at either end; only in the middle position, between these opposites, does a certain amount of consciousness and with it of individual freedom seem to be possible.

Another oversimplification in sociological literature is the statement that the "we" came historically before the "I." This seems to be true only insofar as collective consciousness (group consciousness with its rules of behavior) seems to be historically older than "ego consciousness"; it does not apply to the pair of opposites "group-individual," for individuality is not identical with ego consciousness. A small child, for instance, or an animal, can display a lot of individuality before developing any stable ego consciousness. The group-versus-individual polarity exists already in the animal world. The zoologist Adolf Portmann has pointed out that among groups of animals *creative changes of behavioral patterns can only be initiated by individuals*. For instance, an individual bird of a flock of migratory birds decides to stay in the same place in winter. If it succumbs, nothing more results; if it survives, however, a few more birds may stay with it the next winter, and thus slowly the whole group sometimes changes its habits.

We have therefore to reckon with two pairs of opposites:

(1) collective consciousness (the "we" or "us") versus ego consciousness, and (2) group (conscious plus unconscious) versus
individual (conscious plus unconscious). Modern sociologists
generally evaluate collective consciousness more positively than
ego consciousness, the former being more "normal," the latter
tending to exhibit asocial "outsider" characteristics. But we
have to consider the fact that this is not generally valid.[2] Just
as in a single individual, the conscious attitude of a whole
group can deviate from its instinctual roots and become neurotic and can then collide with the healthy ego of an individual. I have often observed that a whole neurotic family group
will fight its only healthy member. In Nazi Germany anybody
who tried to keep his balance was persecuted. Therefore we
must ask the question: What is normal? When is the collective
"we" more normal than the outsider-ego, and when not?
There we get into deep water. Groups can also definitely display typological one-sidedness. In certain American groups an
introvert is automatically labeled abnormal, while in the Far
East I sometimes saw how the enterprising extravert behavior
of a person was met by great distrust. If we stand naked on
one leg on Fifth Avenue in order to honor God, we will end
up in a psychiatric ward, but if we do the same thing in Cal-
cutta we will be respected as a saint. Where are the ultimate
criteria for what is normal or the reverse? Is social adaptation
the only important thing? What if the society has become neurotic? Is social adaptation still recommendable, or should the
individual find the courage to resist it alone? Where is he to
get that courage? These questions are not yet answered in
modern sociological theories. As far as archetypes are concerned, this too leads to further unanswered questions. Raymund Battegay observed with his patients that his therapeutic
groups always desired to have "their own room" in a manner

similar to an animal's attachment to its territory and similar to the territorial attachment of tribes and nations.[3] This territorial attachment is derived from the mother archetype, and with it one has observed that people tend to project the "mother" onto their group, a fact which often leads to all sorts of infantile regressions. But this is not the only possibility: among the Jews living in exile, the Law replaced the territory and proved just as efficient in keeping a group together. In fraternities, bands of warriors, and the like, it is more a common "spirit" or "idea," i.e., the father archetype, which unites people. Such aspects also can change in the course of history. Hans Marti has shown, for instance, that the Swiss Democratic Constitution was first based more on the patriarchal image of a *contract social* of men, the Father State, but nowadays has changed more and more into an image of Mother Helvetia, who nourishes her children and who owns the woods, lakes, and earth—all maternal symbols. These two parental images, however, are still not the only possible centers around which human beings assemble. There are many others also.

Sociology has discovered that all groups gather around some kind of a center, which is defined as being concentrated onto a group theme, a group purpose, or a group aim. From this center the existence of all groups depends.[4] Either the center has a purely rational purpose, as in sport, commercial, and political groups, or it belongs to a higher order, such as the totem in primitive tribes, or the symbols of religious societies,[5] where the center satisfies "a need for transcendental experience." In sensitivity groups and therapeutic groups, the center consists in the goal of supporting healing tendencies and tendencies of becoming more conscious of one's social behavior, and of the mutual effects we have upon one another in relationships.

In these descriptions a factor has again been overlooked: the effect of the archetype. Some groups, such as commercial or sports groups, or even some political groups, have only conscious rational aims, but as soon as some hidden or open ideological factor comes into play even they become "emotionally" bound and reveal by that fact that they are under some archetypal influence. The greater the emotional influence of an archetype, the greater becomes the coherence of the group. National Socialism and Communism show this very clearly, the former having been a revival of Wotanism and the latter containing a distorted Savior myth.[6]

With greater coherence there is always also a greater aggressiveness against outsiders and against "unbelievers." Such political groups approach the pattern of the groups with greatest coherence: the religious communities which gather around a transcendental center. As we see from the so-called world religions, like Christianity, Buddhism, and Islam, a "transcendental center" can hold much larger societies together than groups with only a rational or semirational purpose. The reason is to be found in the fact that *the archetype of the Self is a more powerful archetype than all the others.* It manifests itself in monotheistic God images or concepts of the basic Oneness of Being (Tao) or even more frequently in the images of a cosmic man (Anthropos) or God-Man or of a *mandala* as a symbol which unites the opposites (for instance the Chinese T'ai-chi-t'u).

Until the Greeks came in touch with India, even Buddha was never represented in human shape, but as a twelve-spoked wheel of stone. To a certain degree the totem symbols of primitive societies represent anticipations of these great God-Man symbols which became internationally uniting forces, and often overlaid or absorbed the local former polytheistic archetypal images. They brought them together in a symbol of "Oneness-plurality" which unites in a paradoxical form the many archetypes and the oneness of the collective unconscious within *one* form. But these God-Man symbols and *mandala* images unite a plurality of forms not only in this respect; they also unite a multitude, insofar as the Self within each individual is its own unique Self *and* the Self of all other human beings as well. This paradox is expressed in Hindu philosophy by the identity of the individual *atman-purusha* with the cosmic *Atman-Purusha*. The same holds for the "Buddha" or rather "Buddha-Mind" in Zen and other forms of Buddhism. In our hemisphere the collective aspect of the Self symbol is represented by the idea of "Christ in us," and in the *filiatio* through the pouring out of the Holy Ghost, and in the idea that the multitude of believers forms the visible Body of Christ, the Church. Christ has therefore been until now our "group dynamic center," a fact which is expressed in the allocution of the early Christians who called each other "brother and sister in Christ."

In the early Church, the psychic life of this archetypal group-center was not only based on conscious tradition but was also kept alive by the inner experiences of individuals, such as the conversion experience of Saint Paul or Saint Augustine, the visions of the martyrs and saints, and the experience of miracles among the simple people. But in the later development of the Church, a tendency to "censor" such experiences prevailed more and more, and collective conscious norms were imposed upon the inner life. This led to splitting up into all sorts of movements which began to cluster around new group centers.

Today we could describe our situation as follows: the most universal groups are Christianity with its God-Man symbol, Christ; Buddhism with its symbol of the universal Buddha-

Mind; Hinduism, Islam, and the Marxist movements. The official Christ image suffers from a lack of including the feminine principle, evil and matter, and the Buddha-Mind symbol from a lack of including the real earthly life of man. Both systems reject the symbol-forming activities of the unconscious in man which express themselves in dreams. In Christianity dreams are looked upon as dangerously mystical and heretical, in Buddhism as belonging to the world of illusion. Marxism has also its symbol of a perfect man or Anthropos, but it appears projected not onto one individual but onto a whole class. (The tendency to project it onto a single man turns up in the forbidden cult of persons.) According to Karl Marx, the labor class represents the true man who is solely in harmony with nature, altruistic, creative, and not neurotically degenerated.[7] What is psychologically wrong about this Marxist Anthropos symbol is the fact that it is only earthly material and only collective, even a collectivity itself, with no opening toward any individual transcendental inner experience. Maoism is still a riddle for us because, as Jung pointed out, how Marxism will be assimilated by the highly cultured Chinese mind cannot yet be predicted.

The decay of the great international religious centering systems and the unsatisfactory one-sidedness of the compensatory Marxist Anthropos symbol have led modern man into a deep inner isolation and loneliness and evoked a great need in him for social contacts. This, no doubt, has called up the new fashion of group experiences and experiments of most diverse forms. As early as 1923, Jung predicted in his seminar in Cornwall that if the Christian system continued to decay, there would be a regression toward totemistic groups. Some would resemble the Mithraic clubs, and "there would be much bull roaring." Others would have a lamblike character and play the

innocent victim. We now see this realized in the criminal ter-
rorist gangs and in the "innocent" promoters of peace.

Realizing the need of modern man to get out of his urban
isolation, the Churches on one side, and the left wing movements on the other, try to ride the wave and offer group experiments of all sorts. This, however, is *putting the cart before
the horse and can only lead to disaster because it prevents the one
inner saving event from taking place: the individual's experience of
the Self.* The latter can only be found alone, for, as Jung writes:
"The patient must be alone if he is to find out what it is that
supports him when he can no longer support himself. Only
this experience can give him an indestructible foundation."[8]

The responsible analyst "therefore prefers individual treatment to collective ameliorations; this accords with the experience that social and collective influences usually produce only
a mass intoxication, and that only man's action upon man can
bring about a real transformation."[9]

At first it seems a great relief for the individual to feel protected by a group and removed from himself. In the group,
therefore, the sense of security increases *and the feeling of
responsibility decreases.* Suggestibility also increases enormously,
a fact which includes, however, a loss of freedom, because one
falls into the hands of good or evil environmental influences.
Even a small group is dominated by a suggestive group spirit.
If the latter is good, it can have positive social effects, but this
is paid for by a decrease of the mental and ethical independence of the individual. As the group reinforces the ego, one
gets more courageous, or even impertinent, but the Self is
pushed into the background. That is why weak and insecure
people want to belong to big organizations. Then one feels big
oneself, but one loses the Self (the devil catches one's soul) and
one's individual judgment. The leveling down is generally com-

pensated by the fact that one person identifies with the group spirit and tries to become the leader. That is why groups are always full of struggles for power and prestige. These battles are based on the heightened egoism of collective man.[10]

In a letter in which he deals with this theme Jung adds that he has no objection to group therapy, any more than to Christian Science or the Oxford Movement; it constellates and educates the social behavior of individuals, which sometimes does not come up sufficiently in personal analysis. But because man is always inclined to cling to others, or to "isms," instead of seeking independent strength in himself, the danger arises that one makes a father or mother out of the group and remains as infantile and insecure as before. If society consisted of highly valuable individuals, it would be worthwhile to adapt to it, but generally it is dominated by weak and stupid people, and thus suffocates all higher individual values. Even if socially positive effects are for the moment achieved, they must be paid for later and then very dearly.[11]

If we think over these reflections of Jung's, we must ask: Is our present society at a level on which one would wish to adapt to it? Do we not rather live in an era where it is especially important that independent individuals can resist the stupidity and generally neurotic tendencies of our societies?

It has been objected that if an individual is simultaneously in a personal analysis, the group experiments complement it. I have myself seen, however, and it has been confirmed to me by others, that participation in group experience more often disturbs the individual analysis than helps it, because it stirs up problems *at the wrong moment*, while in individual analysis the unconscious can "time" their constellation. And with all such individuals who are already socially overadapted (as happens often, for instance, with parsons, managers, and social workers), their dreams show openly that group experiences are obnoxious to them. When urged to participate in a group experiment, one of my analysands dreamed that he was forced to expose his girlfriend naked to a dirty old voyeur. Later he dreamed that the waters of his unconscious had been polluted by others; finally, when he left the group, he dreamed that he had extricated himself from a cheap show! Considering these facts, *group experience should never be compulsive.* The learning of social adaptation for people who by any chance lack it could be quite sufficiently practised by participating in freely informed (unanalytical) social groups, such as have existed for a long time among clubs in most countries. Whoever, therefore, supports compulsory group experience has departed from the basic values of Jungian psychology.

Who, we must now ask, are the analysts who like to conduct group experiments? They very often find their motivation in the fact that one earns more money with less effort, as some have openly admitted to me. Another motivation lies in the fact that some analysts cannot cope with passionate and demanding transferences of their patients. It is generally admitted that the transference phenomena are weakened in group situations, and the latter thus help to lessen the pressure of the transferences. Jung has shown, however, that transference is *the* vehicle of the process of individuation, and with it all of healing transformation of the individual.

The individuation process, based on the vehicle of transference, is the *conditio sine qua non* of *true* social behavior, for if individuation is not consciously realized "it takes place spontaneously in a negative form, i.e., in the form of a *hardening* against our fellow men." The conscious achievement of inner unity needs human relationships as an indispensable condition, for without the conscious acknowledgment and acceptance of our kinship with those around us, there can be no synthesis of the personality. "That is the core of the whole transference phenomenon and it is impossible to argue it away, because relationship to the Self is at once relationship to our fellow man and no one can be related to the latter until he is related to himself."[12] The reducing effect of group therapy as regards the transference is plainly detrimental. It only helps the analyst to evade the problems which any powerful transference poses for him.

But there are other motivations for which we have to look briefly into the history of psychotherapy. The roots of both priesthood and psychotherapy lie in the primitive phenomenon of shamanism and the existence of medicine men. The shaman or medicine man is *mainly concerned with the fate of the individual soul*, its preparation for death, its protection after death, and its protection against states of possession by ghosts and demons—i.e., by archetypal powers. He can do this because during his own initiation he has suffered such states of possession and found ways of curing himself.[13] The initiation experience of such shamans and medicine men coincides with what we now call the process of individuation.

After this process has taken place, the shaman wins natural authority within his tribe because he represents its most individuated and conscious individual. But already in this early stage we also find the shaman's shadow, the neurotic (or even psychotic) black magician. The latter *demands* collective authority on account of his experiences of the ghost world (i.e., the collective unconscious); in doing so he proves to be mentally sick. (Modern examples would be Rasputin and Hitler.) *Individuation is ultimately incompatible with any demands for collective power*, even if it is veiled by the attitude of a well-meaning, liberal, modest, and moderating group leader! For only the

Self can give us *natural authority* which has not been asked for by the ego. In the early Christian Church the leaders were people of natural authority, which they had acquired by their individual inner experiences and their Christian conduct of life. With the forming of the Church as a collective outer institution, the leaders more and more became people who *demanded* authority and power, and superimposed collective conscious rules over the spontaneous inner religious life of people. The confessions, as Jung points out, thus began what he calls "the game of shepherd and sheep."[14] "The flock of harmless sheep was ever the symbolic prototype of the credulous crowd."[15] But the blind trust of such a multitude can just as easily be taken in by a wrong goal as by a right one. We see therefore that Communism is more widespread in Catholic countries than in Protestant, because the Church had had a stronger hold upon them before. In contrast to this, in the past, stood the search of the alchemists for Christ or Mercurius as a symbol of the "true man" within. Jung says:

> The "true man" expresses the Anthropos in the individual human being compared with the revelation of the Son of Man in Christ. This seems a retrograde step, for the historical uniqueness of the Incarnation was *the* great advance which gathered the scattered sheep about one shepherd. The "Man" in the individual would mean, it is feared, a scattering of the flock. This would indeed be a retrograde step, but it cannot be blamed on the "true man," its cause is rather all those bad human qualities which have always threatened and hindered the work of civilization . . . the "true man"[16] has nothing to do with this. Above all he will destroy no valuable cultural form since he himself is the highest form of culture. Neither in the East nor in the West does he play the game of shepherd and sheep, because he has enough to do to be a shepherd to himself.[17]

NOTES

1. Cf. Raymund Battegay, *Der Mensch in der Gruppe*, vol. 1 (Bern, 1967–72), pp. 10–16.
2. As Clovis Shepherd, in *Small Groups* (Chandler M. Francisco, 1967), points out, too many modern sociological theories are biased by unconscious emotional prejudices of their authors.
3. Battegay, *Der Mensch*, vol. 1, pp. 32, 40f.
4. Cf. ibid., p. 32.
5. One distinguishes, therefore, structured groups from focused groups (cf. Shepherd, *Small Groups*, p. 3).
6. Cf. C. G. Jung, *Man and His Symbols* (New York: Doubleday, 1964), p. 85.
7. Cf. Robert Tucker, *Philosophy and Myth in Karl Marx* (Cambridge: Cambridge University Press, 1963).
8. Jung, *Psychology and Alchemy*, CW 12, para. 32.
9. Jung, *Mysterium Coniunctionis*, CW 14, para. 125. Cf. also Jung's footnote, ibid.
10. Jung, letter to Hans Illing, 26 January 1955, *Letters*, vol. 2, pp. 218–19.
11. Ibid., p. 453. Cf. the confirmation of these statements by Jung in Kurt W. Back, "The Group Can Comfort, but It Can't Cure," *Psychology Today*, December 1972, pp. 28ff.
12. Jung, "Psychology of the Transference," in CW 16, para. 445.
13. Cf. Mircea Eliade, *Shamanism* (Princeton: Princeton University Press, 1964), chap. 1, pp. 8, 14f.
14. Jung, *Mysterium Coniunctionis*, CW 14, para. 491.
15. Ibid., para. 347.
16. Jung means the Anthropos, or the Self. "The alchemical Anthropos shows itself to be independent of the dogma," Ibid., para. 492.
17. Ibid., para. 491.

DRUGS IN THE VIEW OF C. G. JUNG

The flood of drugs that is rolling over our world today was not yet widespread at the time of Jung's death. Jung therefore was only familiar with the effects of mescaline (especially through Aldous Huxley's description) and only knew that such pharmaceuticals were beginning to capture attention in psychotherapy.[1] He admitted in a letter of April 1954 that he was not sufficiently acquainted with the psychotherapeutic value of such drugs for neurotic and psychotic patients to be able to form a conclusive judgment.[2] He was profoundly disquieted, on the other hand, by our modern tendency to exploit such discoveries out of idle curiosity, without recognizing the growing moral responsibility that we incur:

> This is really the mistake of our age. We think it is enough to discover new things, but we don't realise that knowing more demands a corresponding development of morality. Radioactive clouds over Japan, Calcutta, and Saskatchewan point to a progressive poisoning of the universal atmosphere. . . .
>
> I am profoundly mistrustful of the "pure gifts of the Gods." You pay dearly for them. *Quidquid id est timeo Danaos et dona ferentes.*[3]

Drugs (hashish, mescaline, LSD, opium, heroin), generally speaking, bring about a decay of apperception, that is, a decomposition of the conscious synthesis and perception of gestalts (in the sense of Gestalt psychology), and thus cause the appearance of the normal perceptual variants—innumerable nuances of form, meaning, and value—that normally remain subliminal. This means above all an enriching of consciousness. We come into contact with "the sphere where the paint is made that colours the world, where the light is created that makes shine the splendour of the dawn, the lines and shapes of all form, the sound that fills the universe, the thought that illuminates the darkness of the void."[4] This is an experience of the collective unconscious. If this experience were to be a God-given gift without a hidden counterpoison, then it would mean a tremendous enrichment, an expansion of consciousness by which we are naturally fascinated. But it is just this expansion and enrichment of consciousness that make integration and moral processing of what we see and hear in this state impossible. Therefore Jung says:

> If you are too unconscious it is a great relief to know a bit of the collective unconscious. But it soon becomes dangerous to know more, because one does not learn at the same time how to balance it through a conscious equivalent. . . .
>
> There are some poor impoverished creatures perhaps, for whom mescaline would be a heaven-sent gift without a counterpoison."[5]

The world of the collective unconscious, which Jung, without drugs, was the first to discover in its essence as the primordial creative ground in every human being,[6] is something alive that does not allow itself to be subjugated without an equal reaction. For this reason I have been occupied for a long time with the question of how the unconscious itself reacts to the taking of drugs. What do the dreams of addicts have to tell us about this problem? A young man, for example, who was a heroin smuggler and also frequently took LSD had the following dream:

> I am in Tahiti on the sun-bathed beach. I have built myself a little straw hut under the palms and live by fishing in the sea. It is magically beautiful. Suddenly a tremendous storm tide comes and washes everything away. I am sucked under water and find myself suddenly in the depths of the sea, standing in front of a big writing desk at which the "Lord of the Sea" is sitting. He is a giant man-o'-war jellyfish who looks at me angrily, and it dawns on me that he is the one that sent the storm tide. "Yes," says the man-o'-war, "I am angry at you and am going to completely destroy you." Then I wake up with a shock.

The magical, primitive land of innocence amid the paradisiacal beauty of nature with its happy life, devoid of responsibilities—that is what the drug user really is seeking. He is alone there, without social or emotional human obligations. Earlier on, it was military deserters in our culture who actually did flee to such countries in reality. However, the "Lord of the Sea" is infuriated about this. The big, round man-o'-war is what Jung described as a *mandala*, a symbol of the Self, that is, of the ultimate regulatory transpersonal inner-psychic center. And this divine soul guide is angry at the dreamer and wants to destroy him. Thus the unconscious reacts negatively to the irresponsible penetration into its sphere. And in fact, soon after this the dreamer went to pieces and was lost.

In another case, a slightly different picture emerged. A young man, who came from a ghastly family situation, was regularly taking LSD. He was perhaps one of those "impoverished creatures" mentioned by Jung for whom the drug contained no counterpoison. In any case, he always had a "good trip" with apparently no unfortunate consequences. But since this nevertheless did not solve his problem, he decided to undertake analysis, which guided him gradually and responsibly to the world of the beyond. At that point, he decided to take LSD again. He not only had a "bad trip" with psychosis-like anxiety states, but he was left from this trip with a nervous twitching of the head that lasted for months and frightened him a great deal. Evidently drug trips had now somehow become illegitimate, now that he knew of a better path to the unconscious. And the unconscious itself beneficently frightened him off. He never took LSD again, but he developed inwardly in a very rewarding fashion and turned himself toward life.

In a further case, a slightly different picture emerged. The person in question here was a young woman who was highly gifted artistically but had been greatly restricted psychically by an inculcated conventional outlook. Once, out of curiosity, she took LSD. After this, she dreamed that she had had a lovely trip but now she had to adopt a different approach. She saw her analyst standing in front of her with a playful-looking fool's cap on. The unconscious was obviously saying to her that she needed more creative "tomfoolery" and should acquire this through analysis (that is the reason why in her dream it was the analyst wearing the fool's cap), not only through drugs. The drug had indeed opened up to her the realm of unconventional experience, but now this had to be consciously and morally followed up.

A doctor who had taken LSD experimentally and who afterward was reflecting intensively on his experience, because he had been amazed by the strange personality change during the intoxication, had the following dream:

> I'm standing on a beautiful, broad plain. Above me in the sky I see strange, fantastic cloud formations. Before my feet lies a

round, very deep well shaft. I look down and see similar fantastic cloud structures in the water. Then I realize that it is my duty, and therefore a matter of life and death, to get a bucket and draw these cloud structures, which are real things, out of the well. I wake up looking for a bucket.

Up till now, humanity has always projected its inner psychic contents onto the sky as "signs from heaven." But now the dreamer catches sight of similar things in the depths of his own psyche. The contents turn out to be no mere reflections, as one might think, but they have their own reality. One has to draw them out of the well and work with them creatively, otherwise they are obviously dangerous in some way. One could hardly convey what is at stake here better than this dream does. Jung writes in the same letter cited above:

> I only know there is no point in wishing to know more of the collective unconscious than one gets through dreams and intuition. The more you know of it, the greater and heavier becomes your moral burden, because unconscious contents are transformed into your individual tasks and duties as soon as they begin to become conscious. Do you want to increase loneliness and misunderstanding? Do you want to find more and more complications and increasing responsibilities? You get enough of it. If I once could say that I have done everything I know I had to do, then perhaps I should realise a legitimate need to take mescaline. But if I should take it now, I would not be sure at all that I had not taken it out of idle curiosity. . . . This is not the point at all, to know of or about the unconscious, nor does the story end here; on the contrary it is how and where you begin the real quest.[7]

Thus in this case the doctor in question now had to learn consciously to disengage himself from familial convention and to develop the contents of the psychic depths creatively through hard work. The "trip" had shown him a goal, but the dream insisted on going through a creative process to reach it. And finally, here is the dream of a young user of hard drugs:

> I am in a rowboat alone on the sea. The sun is shining brightly, and the surface of the sea is completely covered with magnificent flowers exuding a wonderful overpowering scent. I dip my arm in the water, and when I pull it out again, to the point it had been stuck into the water, it has disappeared! It has been eaten away by the water and is no more than a stump! As I look at it in terror, my boat capsizes and I awaken with a cry of fear.

The dreamer had gone out onto the sea — into the collective unconscious. The magnificent flowers symbolize the beauty and sweetness of the drug experiences. "Morphine gives me such sweet dreams," he would often say. But — and this is what the dream showed him — behind that lurks deadly decomposition, an annihilation of the personality and of life!

One could not say any more clearly than the unconscious has here what the use of morphine means. The dream is after all not the reaction of a moralistic person but rather a message from the transpersonal ground of the psyche.

That the drug experience is a substitute for a Dionysian experience of the Divine is generally accepted today. The Christian image of God has lost its effectiveness for many people, and in this way the objective psychic intensity or energy that was formerly invested in it has become free. "God" is no longer to be found outside. Through our scientific intellect, we have divested the external world of its soul. Jung, however, stressed that this has certain psychological consequences:

> The materialistic error was probably unavoidable at first. Since the throne of God could not be discovered among the galactic

systems, the inference was that God had never existed. The second unavoidable error is psychologism: if God is anything, he must be an illusion derived from certain motives—from the will to power, for instance, or from repressed sexuality.[8]

Through this, the person for whom "God is dead" will usually immediately fall victim to an inflation, that is, end up in an overblown dissociated state in which he feels himself to be the "new God," as the example of Nietzsche shows us.[9] Or else he will be overrun by some urge or craving, one that will now exhibit the same intensity as the image of God had done previously.

Here it must be mentioned that intoxicating substances are not the only dangerous addiction of our times. Another dangerous form of addiction is ideological possession, which can make the individual just as "drunk," puffed up, and dissociated as a drug, and in addition misleads him into wanting to impose his ideas on society through force. The energy that previously was invested in the idea of God is poured into the ideological, political, or sociological doctrine, which is then fanatically believed in. It is usually the extravert who has recourse to this form of intoxication, whereas the introvert prefers to pursue inner images with the help of drugs. The danger in both cases lies in the lack of spiritual freedom of the individual who is overrun by overwhelming unconscious fantasies. Jung says:

> The strongest and therefore the decisive factor in any individual psyche compels the same belief or fear, submission or devotion which a God would demand from man. Anything despotic and inescapable is in this sense "God," and it becomes absolute unless, by an ethical decision freely chosen, one succeeds in building up against this natural phenomenon a position that is equally strong and invincible.[10]

This counterposition would correspond to a free choice through a moral decision in favor of a spiritual God who is experienceable within one's own psyche. "Man is free to decide whether "God" shall be a "spirit" or a natural phenomenon like the craving of a morphine addict, and hence whether 'God' shall act as a beneficent or a destructive force."[11] This God would be that ultimately unknown something that Jung calls the Self. Serving it does not amount to egocentricity, but, on the contrary, is a self-limitation through which inflation and dissociation can be avoided. Serving the Self is a long, hard labor on oneself, but one which is rewarding, for the inner richness of the psyche that reveals itself through this is the only possession in this uncertain world that cannot be taken away from us.

Mankind often proceeded to new realizations by passing through errors. It seems to me very understandable, and more than pardonable, if many people in the younger generation are unable to bear the intellectual vacuity and soullessness of our technical nonculture and therefore have recourse to drugs. But then for every individual the hour of destiny strikes in which he must decide whether he wants to sink forever into this meaninglessness, or pass through it as through a gate and go on to the great work of objective self-knowledge.

NOTES

1. Aniela Jaffé, *The Myth of Meaning* (New York: G. P. Putnam's Sons, 1971), pp. 72ff.
2. Ibid., p. 72.
3. Ibid., p. 73. [The Latin maxim at the end of this citation is the one that has become familiar in English as "Beware of Greeks bearing gifts." — Translator]
4. Ibid.

5. Ibid.

6. For Sigmund Freud, as is well known, it is simply "archaic residues."

7. Jaffé, *The Myth of Meaning*, pp. 72–73.

8. C. G. Jung, *Psychology and Religion*, CW 11, p. 85.

9. Ibid., p. 86.

10. Ibid.

11. Ibid.

THE RELIGIOUS BACKGROUND OF THE PUER AETERNUS PROBLEM

The term *puer aeternus*, "eternal youth," is often used in psychology to denote a particular form of neurosis in men, which is characterized by a tendency to remain stuck fast in adolescence as a consequence of an overly strong mother attachment. Its chief hallmarks, therefore, as indicated by C. G. Jung's remarks in his essay on the significance of the mother archetype, are homosexuality and Don Juanism. Both of these types of men show a weak emotional relationship with women of the same age.[1] However, all other typical adolescent features can also be observed: the tendency toward adopting a highly provisory lifestyle, dreaming at the same time the fantasy of a "real" creative life, but undertaking very little to bring it about. Savior ideas usually play a major or minor role in this. These might take the form of a man's thinking that he is a messiah who is going to save humanity, or at least that he is on the verge of being able to utter "the last word" in matters of philosophy, art, or politics. Reality as it is he experiences as unacceptable. The patience-exacting humdrum of everyday life as well as sustained efforts toward achievement are avoided, and everywhere—in the man's profession, with the woman he lives with, with his colleagues—he finds a "hair in the soup," as a result of which again and again a sudden and arbitrary breaking off of all relations can be observed. Usually, it is not only the speculative ideas and plans of the *puer aeternus* that are high-flying, but he often actually chooses aviation or mountain-climbing for his main sport. In this there is often a strong conscious or unconscious suicidal tendency at play, which leads to many accidents and crashes. Sometimes, however, the "winged youth" does not have an actual physical crash, but rather a psychic one in which, as part of a sudden crisis, he denies all his earlier ideals and then either dries up and plods along as a petit-bourgeois cynic or becomes a criminal and thus gives vent to his previously repressed realism in a kind of short-circuited form.

By and large, it appears at present that this form of neurosis is on the rise in our Western culture. The literary works of the well-known author Antoine de St. Exupéry reflect the French form of this problematic. The school of Stefan George and its admirers as well as many other in Germany, the "angry young men" in England, in Spanish poet Federico García Lorca, to mention only a few, belong in this category. The same thing holds true for America. The well-known psychologist Henry Murray in Boston has noted the enormous increase in the incidence of this *puer aeternus* problematic there and is working—I thank his assistant Dr. Greer for this information—on a major study of this problem. The artist George Rimmer or the poet John Maggee would be typical representatives of this type among the young people of America.

As long as we are only talking about individual cases, the problem can be explained and treated in connection with the personal mother attachment. But beyond this, the question now arises of where the collective increase in this neurotic constellation that we now seem to be faced with comes from. We know that the necessity and difficulty of disengagement from the mother represents a universal, one might even say "normal" problem, which is dealt with, for example, among all primitive peoples through male initiation ceremonies. The Protestant and Catholic confirmation ceremonies *mutatis mutandis* still evince weak vestiges of such initiations. In certain Italian towns, priests still give youths at their confirmation a hefty slap in place of the symbolic touch—a small remainder of ordeals of manhood. And in Switzerland, it is often at this time that the young man receives his first long pants and a watch—he leaves behind the dream of childhood and crosses over into time consciousness and manhood. The weakening of Christian faith that is more and more on the rise in many milieus could well be considered a contributory cause of this modern problem; for, after all, the Christian tradition is a patriarchally-spiritually oriented one and therefore represents a protective shield against the mother world and matter. However, this observation is not enough. We must penetrate more deeply into the background.

When we study the evidence of modern literature, which has left behind many typical examples of this psychic constellation, we see two archetypal images coming particularly strongly to the fore: a child god or divine boy or youth associated with light, on the one hand, and a strict, cynically hard father caught up in the psychology of power, a tyrant, or a boss, on the other. The latter is sometimes glorified in literature as an ideal leader of men, sometimes negatively represented as the enemy of "romantic youth."

Goethe depicted this opposition in a moderated form confined to the personal level, that is, conceived in less archetypal terms, in the conflict between Torquato Tasso and Antonio. In *Werther* he pours out his own *puer* problem straight from the heart; and then in *Tasso* he goes so far as to reconcile the ingenious youth Tasso with the fatherly and responsible but all too realistic and prosaic Antonio: "Thus the sailor in the end holds fast / To the rocks against which he might have crashed!" This reconciliation happens in Goethe through the mediation of the feminine principle, that is, the anima.[2]

In more recent literature the same opposition appears in a far more archetypal form. The figure of the child god has perhaps been most purely portrayed—though not without an unpleasant sentimental-infantile tinge—in Antoine de St. Exupéry's *The Little Prince*. The little prince comes from the stars, because there he has had a falling out with his beloved, the rose. On earth he learns from a fox the first secrets of becoming a human being. But all the same he does not enter into close relationship with the earth; instead he is liberated from life by the wise serpent and its deadly bite and returns again to his star. The type of the antagonist is split in this little work into many different figures, all of whom embody the "grownups" who do not understand, whom St. Exupéry had already held up to derision in his introduction to *The Little Prince*. There is the money-counting merchant, the power-hungry king, the cynical and despondent sot, the quixotic lamplighter, and so on. The little prince from the stars does not take up contact with these figures but passes them by, untouched. In a certain sense, the serpent also represents a primary antagonist of the little prince. He is old, wise, hostile to life, and teaches the sweet suicidal temptation of freedom in death. In other works of St. Exupéry's, the boy's antagonist is more clearly drawn, and one can see in these works that the writer is in quest of a positive relationship with these adversarial figures. Thus we have the airline boss and organizer Rivière in the novel *Night Flight*, who—strict, earnest, true to his duty, but hard—sends his "children," the pilots, to their deaths; or the sheik in *Citedelle*, who rules in a paternally strict, responsible, and order-loving fashion, but who, for example, does not hesitate to condemn a woman to a gruesome death from thirst in the desert for a humanly understandable erotic transgression.

The image of the ideal leader-dictator or father of the country that dominates past and present political constellations is based, in my opinion, in part on a projected version of such an "antagonist" image.

In the dream series of a typical *puer aeternus*, characteristically, the Russian secret police, who want to torture the dreamer, appear as the embodiment of such a negatively perceived order-related paternal power figure. Functioning as the representative of this police power in the dream is an old woman, who hits the dreamer on the frontal sinus. The unresolved mother complex often contributes to the formation of a dictator ideal, for the mother attachment keeps the young man infantile, socially irresponsible, and disorderly, which then of course almost inevitably calls forth such a brutal counterposition as is represented here by the Russian secret police. This is surely also the case on a larger scale, politically.

A most vivid literary depiction, it seems to me, is the archetypal background of the *puer aeternus* problem in Bruno Goetz's occult novel of 1919, *Das Reich ohne Raum* (The Kingdom without Space). C. G. Jung often mentioned this novel as a prophetic anticipation of National Socialism and also interpreted the destructive troops of boys that appear in it as a nefarious aspect of the *puer* or divine child.[3] In this novel, the hero of the story, by the name of Melchior von Lindenhuis, comes between two hostile parties: that of the divine boy Fo (= Buddha) and that of Herr Ulrich von Spät, who is pursuing him. Fo is accompanied by an ecstatic troop of boys who trigger upheavals and "liberational" mass eruptions of savagery in every city. Fo is a moon and water spirit, a son of the mother goddess Earth, who protects him in the form of an apple woman. Grapes, wine, Pan flutes, animals, roses, and fire are his elements. He proclaims an eternal change of forms through many rebirths, advocates abandoning oneself to life and death, seeking and wandering, dancing and ecstasy. His pursuer and enemy Ulrich von Spät (*Spät* in German means "late"), by contrast, is the ruler, with his "glass lords," of a crystal-clear transcendental realm among the stars. Order, ethics, and pure spirituality are the goals he proclaims to humanity. For the most part Herr von Spät appears as a power-hungery sorcerer, but in his rare better moments, his face reveals itself as "the noble suffering face of a god." On account of this nobler aspect, the hero of the novel, Melchior, can never completely abandon him, although his heart belongs more to Fo and the boys. Only at the end of the novel does his shadow help to kill the shadow of Ulrich von Spät, and then Melchior himself is united in death with the divine boy Fo, who appears to him surrounded by bunches of grapes. The latter recalls Goethe's Euphorion in many respects and the boy guide in *Faust*, or Stefan George's Maximin. Ulrich von Spät, on the other hand, could be compared to a figure like Klingsor in Wagner's *Parsifal*. Herr von Spät represents, as it were, the mighty pressure of tradition and the past, which, as Jung once said, "buries the gods in marble and gold." The boy Fo, by contrast, lies behind the National Socialistic excesses. We can really apply to him Rabelais's remark that "*La verité dans sa forme brute est plus fausse que le faux.*"[4] Since, in contrast to Goethe's *Tasso*, here the weak anima figure cannot play the role of intermediary, in Bruno Goetz's novel we find neither a transformation of the adversary nor reconciliation with him. But what does the opposition between this severe father figure and the winged boy god mean? Is this the problem that the philosopher Klages called "the spirit as the enemy of the soul"?

The most apt mythological analogues to these two contending figures are to be found in the symbolism of alchemy: the chief-dictator-father spirit corresponds there to the arcane substance known as the "old king"; whereas the *puer aeternus* seems to correspond to the *mercurius infans* or *filius regius*, which is also sometimes personified as a winged youth, *juvenis alatus*.

In *Mysterium Coniunctionis* Jung gives a detailed commentary on the figure of the old king, who represents the arcane substance and is usually portrayed by the alchemists at the beginning of the process as defective, unredeemed, rigidified, sick, or even evil. The defective quality corresponds to an intensified egotism and hardening of the heart that must be broken down in the alchemical bath. Power hunger and concupiscence often also ingloriously characterize the old king. Similarly the boss, Rivière, in St. Exupéry's *Night Flight* and Ulrich von Spät in Goetz's *Reich ohne Raum* embody a pure attitude of power and are characterized by a total lack of eros. The spirit, which in itself is no "adversary of the soul," degenerates in such personifications to the level of intellect, and in this contracted and rigidified form stands in the way of all the psyche's fertile and creative impulses. It is an enemy of emotionality and instinct, but precisely for this reason it secretly lets itself be negatively influenced by primitive impulses.

On the other hand, the *puer aeternus*, understood as an alchemical image, is, vis-à-vis the old king, the element that is destined to replace him. This is a symbol of the renewal of life or the reunion of separated opposites, the "new inner man," or the arcane substance resurrected, a more complete renewed symbol of the Self.

Seen in the light of alchemical symbolism and Jung's remarks on the subject, the father image of the old ruler and the winged son are not only not real opposites but have a single nature. Therefore the alchemists referred to their substance as *senex et puer*. Christ was also called upon in the same terms, since he himself is the "Ancient of Days" who was reborn as a child through Mary. Through the fusion that takes place in the alchemical *opus*, whether in the fire or the bath, through dissolution into chaos or mutilation, in one way or another the old man is transformed into the son. Thus, when in modern variants father and son figures stand opposed, we can only conclude that something must have gone awry psychologically. Somehow or other the transformational process has gotten stuck.

However, in this regard Jung showed that the old king represents not only a tradition-bound, excessively egoistic, stick-in-the-mud principle of consciousness, but rather ultimately the collective God image itself. Therefore when it is said that the king is in need of transformation, it is ultimately our conception of the Divine that needs transforming, and it is clear that such a process is only possible within the psyche. In other words, the only thing we can do is orient ourselves toward the unconscious if we want to find out in what way our prevailing conscious dominants must change so that our image of the divine may once again be transformed, as Jung puts it, "into a real and workable whole, whereas before . . . [it] had only pretended to wholeness."[5]

The archetypal image of the puer aeternus represents such an experience of the divine that renews the image of God. Now, if this whole process of the renewal of the king that Jung described and interpreted in detail in *Mysterium Coniunctionis* is not consciously realized, it seems simply to go on anyhow, but then in a negative fashion. Particularly interesting in this connection is the unfolding of events in *The Little Prince*. The boy from a star voluntarily permits himself to be killed by the serpent, a yellow sand viper, so as to be able to return to his star and the rose he has left behind there. Not too long after writing this, the author, St. Exupéry, himself followed the little prince into death. He was shot down by German pilots over the Mediterranean.

In alchemical symbolism, the serpent is identified with the *filius regius*, that is, with the star prince. The serpent is, as Jung says, "the lowest, most inchoate form" of the king in the process of renewal, "at first a deadly poison but later the alexipharmic [counterpoison] itself."[6] The serpent represents the dark side of Mercury, a Hermes Katachthonios. It is said that when the light of a hero's life is extinguished, he goes on living in the form of a serpent.[7] In the life of St. Exupéry, the serpent actually took on its full deadly significance, as it always can whenever a person is identified with the archetype of the *puer,* because in this way he participates in the transformation of the archetype *in concreto*, and thus himself disappears into chaos, mutilation, and death. It is from this that the suicidal tendencies and proneness to death of human *puer aeterni* derive: the alchemical mortification of the arcane substance takes the form of their own personal death.

In this perspective, the mother complex that is coming to dominate modern society (I recall Philip Wylie's book *Generation of Vipers* and its derision of "momism") acquires a new significance. Attachment to the mother is conditioned by the fascinating power of attraction of the collective unconscious as the locus and matrix of the "renewal of the king." The collective unconscious is the womb of the *prima materia*, the dark primeval state that the alchemists call "chaos," the *massa confusa* in which the old man transforms into a youth. Women who no longer have a religious orientation and whose life has therefore become without content involuntarily identify themselves with this magic role of the Great Mother and then project the archetypal image of the hero or *filius regius* on their son—to the point of even preferring his death to the possibility that he might lead an ordinary human existence.[8] Once a woman who was showing me the deathbed photograph of her drowned only son said to me verbatim: "I would rather have it this way than have him alive and have to give him away to another woman"!

The son, on the other hand, falls under the spell of the maternal principle because he is identified with the *filius regius*, and the *filius regius* is attracted with tremendous passionate force by the matrix of the unconscious, since ever and again this is what he transforms into. This is even more powerfully constellated in Protestant regions, since the archetypal mother image is missing from the religion. Thus either the entire power of fascination of this archetypal image falls upon the personal mother, or there develops such fear and alienation vis-à-vis the feminine principle that the maculine consciousness closes itself off from all feminine influences and, with them, from the influence of the unconscious; in this way it withers into reasonableness and historical retrospection. In this way there arises the attitude of consciousness of Herr von Spät, that is, of the aging king who has withdrawn from the transformation process.

In Bruno Goetz's *Reich ohne Raum*, von Spät appears as the childhood friend of the leading female character of the novel, Sophie (Melchior von Lindenhuis's wife). Thus von Spät is also a personification of the animus in the woman. In this connection, I have often seen mothers using the argument of traditional "positive Christianity" against treatment of their sons, or wives using it against the Jungian analysis of their husbands; the secret motive behind their action was by no means Christian love but rather envy and lust for power. In other words, both the father and boss type—"Herr von Spät"—and the *puer aeternus* are archetypes that can also crop up as animus personifications in the female psyche. In an interesting work, Else Hoppe has explored the *Typus des Mannes in der Dichtung der Frau* (The Masculine Type in the Literary Works of Female Authors),[9] and the opposition of *puer* and *senex* stood out clearly in the way women portrayed men in their writings.

I have often been asked about the psychology of the *puella aeterna* and if there is such a thing. Indubitably there is, as I see it. The *puella aeterna* would be the "eternal daughter" type of woman, one who is unconsciously identified with the anima of the father. Such a woman lives, as does the young man of the *puer* type, in an archetypal role. She is a Kore, the numinous *anima mundi*, a goddess of light. The female type corresponding to Herr von Spät is the bitter, often scheming old woman who clings to tradition and hard-value possessions such as money, furniture, houses, fur coats—an old witch, incapable of love. Also the department-store hyenas that Philip Wylie so aptly portrays belong to this category. Greta Garbo definitely experienced the fall from the Kore role with particular intensity and—at least so I believe—survived as a human being. Grace Kelly also found a way out of the pure anima identification that her career forced on her. On the other hand, Brigitte Bardot, for example, continued to live the *puella* role in her films, which often indicates a hermaphroditic-boyish secondary nuance, since in alchemy the *filius regius* and his bride are secretly identical. Fashion, the film world, and the anima possession of men reinforce the temptation for women to play the *puella* role, just as the animus possession of mothers and women makes young men into "eternal youths." At the same time, so much genuine spiritual, religious, and romantic longing and creative emotion is invested in this identification that it is understandable that those who have it do not want to give it up. After all, it appears to them that there is no other alternative beside the sterile tyranny of Herr von Spät or of the disillusioned old woman, because they do not know where and how an inner transformation of these figures might possibly occur.

In the spiritual revolution of Protestantism, a step was taken in the direction of no longer seeing religious images as external and of no longer assimilating the religious function of the psyche to the function of a visible church. But if one says *A*, one must also say *B*: if the images are no longer "outside" or to be found in a "dogmatic metaphysic," then they must be in us — not in the subject, but in the objective psyche. Fully taking this necessary next step is what Protestantism did not dare; it is precisely at this point that the transformation of the "old king" stuck fast. If this next step had taken place, then a reconciliation of Protestantism with the introverted wing of the Catholic Church — that is, with its mystics — would have been conceivable. In this way a bridging of the schism through the eros principle and through the acknowledgment of the religious function of the unconscious would have been possible.

The reality of the unconscious psyche has for the most part been personified in mythology by the spirit in the nature of matter, by the mother, by the *anima mundi*, or by the "eternal feminine" in Goethe's *Faust*. As this feminine power is not being acknowledged today in our Western culture, there has developed in its place, on the one hand, this increase in a highly regressive-seeming "momism" and in homosexuality, and on the other, a rigidification of consciousness that finds its immediate expression in an increase in the formation of police states. I have even been able to observe directly in individual cases how in dreams the image of the "old God" (in the case of the Germans, Wotan, in that of the Jews, Yahweh) and that of the police power or the dictator replace each other as motifs or else appear as identified, for the God image withdrawing from transformation, or the old consciousness dominant, does not merely remain as it is when the process fails to continue, but plainly regresses into old, primitive forms. Especially interesting for us today is the increasing importance everywhere in the outer world of secret police and spy networks. In their concealment they more or less directly embody the secret workings of the unconscious in an aspect that, on the one hand, is undermining and revolutionary, and on the other, is regressive and serves Herr von Spät. Without possessing any ideal goal of their own, these organizations serve to strengthen the power of the various dominating principles. In most cases their figurehead is material security, that is, the archetype of the *mater materia* is the principal motif that seduces them to action, either that or the conviction that strict "law and order" is necessary to keep down the chaos of the masses — in other words the boss-dictator or "old king" image. On the other hand, those possessed by the *puer aeternus* archetype are usually without political interests, and this goes to the point of social irresponsibility; they just get caught up in every exciting emotional mass movement that comes along, regardless of where it came from and where it is going. Of course, the two types of possession play into each other's hands. *Les extrêmes ne se touchent pas seulement*;[10] they are often even identical.

Even the rocket and flight attempts of the Eastern and Western groups can be seen in this light. Thus the American aviator-poet John Maggee writes about the ecstasy of his high flight in an open airplane that he "put out [his] hand and touched the face of God." And touched the face of God! So God is still in the outer world somewhere in space or—if that is only a poetic metaphor—only attainable through outward-oriented aviational technology and acrobatics, not through searching within oneself. The ecstatic inflation that is associated with the experience of flight, is here incredibly naively spelled out. Soon after composing this poem, John Maggee died in a plane accident. He, too, was bitten by the spirit of earth, the deadly aspect of the Mercurius, the serpent, just like the little prince from the stars.

It had already emerged from Goethe's *Tasso* that the woman and the differentiation of the anima in the man play a crucial role in the transformation of the *senex* to the *puer* as well as in the integration of the whole problem. Here it seems to me, addressing now the female side of the problem, that the indefiniteness and passivity of women presents essential difficulties. If one analyzes women who are identified with the Great Mother, they often seem like an imposing *massa confusa* of emotions, unconscious scheming, animus opinions, and so on, behind which, however, one finds a very small, sensitive, childish ego. And women who are identified with the anima role, though they come off as original and definite when the presence of the male projection is giving them a shape, when they are alone face to face with another woman, all this dissolves into a big sense of emptiness and uncertainty. And when for once one encounters a woman who is definite and formed and knows what she wants, it is unfortunately for the most part her animus that is bringing this about and not her own character. The spinning of schemes and intrigues is also closely connected with this indefiniteness: One does not make decisions, but instead hopes and wishes and keeps an eye on which way "the cookie is crumbling," then very gently nudges the forces of destiny along a little bit. A little slander here, a little show of inauthentic emotion there, a not entirely unconscious mistake in the right place—all can help the course of things along without one's having to take any responsibility for it. Another possibility lies in an upright and unscheming but entirely rigid male-like identification with the old collective values—Herr von Spät or the old king. In this case, the indefinite, scheming, and vague woman is to be found in the shadow. Sometimes these two types of women have a homoerotic attraction to each other, just as the two male types do, precisely because in fact (but of course inwardly) they must be united.

Only greater definiteness and very clear definition of character such as result from the integration of the animus can counteract this, because then an objective eros becomes possible that submits to the Self and at the same time can love the other as he is. This goes hand in hand with a renunciation of the archetypal role of the Great Mother or of the "Goddess Anima" and a return to humble humanness, just as must be made by the male *puer*. The important thing that Jung has done for us in respect to this situation is to show us a way to find this humility without tumbling into banality, without a return to Herr von Spät, without loss of the creative *mana*, the emotions, and the glamor that surround the figures of the *puer* and *puella*. On the contrary, when the *puer* and *puella* are understood as the Self and as non-ego, that is when they first begin to bring forth their secret redeeming and liberating effects and to lose their poisonous effect—that of making the ego unreal. Without this acknowledging insight, however, the *puer* archetype becomes nothing less than a demon of death.

Bruno Goetz introduces his novel with the following poem to the divine boy Fo:

Als nicht vom Himmel wich
die schwere Wolke
und allem Volke,
die Sonne blich,
da kam aus Tiefen
das neue Licht uns nah.
Wir schliefen
und wussten: "Du bist da."
O Sonnen
aus Deiner Augen Grund
Springende Bronnen
der Liebe aus Deinem Mund.
Funkelnder Geist
Deiner Glieder im Aethermeer —
über die Wellen
Lockst Du zu lohem Mut.
Ewiger Knabe
umspielt von der Sterne Getön
Spender der Labe
Brausend und frei und schön:
Männer und Frauen schwingen in Deinem Schein,
treiben in Tod hinein
neu Dich zu schauen.
Immer ins Helle, ruft Deine weisse Gestalt.
Welle um Welle
nie sind wir alt!

(When the clouds failed to vacate the heavens
and for all the people the sun grew pale,
then, from the depths, the new light came near.
We went to sleep knowing, "You are here."

O suns from the depths of Your eyes,
welling springs of love from Your mouth,
Sparkling Spirit, with Your limbs in the ether sea
across the waves You lure us to blazing courage.
Eternal Boy, around whom the music of the spheres plays,
Giver of refreshment, rousing, free, and beautiful—
men and women resonate in Your light,
rush into death to see You anew.
Your white figure calls us ever into brilliant light.
Wave after wave, never are we old!)

Men and women rush into death to see you anew! That is surely the most dangerous side of this archetypal image of divine renewal. If this renewal is not consciously realized, the *puer* image exercises a mighty seduction toward death. In our time this could even become the motive for an unconscious mass suicide. What the increase in the *puer* problematic could mean for us in view of the current world situation is more than frightening and shows how urgent it has become for individuals to accomplish the step toward inner psychic realization of relationship with the Divine.

Since, as I presume, Herr von Spät, or the alchemical *senex*, and the *puer* or *infans mercurius* are archetypal powers that are constellated in the background of the events of our time as the authors of possession and projections, I believe that we here must keep watch for how these powers might possibly take hold of us or for how they perhaps already have. It seems to me that among analysts, two tendencies that correspond to them have made their appearance. One is a conventionality that wants to make Jung "academic" or "medical" or make him "conform" in some other way. Following this tendency we end up, for example, in "neo-Freudian" fashion with Herr von Spät. The other tendency is that, in *puer*-like fashion, we would like to "go beyond Jung and have the last word," little caring whether what we then say is scientifically accurate or not. That these tendencies are secretly identical is demonstrated, for example, by a "*puer*" like Ira Progoff, who promises as a great innovator to develop Jung further for us—and ends up in Otto Rank's camp!

We could adduce further examples, *sed nomina sunt odiosa.*[11] We can only save ourselves from these tendencies through greater humanity, that is, by seeing and acknowledging that the two archetypal images can only exercise their effects of negative possession on us to the extent that our own experience of the Self has not yet gone far and deep enough.

NOTES

1. C. G. Jung, "Psychological Aspects of the Mother Archetype," in CW 9/i.
2. The author is referring here to Goethe's famous early novel *The Sorrows of Young Werther* (1774) and to his classical drama *Torquato Tasso* (1790).—Translator
3. C. G. Jung and C. Kerényi, *Essays on a Science of Mythology* (Princeton: Princeton University Press, Bollingen Series, 1973), p. 78.
4. Truth in its crude form is falser than falsehood.—Translator
5. Jung, *Mysterium Coniunctionis*, CW 14, p. 360.
6. Ibid., pp. 335–36.
7. Ibid., para. 340.
8. Ibid.
9. My thanks to René Malamud for his kindness in letting me know about this book.
10. "*Les extrêmes . . .*": The extremes do not only touch each other.—Translator
11. *Sed nomina sunt odiosa*: But names are odious.—Translator

INDEX

acting out, 186–187
active imagination, 8, 141, 146
    absolute freedom of, 158–160
    borderline cases and, 168
    dangers of, 155, 248–249
    difficulty of, 148–149
    four phases of, 163–169
    individuation process and, 157–158
    liberating effect of, 151, 153–154
    magic and, 175–176
    versus passive imagination, 2
addicts. *See* drugs
Aelian, 157
alchemical literature, 191
alchemical mythology, 188–189
alchemy, 165
analysis, role of body in, 165
analysts
    choice of, 38–39
    collective unconscious and, 276
    compassion of, 273
    creativity and, 281
    demands on, 280–281
    dream of, 268–270, 271–272
    emotional reactions of, 180
    four functions of consciousness and,
        273–274
    individuation, 9
    individuation and, 278
    inner development of, 271
    mother complex and, 268
    mythological knowledge of, 272
    qualifications for, 267–268
    See also transference
Andreae, 252
anima, 24, 319
    description of, 251

animal behavior, 31–32
animus, 315–316
    description of, 251–252
"anticipated psychosis," 147
archetypal complexes, 264
archetypal contents, 186–187
archetypal dreams, 4, 203–204, 270
archetypal fantasies, 73
archetypal images, affect-laden, 203
archetypal motif, 215
archetypal symbol, 206
archetypes
    father, 287
    fool, 22
    "Great Mother," 153–154
    healer, 268
    human relationship, 284
    mother, 287, 306, 315
    puer aeternus, 313–314
    self, 158
Ares, 215–217
artists, 100
atheism, 11
attitudinal types, 20–21
    See also types
Atum, 6

Battegay, Raymund, 286–287
benbenet, 7
ben-ben stone, 6–7
Boehme, Jakob, 103–104
bolts symbol, 6
Bon, Gustave le, 284
borderline cases, 168
bread symbol, 5–6
bush manners, 124–125, 127–128, 129–
    130

C. G. JUNG FOUNDATION BOOKS

Absent Fathers, Lost Sons: The Search for Masculine Identity, by Guy Corneau.

Creation Myths, Revised Edition, by Marie-Louise von Franz.

Ego and Archetype: Individuation and the Religious Function of the Psyche, by Edward F. Edinger.

The Female Ancestors of Christ, by Ann Belford Ulanov.

The Feminine in Fairy Tales, Revised Edition, by Marie-Louise von Franz.

Gathering the Light: A Psychology of Meditation, by V. Walter Odajnyk.

The Golden Ass of Apuleius: The Liberation of the Feminine in Man, Revised Edition, by Marie-Louise von Franz.

A Guided Tour of the Collected Works of C. G. Jung, by Robert H. Hopcke. Foreword by Aryeh Maidenbaum.

In Her Image: The Unhealed Daughter's Search for Her Mother, by Kathie Carlson.

Knowing Woman: A Feminine Psychology, by Irene Claremont de Castillejo.

Masculinity: Identity, Conflict, and Transformation, by Warren Steinberg.

*Psyche and Matter, by Marie-Louise von Franz.

*Psychotherapy, by Marie-Louise von Franz.

Shadow and Evil in Fairy Tales, Revised Edition, by Marie-Louise von Franz.

The Way of All Women, by M. Esther Harding. Introduction by C. G. Jung.

Transforming Sexuality: The Archetypal World of Anima and Animus, by Ann Belford Ulanov and Barry Ulanov.

Witches, Ogres, and the Devil's Daughter: Encounters with Evil in Fairy Tales, by Mario Jacoby, Verena Kast, and Ingrid Riedel.

*Published in association with Daimon Verlag, Einsiedeln, Switzerland.